Immigrant Success Planning

A Family Resource Guide

Immigrant Success Planning

A Family Resource Guide

Atta Arghandiwal

with Eileen Figure Sandlin

First Published in Canada 2014 by Influence Publishing

Book Design: Marla Thompson
Typeset: Greg Salisbury
Author Photographer: Edreece Arghandiwal

DISCLAIMER: This resource guide is designed to provide generic definitions, best practices, and helpful tips based on extensive hands-on experience and knowledge of the author as an immigrant. The book is being published with the understanding that the author and the distribution company have not and will not be engaged in providing legal, professional, or financial advice. Any legal, financial, and professional advice or services must be sought through proper and professional resources.

With much love and admiration, I dedicate this book to humanity.

"This comprehensive book provides proven guidelines for immigrants and refugees, from their inception and resettlement to full integration. The lessons learned and the best practices compiled in this book will help immigrants and refugees take control of and lead successful lives."

Ambassador Waheed Waheedullah, Ph.D

Acknowledgements

I wish to express my sincere thanks and profound gratitude to the people without whose invaluable assistance and generous contribution this book would have not been successfully accomplished.

My special thanks go to Edreece, my son, who devotedly assisted me and stood firm by my side for several years to complete this project. He has been my closest companion, co-worker, and advisor throughout the process in all aspects of the mission, from the inception of the book to the final stage of its production.

I am profoundly grateful for the sterling contributions of my co-author, Eileen Figure Sandlin, and my editor, Marla Markman, for their highly professional skills and input in making it possible for all immigrants to understand and easily digest the book's substance and purpose.

My sincere thanks and heartfelt gratitude also goes to Julie Salisbury and her team at Influence Publishing for their hands-on and strategic approach; my very talented and close friend, Shafiq Ahmadi, for his great ideas and creative marketing designs; and to my highly tuned intellectual friends and associates, Rahim Aurang and Husna Mohammadi, for their precious insight and instructive tips.

And finally, I extend my very special thanks and gratitude to my best friend, scholar, and educator, His Excellency Ambassador Waheed Waheedullah, the latest recipient of the Mother Teresa International Peace Award, for his valuable time and thoughtful contributions, including writing the book's foreword and his conceptual input on the book's cover image and title.

CONTENTS

Foreword

As a long-term conflict manager and trouble shooter at the United Nations, one of the major issues I have always dealt with is the voluntary or non-voluntary movement and immigration of peoples within our globe. Erupting conflicts and wars give birth to short-term, medium-term and long-term political, social and economic chaos and disorder. One of the many ways that people escape from such chaos and disorder is by taking refuge in more peaceful or safer locations and to immigrate there accordingly. As such movements are often triggered by wars and conflicts, the United Nations has found it impossible to cease, control, or prevent the movement and immigration of peoples taking place around the globe. The United Nations has kept trying to do its best to find the most effective ways and means to help facilitate a voluntary, safe and dignified re-location or immigration of people in need. It was the result of such efforts which gave birth to the UNHCR and IOM, two major global organizations specifically mandated to deal with the management of Internally Displaced Persons (IDPs), refugees and immigrants, at the local, regional and global level. The world, no doubt, admires the influential role that the UNHCR and IOM have played in the management, the humanitarian organization, and the international regulation of migration and refugee-related affairs thus far. However, it must be sincerely admitted that these organizations have also fallen short of suggesting any effective ways and means leading to successful planning for the future life of emerging immigrants and refugees, of either voluntary or non-voluntary nature.

It is, indeed, this very significant gap, which the book *Immigrant Success Planning* fills in and addresses for the first time as a unique family resource guide. The book provides a comprehensive set of proven guidelines for immigrants and refugees from the very inception point of their pre-settlement, to proper resettlement, and from there to full integration, all the way to the highest stages of educational, professional and career development. The practical lessons learned and best practices compiled in this book by a distinguished and renowned author, the Honorable Atta Arghandiwal, will help immigrants and refugees to effectively take control of their own lives, and to automatically turn from being event-driven people into those who can drive events in their own legitimate best interests. The book will help immigrants and refugees to develop an effective plan for their short, medium and long-term successes. As a family resource guide, it will help them plan their successes for the future, nonetheless, they should always remember that no one plans to fail in their life, but many are simply failing to plan.

Ambassador Waheed Waheedullah

Preface

The idea for this resource guide evolved over a long period of time. Like every other immigrant, when I first came to the United States I needed a lot of information to make a life here. I looked for a simple guide that would help me navigate through my new life and environment, but I could never find one. Many self-help books focused on just one or a few topics, while others focused on such complicated matters that it was discouraging rather than helpful to read them. In addition, because this was before the internet, it took a lot of time and patience to find out what I needed to know.

I often thought about creating a condensed lifestyle guide geared toward immigrants—a road map, if you will—but over time I got busier and busier. So I am now delighted to have finally succeeded in creating the best practices/success resource guide for immigrants that you're now holding.

This guide is the product of years of knowledge, real-life practices, and proven ideas. It was developed based on core principles of and input from various groups of immigrants I've met from all walks of life, including parents, students, teachers, social services experts, entrepreneurs—in short, anyone who had best practices to share. The result is a guide for immigrants that focuses on the entire family. Chapters include useful details, best practices, and success tips that can be used throughout the life cycle, from the birth of a child through retirement and beyond. You could say that the information it contains never expires and provides the foundation for a successful and powerful way of life.

Despite the amazing life full of joy, hard work, love of family and friends, and success I have enjoyed, I truly consider this book to be my biggest achievement in life and my personal gift to humanity. I hope it gives you as much pleasure.

Chapter 1: Welcome to a Whole New World

From sea to shining sea, North America is a unique place filled with breathtaking beauty, abundant natural resources, diverse people, personal freedom, and unparalleled opportunities. North America encompasses three nations: the United States of America (also known as "America" or "the U.S."), Canada, and Mexico. Due to space restrictions, this book covers only the United States and Canada.

Unless you're from Russia, the world's largest country, chances are you've never seen countries as large as Canada (the world's second largest country) or the continental United States (the third largest). Depending how you measure her, America stretches 3,300 miles on the diagonal from Seattle, Washington, to Miami, Florida; or 2,790 miles from Los Angeles to New York City. The distance from coast to coast is about two thousand miles and the landmass is 3,639,475 square miles.

At 3,851,809 square miles, Canada is slightly larger than the United States. If you could drive the country's extreme width (between the furthermost points)—and you can't, because the terrain is too rugged in certain areas—you'd cover 5,780 miles. The "Great White North," as she is affectionately called, has more than two million lakes, which is more than the lakes in all other countries in the world combined. Here some additional facts about your new homeland.

AMERICA THE BEAUTIFUL

America is divided into 48 contiguous (adjoining) states and the District of Columbia (DC), which are collectively referred to as the mainland; plus the two outlying states of Alaska and Hawaii. The capital of the United States is Washington, DC.

America has every terrain imaginable: forests and flatlands; plains and mountains; rivers and valleys; volcanic topography and deserts. She also experiences virtually every type of weather phenomenon, from hurricanes to earthquakes, and has the most tornadoes in the world (an average of more than a thousand annually, according to the National Climatic Data Center). Interestingly, Canada has the second most tornadoes worldwide, with just a hundred.

While the most prevalent language in the United States is English, the country actually doesn't have an official language. The second most prevalent is Spanish, but dozens of other languages are also spoken here.

According to the CIA's (Central Intelligence Agency's) *World Factbook* (cia.gov/library/publications/the-world-factbook/), the United States' predominant industries include high-tech (for which she is considered the world leader); and petroleum, steel, motor vehicles, aerospace, telecommunications, chemicals, electronics, food processing, consumer goods, lumber, and mining. Her agricultural output includes wheat, corn, other grains, fruits, vegetables, and cotton; and beef, pork, poultry, dairy products; fish; and forest products like timber.

OH, CANADA

Canada is also a land of abundance. Besides great natural beauty, she has plains, mountains, and lowlands, as well as natural resources that include timber, fish, wildlife, petroleum, natural gas, and precious metals. The country consists of ten provinces: Alberta, British Columbia, Manitoba, New Brunswick, Newfoundland and Labrador, Nova Scotia, Ontario, Prince Edward Island, Quebec, and Saskatchewan; and three territories: Northwest Territories, Nunavut, and Yukon. The capital of Canada is Ottawa, located in the Province of Ontario.

Canada has two official languages: English and French. In fact, the Province of Quebec has more French speakers than English.

The country's main industries (per the CIA *World Factbook*) include transportation equipment, chemicals, processed and unprocessed minerals, food products, wood and paper products, fish products, petroleum, and natural gas.

WE THE PEOPLE

The United States and Canada have the most diverse populations in the world. In particular, the United States is a melting pot of various cultures. Over the past four hundred years, people from around the world have flocked to the United States, with most coming from Europe. According to the U.S. Census Bureau, the keeper of official population statistics, the United States has six racial categories: white American; American Indian and Alaska Native; Asian; African American; Native Hawaiian; and Other Pacific Islander. White Americans make up 72 percent of the population, according to the 2010 Census.

In Canada, people of British Isles origin are the majority population at 28 percent, followed closely by people of French origin at 23 percent. People from other European countries, people of Amerindian heritage, and others make up the remaining population. Statistics Canada, which collects statistical information about the people of Canada, says that more than 20 percent of the Canadian population is foreign-born.

Both Canada and America have large indigenous (native) populations of Native Americans (also known by the disliked term "Indians"). There are 566 Native American nations in the United States, according to the United States *Federal Register*, and more than 630 "First Nations" bands in Canada (not counting the Inuit and Métis aboriginal people). Many of these indigenous people have moved away from the reservations, or tribal homelands, but reservations do exist in both countries, mostly in the west. The native people preserve their heritage through gatherings known as pow wows, which are open to the public and include native dancing, music, food, and crafts. The indigenous nations have also flexed their economic muscles by establishing native-run casinos, bingo halls, and other gaming operations on tribal or native-owned land. In North America, there are nearly five hundred gaming operations run by nearly twenty-five nations, and the number continues to grow.

NOTABLE NORTH AMERICANS

Americans and Canadians have contributed much to western culture. Prominent Americans have included statesmen such as George Washington and Abraham Lincoln; pioneers such as Thomas Edison and Henry Ford; innovators such as Steve Jobs and Bill Gates; architects and artists such as Frank Lloyd Wright and John Singer Sargent; humanitarians such as Eleanor Roosevelt and Martin Luther King; scientists such as Jonas Salk and Robert Oppenheimer; and writers such as Mark Twain, Ernest Hemingway, and Elmore Leonard. If you're familiar with popular culture, then you probably know famous entertainers such as Elvis Presley, Michael Jackson, Sandra Bullock, Jennifer Lawrence, and Tom Cruise.

Notable Canadians have included prominent architects and scholars; musicians and scientists. Canadians have won sixteen Nobel prizes. Frederick Banting was one of the co-discoverers of insulin and was knighted for his achievement. Captain Roy Brown of the Royal Naval Service was a World War I pilot credited with shooting down the Red Baron. James Gosling invented Java computer language, while James Naismith invented basketball. Chris Hadfield was the first Canadian to walk in space and to command the International Space Station. And you're probably familiar with many Canadian-born entertainers, including Jim Carrey, Michael J. Fox, Ryan Gosling, Avril Lavigne, and Sandra Oh.

FREEDOMS

It's probably safe to say that the main reason why people emigrate to North America is because of the many freedoms offered here. Four core freedoms are guaranteed in America's Constitution: freedom of speech, religion, press, and assembly. Everyone within her borders, including native-born people, immigrants, and visitors alike are protected. Likewise, the Canadian Charter of Rights and Freedoms, which is part of the Canadian Constitution, guarantees certain civil and political rights to citizens and others. This is the kind of freedom people in oppressed nations dream of—and it's yours now that you're here.

Learn all you can about your new home. Take a history class, read a book, or peruse the internet. And look around you to discover the beauty and advantages to be found in your new home. Much awaits you.

Welcome to North America. We're glad you're here.

ATTA'S LESSONS

I landed in Germany as a refugee in August 1980. It was a time of great fear and uncertainty for me. I remember leaving my room at the Schoneck refugee camp one cold day and going for a long walk around the big field across from the camp compound. It was a dark, cloudy day, but I looked up and saw the clouds moving overhead. It made me realize that this was a time for me not to sit idle, but to move on.

So I organized a group that consisted of at least one member from each family in the camp. Instead of being confined inside our rooms, we worked together to identify our most pressing challenges as refugees, including language/communication issues. We also developed a shopping guide, and set up sports and fun activities for everyone.

The lesson I learned during my six months at Schoneck was that fear of unknown should never stop you from leading a productive life, and living in the past keeps you from taking control of your own destiny. Instead, if you wish to achieve success as an immigrant, you need to recognize that your new life is not just a change but a transformation.

Chapter 2: Entering the United States and Canada

As with anything worth having, the process of being admitted and establishing permanent residency in North America is time-consuming and takes a lot of paperwork. This chapter covers some of the common procedures and documents you'll encounter on the road to gaining legal status, working in your new country, and becoming a permanent resident. The United States and Canada are discussed in separate sections.

UNITED STATES

Form I-94

Naturally, if you're reading this book from your new home in the United States, you've successfully entered the country using this form. But if you're set to embark on an exciting new venture to North America, here's what you need to know.

The I-94 form is the official record of admission used by the U.S. Customs and Border Protection (CBP) to document arriving and departing aliens (foreign visitors) at American ports and borders of entry. This form is filed electronically, and in its place, you'll receive an admission stamp on your travel document verifying your entry or departure. If you need a copy for any reason, such as to verify alien registration, you can obtain one at i94.cbp.dhs.gov/. You can also obtain your I-94 admission number at this site.

The admission stamp will show the date of admission, class of admission, and mandatory departure date. If you wish to extend your visa, the CBP will confirm your I-94 electronically, then revalidate it if you meet certain conditions. For more information about automatic revalidation, see cbp.gov/linkhandler/cgov/travel/inspections_carriers_facilities/clp/bulletins/auto_reva.ctt/auto_reva.pdf.

WORK PERMIT

There are several types of work permits available to foreigners who wish to work in the United States. They include the following:

- *H1-B:* This work permit is granted to people who have exceptional skills and abilities in specialty occupations, as well as Department of Defense cooperative research and development project work. Strangely enough, fashion models are also included in this category. Certain talent and educational requirements must be met. For more information, see uscis.gov and search for H1B.
- *Temporary (nonimmigrant) worker:* It's possible to come to the United States to work temporarily, but an employer must file a nonimmigrant petition on your behalf to make it happen. There are more than twenty nonimmigrant classifications, and your spouse and children can apply for a visa so they can accompany you. See uscis.gov, then search for "Working in the U.S.," then "Temporary Workers" for the full list of classifications.
- *Permanent worker:* The U.S. Citizenship and Immigration Services (USCIS) makes 140,000 immigrant visas available to aliens, their spouses, and their children each year. Whether you can obtain one depends on your job skills, education, and/or work experience, as well as on whether there are not enough available, qualified, and willing U.S. workers to fill the jobs. There are additional qualifications as well. To check your eligibility for the five employment-based immigrant visa categories (unimaginatively called EB-1 through EB-5), go to www.uscis.gov and search for "Working in the United States," then "Permanent Workers."
- *Student and exchange visitor:* If you're pursuing full-time academic or vocational studies in the United States, you may be eligible to work. There are three student categories: the F category for academic students; the M category for vocational students; and the J category for exchange students. For more information, visit the USCIS page at www.ice.gov/sevis/.

PERMANENT RESIDENCY CARD ("GREEN CARD")

Known as a permanent residency card, an Alien Registration Card, the I-551, or the "green card," this photo identification card unlocks many benefits for immigrants in the United States. Having a green card (which is not actually green, by the way) allows you to live and work legally in the United States, as well as to travel without a visa and re-enter the United States using the passport from your home country. Because of this, you're required to carry the card with you at all times.

Once granted, a green card cannot be taken away, unless you violate the terms of your stay, such as by breaking the law or staying outside the United States for too long at a time. Typically, acquiring a green card is the first step toward becoming a U.S. citizen.

You can obtain a green card in one of several ways:

1. You wish to join other close family members in the United States who are already U.S. citizens or green card holders. (Once you have your green card, you'll be able to do the same for other family members.)
2. You marry a U.S. citizen.
3. You're the fiancé(e) of a U.S. citizen. You and your accompanying minor children would be admitted as K Immigrants, or nonimmigrants, which speeds up the admission process.
4. You're sponsored by an employer because of specific skills and talents you have.
5. You win a spot in the annual Diversity Immigrant Visa (Green Card) Program. Each year, the U.S. Department of State gives out 50,000 permanent resident visas to natives of a qualifying country; specifically, a country that has had low admission rates to the United States in the previous five years. If you win the lottery, you still have to meet education and work requirements. Specifically, you must have at least a high school diploma or its foreign equivalent, and you must have worked for two out of the previous five years in a job that requires two years of experience. See the U.S. Department of Labor's O*Net Resource Center at onetcenter.org to determine whether the job you hold would qualify. But beware: the Department of State advises that there has been a significant increase in the number of fraudulent emails and letters sent to applicants. They may claim that you've won the lottery, and ask for money to process your claim. This is nothing but a trick to separate you from your money. You will not receive any notifications from the Department of State that your application was successful. Instead, you need to check the status of your application at dvlottery.state.gov. Do

not pay anything to anyone who claims to be from the Department of State.

6. You have alien entrepreneur status; that is, you're someone who wishes to start a new commercial enterprise in the United States.

7. You have *asylee* or refugee status. An asylee is someone who is already in the United States and is unwilling or unable to return to his or her native country because of persecution based on race, religion, ethnic background, political beliefs, and other factors. A refugee is someone who asks for asylum while outside the United States. Both can apply for a green card after one year of residence in the United States.

Most green cards are permanent, and some people who have them never apply for citizenship. But green cards granted through marriage are conditional, meaning they come with conditions (specifically, that the marriage is indeed real) as a way to prevent fraud. The conditions may be lifted on the foreign spouse after two years.

The form to apply for a green card is the I-485, Application to Register Permanent Status or Adjust Status, and is available at uscis.gov/i-485. As part of the application process, you'll be fingerprinted, which is a type of biometrics that analyzes physical characteristics that are unique to you (in this case, your fingerprints). The fingerprints will be kept on file with your application.

Green Card Via Special Categories

Certain qualified relatives of U.S. citizens may petition to come and live permanently in the United States, and thus become eligible to apply for a green card. Eligible immediate relatives may include the citizen's spouse, unmarried children under the age of 21, and parent (but only if the U.S. citizen is over the age of 21). Immediate relatives don't have to wait for a visa to become available, because there is an unlimited number of visas in this category. For more information, see uscis.gov/green-card/green-card-through-family/green-card-immediate-relative-us-citizen.

K Nonimmigrant

There are four types of visas available to help U.S. citizens bring their spouse or fiancé(e) and their children to the United States:

- *K-1* visa allows the fiancé(e) of a U.S. citizen to enter the United States in order to be married.
- *K-2* visa is for minor, unmarried children of K-1 visa holders.
- *K-3* visa is issued to the spouses of U.S. citizens who have filed both a fiancé(e) visa petition and a separate application for entry into the United States.
- *K-4* visa is issued to minor, unmarried children of K-3 visa holders.

V Nonimmigrant

The spouse or child of a permanent resident who wishes to live and work in the United States while awaiting permanent residency status can apply for V Nonimmigrant status. However, this applies only when a petition was filed on their behalf by the permanent resident relative on or before December 21, 2000. For more information, see uscis.gov/green-card/green-card-through-family/ green-card-through-special-categories-family/v-nonimmigrant.

Widow(er) of a U.S. Citizen

An immigrant who was legally married to a U.S. citizen, including a member of the U.S. military, at the time of the citizen's death, may apply for a green card. Numerous conditions apply. For more information, visit uscis.gov/green-card/ green-card-through-family/green-card-through-special-categories-family/ widower.

Special Circumstance Green Cards

U and T Visas

These types of visas were created to help immigrants who are victims of domestic abuse (usually women) and their children eventually qualify for a green card. According to the Immigration Policy Center, immigrant women are often victims of abuse or exploitation because of their low status in society. In some cases, they may even have been brought into the United States illegally by human trafficking networks and are forced to work under threats of physical harm and deportation.

Up to 10,000 U visas are available each year to victims of mental or physical abuse. To qualify for this visa, victims must assist in the prosecution of the person who is criminally responsible for the acts of violence. The visa is valid for up to four years, although after three years, the holder is eligible to apply for permanent residency status.

A T visa is granted to victims of human trafficking, such as sex trafficking, involuntary servitude, or slavery. The United States grants up to 5,000 of these visas annually. They also are valid for four years, and the holder can apply for permanent residency status after three years of continuous residency.

There are other requirements, conditions, and waivers attached to these types of visas. Even so, it's important to know that there is help available if you or someone you know is a victim of domestic abuse or human trafficking. For more information, visit the American Immigration Council website at www.immigrationpolicy.org/just-facts/violence-against-women-act-vawa-provides-protections-immigrant-women-and-victims-crime.

OTHER IMMIGRATION FORMS

Other immigration forms you may need to file include:

- *I-130, Petition for Alien Relative:* When filed by a U.S. citizen or lawful permanent resident, this form is the first step in the process of helping a relative immigrate to the United States. The relative must wait until there is a visa number available before immigrating. For more information, go to uscis.gov/i-130
- *I-864, Affidavit of Support Under Section 213A of the Act:* Most family-based immigrants and some employment-based immigrants are required to file this form to demonstrate that they have sufficient means to support themselves and won't be dependent upon the U.S. government for support. The form can be found at uscis.gov/i-864.
- *I-765, Application for Employment Authorization:* Eligible aliens who are in the United States temporarily and wish to work need to file this document. It is available at uscis.gov/i-765.

There are literally dozens of different forms and nonimmigrant visas available, both for those who are seeking permanent residency status and those who wish to visit our great country. You can see a list at travel.state.gov/visa/

temp/types/types_1286.html. Also, this section is just an overview of the typical forms you might encounter on your way to permanent residency. For more information about your particular situation, go to the U.S. Citizenship and Immigration Services website at uscis.gov.

Citizenship Best Practices

Now that you've decided to become a permanent resident of America or Canada, you should learn more about your new country while respecting the customs of your homeland. Here are some suggestions on how to "meet" your new homeland:

- *Take a course in American or Canadian history.* You can find such courses through adult education programs and online.
- *Improve your English (or French) language skills.* Listen to the radio, watch TV, read signs, and otherwise expose yourself continually to written and spoken English.
- *Read the U.S. Constitution.* It's a great way to understand the many rights and responsibilities of American citizens.
- *Learn about American and Canadian culture while embracing your own.* Blending into your new country doesn't mean you have to give up your heritage. Celebrate them both.
- *Write a "Letter to the Editor" of your local newspaper when you disagree with an issue.* Freedom of speech is one of the most cherished rights in North America, so exercise it.
- *Discuss current events over dinner with your family.* Develop a healthy interest in the events that shape your new community and your world, and share that interest with your family.

CANADA

With a population of just over 35 million people and a lot of wide open spaces, Canada offers many opportunities for immigrants who wish to call the "Great White North" home. Following is information on how to make that happen for you and your family. Please note that this is not an all-inclusive list of the steps you must take, but a representation of what you may need to do or which forms you may need to fill out.

The process to enter Canada as an immigrant is by no means easy. There are a number of rigorous qualifications and requirements that you must meet to become a permanent resident and ultimately a citizen some day.

Immigration Eligibility

Canada has several different programs that determine one's immigration eligibility. The categories have different requirements, but at a minimum, every person who wishes to immigrate to Canada must have English- or French-language skills and will be tested to determine whether those skills are sufficient for admission. The major categories include the following:

Federal Skilled Workers (All Provinces and Territories Except Quebec)

These are people who are eligible to become permanent residents because of their ability to contribute to the national economy. In addition to being evaluated on their language skills, skilled workers must qualify based on their education, work experience, and other factors. People with managerial, professional, and technical occupations and trades are most in demand. You'll also need a degree from a Canadian or foreign university, and age plays a part in the decision.

Canada admits a finite number of federal skilled workers each year. For additional information, refer to cic.gc.ca/english/immigrate/skilled/index.asp.

Skilled Trades

People with certain skilled trades may qualify to immigrate. Some of the trades Canada seeks include industrial, maintenance and operation, technical, and manufacturing. For a complete list, visit cic.gc.ca/english/immigrate/trades/apply-who.asp#nocfor.

Quebec-Selected Skilled Workers

Quebec has its own rules concerning people who wish to immigrate. To be considered, you must first apply to the Quebec government for a *Certificat de sélection du Québec* (CSQ). The next step is to apply to become a permanent resident of Canada (discussed later in this chapter). There's a special program available for people from Haiti. More information is available at cic.gc.ca/english/immigrate/quebec/apply-who.asp.

Canadian Experience Class

This category applies to people who have been living in Canada for a while and have acquired the type of skilled work experience approved by the government. However, the government accepts only a finite number of these applications every year. For information, go to cic.gc.ca/english/immigrate/cec/index.asp.

Provincial Nominees

Occasionally, provinces and territories seek people with certain skills, education, and work experience who can make a contribution to the area economy. These folks are then nominated for immigration. To be considered, you must already have good English- or French-language skills. For a list of provinces and territories with links to their websites where you can view the qualifications, see cic.gc.ca/english/immigrate/provincial/apply-who.asp.

Family Sponsorship

Under the Family Class program, a Canadian citizen or permanent resident can sponsor eligible relatives who wish to become permanent residents. These relatives include a conjugal (married) or common-law partner, dependent child (including an adopted child), and others. Additional information may be found at cic.gc.ca/english/immigrate/sponsor/index.asp.

Live-In Caregivers

This immigration class is for individuals who are qualified to care for children, elderly people, or disabled people in private homes. They are required to live in that home while caring for the individual. Applicants need a Labour Market Opinion from the prospective employer, which is a document verifying that a foreign worker is needed to fill the job because a Canadian cannot do it. There are a number of other requirements, as well. See cic.gc.ca/english/work/caregiver/apply-who.asp for more details.

Refugees

This category is for individuals who fear retaliation, persecution, or personal harm in their home country. Refugees living either in or outside Canada may request refugee status. Canada is world-renowned for its role in offering humanitarian aid to refugees, and Canadian citizens and permanent residents may sponsor a refugee. For additional information, see cic.gc.ca/english/refugees/index.asp.

Come to Canada Wizard

If you're not certain which immigration category applies to you, use the Come to Canada Wizard at cic.gc.ca/ctc-vac/cometocanada.asp. It takes ten to fifteen minutes to fill out the questionnaire, after which you'll have a better idea into which category you fall.

Not everyone who wishes to immigrate to Canada is eligible. Some people are considered "inadmissible" under Canada's *Immigration and Refugee Protection Act (IRPA)*. According to Citizenship and Immigration Canada, the reasons why you might be found inadmissible and therefore denied a visa or entry to Canada include one or more of the following:

- reputation as a security risk
- human or international rights violations
- criminality
- organized criminality
- health grounds
- financial reasons
- misrepresentation
- noncompliance with the *Immigration and Refugee Protection Act*
- familial tie to an inadmissible person

For more information, see cic.gc.ca/ctc-vac/cometocanada.asp.

Biometrics

To apply for a visa or work permit (discussed later), you may be required to provide biometrics information, including a photograph and fingerprints. (It usually depends on your country of origin.) Biometrics is used as a way to prevent anyone else from using your identity fraudulently.

Fingerprinting is done at a Visa Application Centre. You'll find a list of centres on the Citizenship and Immigration Canada website at cic.gc.ca/biometrics. You'll place your hands one at a time, then both thumbs together, on a biometrics scanner, which will capture an image of your fingerprints without the messiness of fingerprints taken the old-fashioned way with black printer's ink.

All the personal information you provide, as well as your fingerprints and photograph, will be encrypted (coded) and stored in a secure Government of Canada database to keep it safe and private.

Temporary Resident Visa (IMM 5256)

This is a document that indicates that you have met the requirements for admission to Canada as a temporary resident. It applies to visitors, students, and workers. The visa must be obtained at a Canadian visa office before you leave your home country. You can apply online at cic.gc.ca/english/information/applications/guides/5256ETOC.asp.

Permanent Resident Card (PR Card)

Once you've immigrated successfully to Canada, your next step is to apply for permanent residency. A permanent resident is someone who has been granted permanent resident status, but still is a citizen of a country other than Canada. This can include anyone except someone who is in the country temporarily, like a student or foreign worker.

Refugees fall into a special category. Refugees who resettle in Canada from other countries overseas become permanent residents through either the Government-Assisted Refugee Program or the Private Sponsorship of Refugees Program. However, acceptance as a refugee is not automatic. The Immigration and Refugee Board must approve the refugee's claim first.

Permanent residents enjoy many personal rights. For instance, they can get most of the same social benefits that Canadian citizens are entitled to, including health care coverage. They are permitted to live, work, or study anywhere they wish in the country. They also can apply for citizenship and are protected under both Canadian law and the Canadian Charter of Rights and Freedoms.

To enjoy these rights, permanent residents are required to pay taxes and abide by all federal, provincial, territorial, and municipal laws. There also are some things they *can't* do. Chief among them is that they can't vote or run for public office, and they can't hold certain jobs that require a high-level security clearance. Those rights are reserved for Canadian citizens.

The requirements to qualify for a permanent resident card include having permanent resident status; actually being in Canada; not having been asked to leave the country; and not being a Canadian citizen or a Registered Indian (Canadian citizens don't need the card and First Nations members have different requirements). Most PR cards are valid for five years and should be carried with you at all times.

Some people choose to become permanent residents of Canada and never go on to become citizens. But if you do choose to become a Canadian citizen one day, you must surrender your PR card at the citizenship ceremony, since Canadian citizens don't need such a card. But it's a good trade-off, since at that point you'll be a full citizen of your adopted land.

RECORD OF LANDING

The Record of Landing (Form IMM 1000) documents received on first entering Canada as a legal resident can be obtained only after you become a permanent resident. You should request a copy of this form as soon as you become a legal resident, because you may be required to show it at times. Apply for one at www.canada.immigrationvisaforms.com/us-visa-application-forms/imm-1000-application-pack.

WORK PERMIT

The Canadian government grants many temporary work permits each year to immigrants as a way of addressing labour and skill shortages. You need a work permit for most temporary jobs in Canada, and you usually have to obtain it before you immigrate. Fill out and submit Form IMM 1295, which you can find at cic.gc.ca/english/pdf/kits/forms/IMM5488E.pdf. If you'll be working in Quebec, you'll also need to provide proof of a valid *Certificat d'Acceptation du Québec*. For more information (in French), see immigration-quebec.gouv.qc.ca/en/immigrate-settle/temporary-workers/index.html.

There are a number of jobs that don't require a work permit. Go to cic.

gc.ca/english/work/apply-who-nopermit.asp for an alphabetical list and check it before accepting a job to make sure you're on the right side of immigration law.

Job Hunting Challenges

Immigrants to North America often find it's challenging to find a job. To begin with, the credentials you have acquired in your home country may not be recognized in the United States or Canada. This is especially a problem when it comes to academic degrees, since foreign university requirements differ significantly from those in North America. In addition, previous work experience may not even be enough to help you qualify for a job in your previous field.

It's slightly more difficult to find employment in Canada because fluency in either English or French is required for most professional or trade jobs, and applicants generally are tested to check their proficiency. In addition, many Canadian employers prefer that applicants have Canadian work experience, in part because they are unable to assess foreign work experience.

To prepare you for working in North America, the Canadian government recommends contacting an organization that provides immigrants with job search assistance; networking; volunteering as a way of building your resume; or starting your own business. This is good advice for job hunting on both sides of the border. In addition, in Canada you can apply to the Federal Internship for Newcomers Program, which provides both temporary Canadian work experience and training opportunities that are beneficial for immigrants who are seeking permanent employment.

ATTA'S LESSONS

Upon arriving in America, I immediately experienced a wonderful feeling of optimism.

My first instinct was that I could do anything and that nothing could stop me from accomplishing my lifelong dreams.

Within a week of my arrival in the United States, I came across an ad for a bank teller position. I had never worked for a bank before but I walked into the bank on Market Street with a sense of confidence and asked the manager for the job. I admitted I had no banking experience, but I asked him to give me an opportunity. I was hired as a teller in January 1982 and moved into a management job within five years. I was a senior regional manager within ten years, all because I had had the courage to ask for a chance.

Everyone has wonderful opportunities to build and achieve amazing accomplishments through drive, commitment, and hard work. Key is to not allow fear, doubt, or procrastination to stop you from moving forward.

Chapter 3: Important Personal Documents

As a legal resident, there are a number of documents you need to have and to safeguard carefully. Some of these documents should remain in your immediate possession, while others can be stored in a secure location, like a safe deposit box at the bank, a fireproof box in your home, or a locking file cabinet. This chapter provides a description of the various documents you need for both day-to-day and occasional use.

BIRTH CERTIFICATE

This document is used to prove your identify, age, and citizenship. In North America, it is issued by the state or province in which you were born and is commonly required when you apply for a Social Security card (discussed later), a driver's license, or a passport, as well as when you apply for admission to a college or university, among other things.

If you were born outside North America and your native language is not English, you should have a copy of your native birth certificate translated into English. It should be translated word-for-word and certified to verify its accuracy. In addition to needing this copy for the reasons stated above, you'll also need it if and when you apply for citizenship. The naturalization services in both the United States and Canada will not accept a document that's not in English. Keep a copy of the translated document with your original birth certificate for easy reference.

Be sure to protect the original copy of your birth certificate. Never carry the original with you; instead, make a few photocopies of it, then stash the original in a safe place. You may also wish to purchase a couple of extra certified copies to have on hand in case the need arises. However, don't give those copies out to anyone. In this age of identity theft, passing out a document with your name and birth date on it is like giving thieves the key to your house. The only time you'll be required to produce your birth certificate is in the instances named above or in other specific situations discussed later.

To obtain a birth certificate for a family member born in the United States, contact your local county office of vital records. In Canada, contact your provincial or territorial government. You'll find links to Canadian government offices at this address: servicecanada.gc.ca/eng/subjects/cards/birth_certificate.shtml. All birth certificates are recorded the same way, including those that document births attended by a licensed midwife.

You may find it helpful to create a worksheet with birth information for every member of your family. Include the full name of each person; the birth certificate number; the issue date; the issuing country, city, and state or province; the name and address of the hospital where the birth occurred; and the date of registration. Print copies of this worksheet and store it with your other important papers.

DEATH CERTIFICATE

It's helpful to keep copies of the death certificates of close family members in case proof is needed, like in the case of insurance claims. Contact the local vital records department in the United States or Service Canada in Canada to request a death certificate.

MARRIAGE CERTIFICATE

Marriage certificates are issued by the county clerk, marriage bureau, or other similar office in the United States, and the provincial or territorial government in Canada. Many jurisdictions will allow you to request a copy of a marriage certificate online, so search the internet for information.

As with your birth certificate, you should have a word-for-word translation created if the document is not in English, then have it certified in case you ever have to show it to an official in the United States or Canada.

DRIVER'S LICENSE

Every person who operates a motorized vehicle on a public roadway in North America must have a valid driver's license.

United States

The laws regarding the licensing age for passenger vehicles vary by state, from as young as 16 in most states to up to 21 in the District of Columbia.

All states have a graduated licensing system, meaning drivers earn their license in stages by meeting certain skill and experience requirements. New drivers are required to take a driver's training course (usually consisting of a certain number of hours of classroom instruction) before earning a learner's permit. In the United States, many states issue learner's permits around the age of 15, although the age range is 14 to 16. The next level is the restricted license, which allows a new driver to take the road only when driving with a licensed driver (usually someone who is aged 25 or older). Finally, a full license is granted in some states to drivers as young as 16, but most states make new drivers wait until age 17 to 18.

If you're an adult, you must complete the same driver's training and meet the same graduated license requirements as younger drivers. You also may be able to take your driver's training online, rather than in a classroom. Check with your state's department of motor vehicles or secretary of state for details.

There are various types of driver's licenses based on the kind of driving you do, including a standard operator's license; a chauffer's license (if you drive a bus or other commercial vehicle); a commercial driver's license, or CDL, which is issued to truck drivers and long-distance haulers who drive 18-wheel trucks; a motorcycle endorsement, and others. See dmv.org for more information by state.

You have to qualify for all these types of licenses, usually by taking both a written and a road test, and completing a vision screening. In the case of a CDL, you also must take an alcohol and drug test. Check with your local licensing authority for details on when and where.

Canada

In Canada, all provinces and territories, except Nunavut have graduated driver's licenses, which are issued through provincial and territorial offices. They have different names depending on where they're issued. For instance, Ontario issues a G license, while Alberta's licenses are numbered Class 1 through 7. Go to servicecanada.gc.ca and search for "driver's license" to find clickable links to provincial and territorial websites where you can find all the information you need.

It's a little easier to get a license in Nunavut, where there are only two steps in the process. You'll earn a Class 7 license after you pass the learner's permit written test, at which point you can immediately take a road test and get the Class 5 full license. There's no waiting period between tests.

Everywhere else in Canada there are a number of different license categories. Here, for instance, is a list of the various licenses available in Alberta:

- Class 1: professional, any vehicle
- Class 2: professional, bus
- Class 3: 3-axle plus
- Class 4: professional, taxi, ambulance
- Class 5: 2-axle, cars, light trucks, motor homes or mopeds
- Class 6: motorcycle and moped
- Class 7: learners, 2-axel and motorcycle and moped

ENHANCED DRIVER'S LICENSE

Four U.S. states and four Canadian provinces offer what's known as an enhanced driver's license, which is identification that allows you to cross the U.S.-Canadian border by land or water without a passport. An enhanced license is less expensive and much smaller than a passport; it's the size of a standard driver's license and will fit into your wallet. If you travel from the United States to Canada or vice versa by air, you will still need a passport.

In the United States, residents of Michigan, New York, Vermont, and Washington are eligible for an enhanced license. In Canada, enhanced licenses are available to residents of British Columbia, Manitoba, Ontario, and Quebec.

MATERIALS AND TESTS IN LANGUAGES OTHER THAN ENGLISH

Some states and all Canadian provinces offer educational materials and tests in languages other than English. You may be able to print them directly from the secretary of state or department of motor vehicles' website, or you may have to visit these offices in person. Go online or call your local office for information. However, your road test may be administered by a person who speaks only English. (Exceptions to the rule may include the southern and western states, where Spanish is commonly spoken as a second language, and in francophone Quebec.) Don't be nervous if you can't understand everything the examiner says. If you studied your instructional materials well and practiced before the test, you should do fine.

INTERNATIONAL DRIVING PERMIT

An international driving permit is a translation of your foreign driver's license into English. Residents of a foreign country that signed the 1949 United Nations Convention on Road Traffic (and its successor in 1968) may drive in the United States and Canada with a valid International Driving Permit and their home country license. It's also recognized by some other countries that were not signatories of the act. For a list of the nations that signed, see www.michigan.gov/documents/Reciprocity_Agreements_and_Underlying_Authority_170819_7.pdf.

Generally speaking, you can use your foreign driver's license for a year in North America. Getting a new license in your new state, province, or territory should be a priority. Americans and Canadians may drive in both countries using their state, provincial, or territorial license. An international driving permit is not necessary. However, you do need a passport, enhanced driver's license, or identification card to enter either country.

PERSONAL IDENTIFICATION CARD

UNITED STATES

If you don't plan to drive, you should apply for a personal identification card (IC), nondriver identification card, or other similar state identification card instead. This card may be presented as official proof of identify when boarding an aircraft, opening a bank account, making a credit card purchase, and other situations. The card is issued by the state, the same way a driver's license is issued. In fact, the card looks a lot like a driver's license, with a unique identification number, a photograph, and the name and address of the individual carrying it. Also like a driver's license, a personal identification card has an expiration date. An enhanced version of the IC is available in Michigan, New York, Vermont, and Washington states, as described above.

You may apply for an IC at your local department of motor vehicles or other licensing authority. Typically you will be required to produce two or three pieces of identification to obtain it, such as your Social Security card, proof of citizenship or naturalization, birth certificate, passport, income tax documents, military identification card, and other materials. Generally, if you are not a citizen of the country in which you live, you can still obtain an IC by showing proof of residency. Acceptable forms of proof are utility bills, a state certificate of title for a motorized vehicle, a mortgage statement for your residence, a property tax bill, and other documents. Again, check with your local department of motor vehicles for a complete list.

CANADA

The Canadian equivalent of the personal identification card is known by different names. For instance, in Ontario, it's called the Ontario Photo Card; in Prince Edward Island, it's the Voluntary ID. Quebec doesn't have a nondriver photo identification card at all. Contact your providence or territory for information on how to obtain the card.

PASSPORT

UNITED STATES

If you expect to travel internationally, including to and from the United States by road and by air, you will need a passport. Obviously, if you are a citizen of a country outside North America, you will continue to use the passport from your native land. But if your children were born in the United States, they must have their own U.S. passport (this includes infants). In addition, if and when you decide to seek citizenship, you will have to apply for a U.S. passport, something that is often done as part of the naturalization process.

U.S. passports are issued by the Department of State. There are ten passport agencies where you can apply in person, including in Arkansas, Buffalo (New York), Colorado, Detroit, El Paso (Texas), Honolulu, Minneapolis, San Diego, Seattle, and Vermont. You'll have to pay an additional expedited delivery fee if you apply in person at any of these agencies.

The State Department has also designated other facilities to accept passport applications on its behalf. They include certain post offices, clerks of court, public libraries, and other state, county, township, and municipal government offices. To find one close to you, use the passport acceptance facility search page at iafdb.travel.state.gov/. You won't pay the expedited service fee at these facilities unless you want to receive your passport faster than normal.

A U.S. passport is good for ten years or five years for minors. As mentioned earlier, if you will be entering the United States and Canada, as well as Mexico, the Caribbean, and Bermuda only by land or sea, you might prefer the less expensive passport card instead. However, the passport card cannot be used for international air travel.

It usually takes four to six weeks during off-peak times to receive your passport or passport card by mail. Paying extra to expedite (rush) delivery will cut the time down to about two weeks.

CANADA

Passport Canada issues Canadian passports. There are four different types based on residency status. They include passports for a Canadian living in Canada, a Canadian living in the United States, a Canadian living abroad, and a non-Canadian living in Canada. (The latter is specifically for refugees, protected and stateless persons, and permanent residents of fewer than three years who don't qualify for a national passport for some reason.) Every Canadian citizen or resident who travels abroad, including children and infants, must have his or her own passport.

Several different types of federal, provincial/territorial/state, and municipal authority identification must be shown to acquire a new passport in Canada. Passports are issued to adults for a period of five or ten years, while passports issued to children under the age of sixteen are good for five years. For more information, visit ppt.gc.ca/index.aspx.

When you receive your passport, sign your full name in ink. You may wish to fill in the emergency contact information in pencil so it can be erased and changed if you decided to name someone else as your contact. Keep your passport in a safe place when you're not using it.

IMMIGRATION PAPERS

UNITED STATES

As you know, there are dozens of documents required before you emigrate to and after you land in the United States. All these forms are available free of charge at the U.S. Citizenship and Immigration Services (USCIS) website at uscis.gov/forms. Some of the forms that you may have filled out already or will need to fill out in the future include:

- I-485: Application to Register Permanent Residence or Adjust Status (Green Card)
- I-94: Arrival/Departure Form
- I-864: Affidavit of Support under Section 213A of the Act
- I-765: Application for Employment Authorization
- I-9: Employment Eligibility Verification
- 1-130: Petition for Alien Relative
- DS Visa and Passport Forms

These forms provide a record of your journey from your homeland to your new country and should be retained indefinitely. As with other records discussed here, you should make copies of these forms and file a complete set in a safe place like a safe deposit box. For more information about immigration documents, go to uscis.gov.

CANADA

Citizenship and Immigration Canada is the keeper of the documents required to become a Canadian citizen or resident. The main document you must complete is the Application for a Permanent Resident (PR) card. In addition, you'll have to choose from among nine different applications that describe your personal situation, each of which includes numerous forms. The application packages include the following:

- Federal skilled workers application package
- Federal skilled trades program application package
- Quebec-selected skilled workers application package

- Canadian experience class application package
- Investors, entrepreneurs, and self-employed application package
- Family sponsorship application package
- Provincial nominees application package
- Live-in caregivers application package
- Refugees application package

Information about each of these application packages can be found at cic. gc.ca/english/immigrate/apply.asp. If you're not sure which program to apply for, visit "Come to Canada" at cic.gc.ca/ctc-vac/cometocanada.asp for more information.

NATURALIZATION PAPERS

UNITED STATES

Your naturalization papers will be among your most important possessions. As soon as you are eligible for citizenship, you can fill out N-400, the first form on the road to citizenship. You'll need to send two identical color photographs (passport photos) and a copy of your Permanent Resident Card with your application.

If you are a U.S. citizen parent of a foreign-born child (either one you or your wife/partner delivered or one you adopted), or you're the foreign-born child of American parents, you'll need to file form N-600, Application for Certificate of Citizenship, to establish citizenship status. See uscis.gov/n-600 for more information.

Your naturalization papers are one-time documents that must be carefully safeguarded. Since the only time you'll need to show these papers is if you apply for a passport, you should make copies of the original papers, then place them in a safe deposit box or a fireproof file cabinet. It's also helpful to maintain a record of all of your family members' papers on a single spreadsheet. Be sure to include information like the full legal name that appears in the document, the certificate number, and the issue date. As with other important papers, file the worksheet with the rest of your copies.

CANADA

The application form for Canadian citizenship is called—not surprisingly—Application for Canadian Citizenship: Adults. If you're filing for citizenship for children under the age of eighteen, you'll complete the Application for Canadian Citizenship: Minors form.

Create a worksheet that captures the main information from the naturalization papers for each member in your family, including the certificate number and issue date. Then keep copies of the worksheet along with your other important papers. Your approved naturalization papers are precious—keep them safe.

SOCIAL SECURITY CARD

UNITED STATES

Every person who lives legally in the United States must have a Social Security Number, including U.S. citizens, permanent residents, noncitizens who are authorized to work in the United States, and children. The nine-digit number that appears on an official Social Security card is unique to you. You'll use it when filling out employment paperwork and income tax returns, and applying for a credit card, car loan, or government benefits. You'll also need it when applying for city, county, and state welfare benefits. Finally, your children need their own Social Security number so you can claim them as dependents on your income tax returns and they will be eligible for free and low-cost Medicaid health insurance, if needed.

If you don't have a Social Security card yet and you're eligible, go to your nearest Social Security office (find one at secure.ssa.gov/ICON) or fill out the paperwork you'll find at ssa.gov/online/ss-5.pdf and mail it in. When applying, you're required to provide proof of identity and citizenship, or immigration status. Documents that are acceptable include a certified original copy of your birth certificate, your passport, or your certificate of naturalization, among others. A noncitizen will need current, unexpired U.S. immigration papers and a foreign passport when applying. These documents will be returned to you after your application is processed.

If you have a baby while living in the United States, you should apply for a Social Security number for your child right after birth. The hospital can help you with the paperwork.

Despite the fact that your Social Security card is so important, you won't have to show it very often. For this reason, you shouldn't carry it with you. Rather, protect it by tucking it away somewhere safe, like a locking file box or safe deposit box.

CANADA

Canada's personal identification card is known as the Social Insurance Number (SIN) card. Every citizen born in Canada, Registered Indian, Canadian citizen born outside Canada, and permanent and temporary resident should have this card. It has a nine-digit identification number and is needed to work in Canada or receive government benefits and services.

Applications for a SIN card are accepted at Service Canada Centres, which you can find by searching for "social insurance number" at servicecanada.gc.ca. You'll need to bring identity documents like your birth certificate and/or passport when you apply.

A newborn registration service is available for children born in Alberta, British Columbia, Manitoba, Nova Scotia, Ontario, Prince Edward Island, Quebec, and Newfoundland and Labrador. If you live in one of the provinces or territories not on this list, application is made by mail. Go to servicecanada.gc.ca/eng/sin/apply/how.shtml for instructions on how to apply.

HEALTH INSURANCE CARD

Health insurance companies commonly issue identification cards to their policy holders. You'll definitely want to carry this card with you at all times, since you usually have to show it when you use health care services, from doctor's appointments to medical tests, and when you pick up prescriptions. Even so, make a couple of copies of your card and keep them with the other personal papers mentioned earlier.

CREDIT CARDS

Also known as bank cards, credit cards are used to make face-to-face and online purchases. In addition to having a long (often 16-digit) number on their face, most cards also have an expiration date, and a number on the back known as the CVV, CSC, or other acronym. This number is unique to the card and is a security feature intended to prevent fraudulent use of your card. The stripe on the back contains encoded information like your card number, name, and address.

Naturally, you'll need to carry your cards with you if you wish to make purchases in stores and other venues. When using the card, carefully watch the clerk who swipes it to make sure it's used only for the purchase you're authorizing. At a gas station, make sure the card swiper is firmly attached to the gas pump, since there have been incidents where scammers have installed temporary card swipers as a way to steal card numbers and other information. After making a purchase, safeguard your card by placing it securely in your wallet or a zippered compartment of your purse.

Bank cards use technology known as radio frequency identification (RFID) on smartcards to encrypt your credit card and to store personal information like your name and card number in the stripe on the back of the card. You'll know if your credit card is a smartcard if it has a horn-shaped symbol on its face in the upper corner. The problem with this technology is that equipment exists that allows scammers to walk to within a few feet of you and capture that information using an RFID reader. They'll then either use your card themselves to make purchases or sell your information to someone else who will use the card. Protect yourself from these scammers by putting each credit card into a Tyvek sleeve, which is an inexpensive sheath that covers your card and blocks RFID signals. You also can purchase an RFID wallet that will protect all your cards at the same time.

MEDICAL RECORDS

Medical information is considered private, and there's even a U.S. law called the *Health Insurance Portability and Accountability Act* (HIPAA) that protects you against discrimination due to medical conditions. It also protects your privacy. So you'll want to do the same by safeguarding your medical records.

Do keep copies of documentation from medical and dental visits for at least three years, or scan them and shred the original document.

PROTECTING AGAINST IDENTITY THEFT

All the personal documents described in this chapter share one thing in common: they can be stolen and used to commit crimes like fraud and identity theft. Identity theft is a growing problem worldwide. In 2012, around 12.6 million people were victims of identity theft in the United States alone, according to a survey by Javelin Strategy and Research. All a thief needs to impersonate you and open accounts in your name, access your bank accounts, or make fake-but-convincing-looking documents with your name on them is your full legal name, your date of birth, and your Social Security or Social Insurance number.

Identity theft can cost you a great deal of money, time, and stress, and recovering from the effects of the crime isn't easy. At best, it can take years to unravel the damage caused by an identity thief; at worst, it can destroy your credit and ruin your good name. So in addition to filing important papers away in a secure location, as discussed earlier, here are some general tips that can help you avoid identity theft and other forms of fraud:

- *Scan important documents and save them to a flash drive that is used only for that purpose.* (Don't save the information on your hard drive, because it can be hacked when you're on the internet.) Password-protect the file so only you know how to access it. Just remember to memorize or write the password down in a secure location so you can open the file again when you need to.
- *Never give out personal information to anyone who calls you, sends you a letter through the mail, or emails you, no matter how convincing the person is or how much he or she offers you.* Check the person's credentials or call the company he or she represents back to make sure it's legitimate.
- *Limit the number of personal items you carry with you when you leave the house.* Naturally, you need your driver's license or personal ID card, as well as a credit or debit card if you're going shopping. Leave all the others you have at home for safekeeping.
- *Limit the number of credit cards you apply for.* Accumulating lots of cards is not a contest; it's a way to increase your odds of being ripped off, as

someone could take the cards out of your mailbox, steal your wallet or purse, or otherwise relieve you of your charge cards.

- *Never carry your Social Security or Social Identification card with you, but do memorize the number in case you need it.* When you're asked for your number when making a transaction, ask if you can provide a different form of identification, like your driver's license. The answer will probably be no, but it's worth asking to keep your number private.
- *Shred financial documents you don't need any more, if they contain personal information.* Never just toss these documents into the trash or a dumpster. Identity thieves often find most of the personal information they need in exactly those places.
- *Remove yourself from the mailing lists of companies that send preapproved credit card offers so they don't fall into the wrong hands (that is, anyone's but yours).* In the United States, call (888) 567-8688 or visit the Consumer Credit Reporting Industry website at optoutprescreen.com[EFS1].
- *Reduce the amount of junk mail you receive by filling out the form found at dmachoice.org or Canada Post's opt-out site* at canadapost.ca/cpo/mc/personal/support/helpcentre/others/opt_out.jsf. It won't completely stop unwanted mail, but it should make a pretty good dent in it.
- *Put all your phones on the National Do Not Call Registry to reduce unwanted telemarketing calls.* In the United States, you can sign up at fcc.gov; in Canada, go lnnte-dncl.gc.ca.
- *Never open email attachments from someone you don't know.* The link could load a virus onto your computer, or take you to a website that looks legitimate but is a front for criminal activity. In fact, in general, you might not want to open attachments at all, since hackers know how to highjack the address books of unsuspecting people, then send emails to everyone in the address book. As a result, you could receive an email from someone you know, then unleash a virus on your poor, unsuspecting computer when you click the link.

For additional information about identify theft, see the Federal Trade Commission Identity Theft Center at ftc.gov. Canadians should view the Royal Canadian Mounted Police's identify theft resources at rcmp-grc.gc.ca.

ATTA'S LESSONS

One of my greatest frustrations during my early years in America was a lack of information about some of the most ordinary day-to-day things. The situation was even worse after my big family arrived. I had so many questions, like what should I do in case of emergency or death of a loved one? Who should I call? It was truly shocking to realize that I didn't know what to do in my new land.

Eventually I created a family planner, kind of like an operations manual. It covered everything the family needed to know, from how to react in a life-threatening situation (like a natural disaster or a health crisis), to where to go for medical help, and even where to go to have fun. I shared my "manual" with the whole family.

Next, I organized our personal documents. I had them translated and figured out where to store them to keep them safe. That way, if we ever needed them, everything would be accessible and ready to use. This made me feel a lot more confident that I was in control of my life.

You should do the same thing. You'll be amazed by how much better you feel knowing you have a plan for every situation.

Family Resource Contact Information

	Name	Phone	Address
Health Insurance			
Health Insurance			
Primary Physician			
Specialist			
Specialist			
Hospital			
Hospital (trauma)			
Pharmacy			
Dental Insurance			
Dental Insurance			
Dentist			
School 1			
School 2			
School 3			
College 1			
College 2			
Post Office			
UPS Store			
FedEx			
Other			
Bank 1			
Bank 2			
Credit Union			
Car Insurance co.			
Home Insurance co.			
Grocery Store			
Library			

Utilities

Utility	Name	Phone	Address
Gas			
Electric			
Water / Hydro			
Trash Collection			
Recycling			
Cable TV / Internet			
Phone			
Cell Phone			
Special Services			
Plumber			
Electrician			
Handyman			
Car Mechanic			

Chapter 4: Becoming a Citizen

If you have been in North America for any length of time, you know that both the United States and Canada offer many freedoms and benefits that you may not have had in your homeland. At some point in your residency here, you may decide that you wish to become a citizen of one of these great lands. Naturally, there are specific requirements you must meet and processes you must follow on the road to citizenship. This chapter outlines all of them for you. Much of the information is presented in list form so you can use this book as a step-by-step guide for becoming a citizen of your new country.

The information for each country is presented in its own section, and most of the information comes directly from the U.S. Citizenship and Immigration Services, and the Citizenship and Immigration Canada websites.

UNITED STATES

The Value of Citizenship

The United States is a nation of immigrants. While the largest wave of immigration occurred in the period from 1881 to 1920, when 23 million people immigrated here, throughout her history America has always welcomed people from other nations who wished to make a new life for themselves here. In fact, the sculptor of the State of Liberty famously inscribed its base with words from a poem by Emma Lazarus: "Give me your tired, your poor, your huddled masses yearning to breathe free." The inscription has come to mean that people of all ethnicities, nationalities, race, color, and age are welcome here. Their contributions are valued and contribute much toward making America a great place to live and raise a family.

When you make that momentous decision to seek American citizenship, you'll join the ranks of many famous people—and the not-so-famous—who have walked that path and added to America's rich heritage. In fact, it's one of the most important decisions you'll make in your lifetime. You can use the information and numerous resources that follow to smooth the way.

Rights and Benefits of Citizenship

- Right to vote, which allows you to have a voice in the government—the embodiment of the expression of "government of the people, by the people, for the people," as found in the *Gettysburg Address* by Abraham Lincoln
- Right to hold an elected office
- Eligibility for federal employment in virtually any position except president and vice president, whom the U.S. Constitution states must be native-born citizens
- Right to public education, scholarships, and grants
- Ability to obtain citizenship for children born abroad
- Ability to sponsor family members who wish to join you in the United States
- Right to travel with an American passport, which allows you to get assistance from the American government when abroad
- Protection from deportation or expulsion from the country against your will
- Access to public assistance

Responsibilities of Citizenship

As an American citizen, you agree to do the following:

- Give up all prior allegiance to any other nation or sovereignty
- Swear allegiance to the United States
- Support and defend the Constitution and the laws of the United States
- Serve the country when required
- Register and vote in elections
- Serve on a jury in a court of law when called

You'll swear to these conditions of citizenship when you take the oath that makes you an American citizen. You'll read about the oath and ceremony later in this chapter.

Eligibility Requirements for Individuals

- Be 18 or older at the time of filing
- Be a green card holder for at least five years immediately preceding the date of filing the Form N-400, Application for Naturalization
- Have lived within the state, or USCIS district with jurisdiction over your place of residence, for at least three months prior to the date of filing the application
- Have continuous residence in the United States as a green card holder for at least five years immediately preceding the date of filing the application
- Be physically present in the United States for at least 30 months out of the five years immediately preceding the date of filing the application
- Reside continuously within the United States from the date of application for naturalization up to the time of naturalization
- Be able to read, write, and speak basic English, and have knowledge and an understanding of U.S. history and government (civics)
- Be a person of good moral character, attached to the principles of the Constitution of the United States, and well-disposed to the good order and happiness of the United States during all relevant periods under the law

Other Paths to Eligibility

- *You're a green card holder married to a U.S. citizen.* If you've been a permanent resident (green card holder) for at least three years, have been living as the married spouse of the same U.S. citizen for at least three years, and you meet all other eligibility requirements, you are eligible for U.S. citizenship.
- *You're a military member and green card holder.* Members of the U.S. Armed Forces (U.S. Army, Navy, Air Force, Marine Corps, Coast Guard, and certain components of the National Guard and the Selected Reserve of the Ready Reserve) who have served honorably are eligible for naturalization under Section 328 or 329 of the *Immigration and Nationality Act*. Under this act, the general requirements for naturalization may be waived. Your spouse and children may also be eligible for expedited citizenship. See uscis.gov/military/

citizenship-military-personnel-family-members/citizenship-spouses-and-children-military-members for more information.

Special Circumstances for Children Born Outside the U.S.

According to U.S. Citizenship and Immigration Services:

United States laws allow for children to acquire U.S. citizenship other than through birth in the United States. Persons who were born outside of the United States to a U.S. citizen parent or parents may acquire or derive U.S. citizenship at birth. Persons may also acquire citizenship after birth, but before the age of 18, through their U.S. citizen parents ... The law in effect at the time of birth determines whether someone born outside the United States to a U.S. citizen parent or parents is a U.S. citizen at birth. In general, these laws require a combination of at least one parent being a U.S. citizen when the child was born and having lived in the United States for a period of time. In addition, children born abroad may become U.S. citizens after birth.

Source: Citizenship & Naturalization, Part H: Children of U.S. Citizens

What this means to you is that if you're already an American citizen and your child is born outside the United States, he or she may already be a citizen. If this is the case, you must apply for a Certificate of Citizenship using Form N-600. You can do this for your child. See uscis.gov/n-600 for eligibility requirements and instructions.

Please note that the information here may not apply to every person. For additional information about these requirements, please visit uscis.gov/citizenship. Information on each of these requirements is also available in *A Guide to Naturalization* , available at uscis.gov/natzguide. In addition, be sure to confirm your eligibility before applying for citizenship, because the USCIS will not refund fees if you're ineligible and your application is turned down.

Dual Citizenship

It is possible to be a citizen of the United States and your home country at the same time. Known as dual citizenship or dual nationality, dual citizenship means you owe allegiance to both countries, you must obey the laws of both countries, and you can carry the passport of both countries. Use of the foreign passport doesn't endanger your American citizenship in any way.

Under U.S. law, you're not required to choose one nationality over the other. However, the U.S. government doesn't encourage dual nationality because it can cause problems. For example, claims of the second country on dual nationals may conflict with U.S. law. It may also limit the U.S. government's ability to provide assistance if you need help while you're abroad.

Once you become an American citizen, you must use your U.S. passport to leave or enter the United States. Your native country may also require you to use its passport to enter and leave, so be sure to check the requirements before traveling.

Applying for Citizenship

Once you've determined you're eligible to apply for naturalization, you must complete and file Form N-400, Application for Naturalization. For assistance during the application process, refer to the USCIS's *Guide to Naturalization* at: www.uscis.gov/us-citizenship/citizenship-through-naturalization/guide-naturalization.

Required Documents

The following documents must be submitted with the N-400 application:

- *A photocopy of both sides of your Permanent Resident Card (green card).* If you have lost the card, you must submit Form I-90, Application to Replace Permanent Resident Card, then submit a photocopy of the form with your application.
- *Two identical color photographs with your name and Alien Registration Number (A-Number) written lightly in pencil on the back of each photo.* For details about the photo requirements, see the instructions in Form N-400. If your religion requires you to wear a head covering, your facial features must still be exposed in the photo for purposes of identification.
- *A check or money order for the application fee and the biometrics (fingerprinting) services fee (see Form M-479, Current Naturalization Fees, for the amount).*

Applicants seventy-five years of age or older are exempt from finger-printing and the biometrics services fee. Write your A-Number on the back of the check or money order. Fingerprinting is also discussed in Chapter 2 and later in this chapter.

If you are applying for naturalization on the basis of marriage to a U.S. citizen, send the following four items with your application:

1. Evidence that your spouse has been a U.S. citizen for the last three years:
   a. birth certificate (if your spouse has never lost citizenship since birth); or
   b. Certificate of Naturalization; or
   c. Certificate of Citizenship; or
   d. the inside of the front cover and signature page of your spouse's current U.S. passport; or
   e. Form FS-240, Report of Birth Abroad of a Citizen of the United States of America; and
2. Your current marriage certificate
3. Proof of termination of all prior marriages of your spouse, including divorce decree(s), annulment(s), or death certificate(s)
4. Documents referring to you and your spouse:
   a. tax returns, bank accounts, leases, mortgages, or birth certificates of children; or
   b. Internal Revenue Service (IRS)-certified copies of the income tax forms that you have both filed for the past three years; and an
   c. IRS tax return transcript for the last three years

If you are currently in the U.S. military service and are seeking citizenship based on that service, send a completed original Form N-426, Request for Certification of Military or Naval Service.

If you have taken any trip outside the United States that lasted six months or more since becoming a lawful permanent resident, send evidence that you (and your family) continued to live, work, and/or keep ties to the United States, such as:

- an IRS tax return "transcript" or an IRS-certified tax return listing tax information for the last five years (or for the last three years if you are applying on the basis of marriage to a U.S. citizen)

• rent or mortgage payments and pay stubs   *Source: USCIS*

To find out where to submit your N-400 and supporting documents, go to uscis.gov/n-400.

Fingerprinting (Biometrics)

The USCIS requires those who are applying for citizenship to be fingerprinted. This is done so the FBI can conduct a criminal background investigation on you. You must be fingerprinted at an authorized fingerprint site. You can find a list of authorized application support centers at egov.uscis.gov/crisgwi/go?action=offices.type&OfficeLocator.office_type=ASC.

The Naturalization Test

Most naturalization applicants are required to take a test on English and civics (U.S. history and government). The English test covers speaking, reading, and writing skills, while the civics test asks one hundred questions. During your naturalization interview, you'll be asked up to ten questions from the civics questions list, and you must answer at least six correctly to pass.

The USCIS's Citizenship Resource Center has many free resources that will help you study for the test. Go to uscis.gov/citizenship/learners for practice questions, videos, and printed and audio materials. Some of the materials are available in other languages. If you prefer to take a face-to-face citizenship class, go to the Literacy Information and Communication System site at literacydirectory.org/ and type in your ZIP code to find a class near you.

If You Don't Pass

The USCIS wants you to be successful and will allow you to retake the test if you fail your initial interview. You'll be retested only on the portion of the test that you failed (either English or civics). You'll receive details about when to retake the test at your interview.

Exemptions from English and Civics Requirements

There are some exemptions from the English and civics test requirement.

For information, go to:
www.uscis.gov/us-citizenship/citizenship-through-naturalization/
exceptions-accommodations.

THE OATH CEREMONY

Once you've passed the test, the final step in the naturalization process is the oath ceremony. During this ceremony, you will take the Oath of Allegiance, which is your promise to the government and the people of the United States that you will do the following:

- support and defend the Constitution and the laws of the United States against all enemies
- support, defend, and obey the laws of the United States
- swear allegiance to the United States
- serve the United States, if required, in times of war or national emergency (you may be allowed to serve in the military or help U.S. military efforts in some capacity)
- give up any prior allegiances to other countries

Another thing you're promising is that you will serve on a jury if called. Jury summons are issued by courts at the local; county, parish, and borough; and federal levels, and American citizens are required by law to serve when called upon. Failure to report for jury duty may result in a fine, jail time, or both. You may be able to get an exemption from jury duty if you are not fluent in English. But you should look at jury duty as a privilege of citizenship and serve with honor and pride.

While not a legal requirement, being an American citizen also means being tolerant of others. As a melting pot comprising many different cultures, America is a nation that embraces people of all ethnicities, backgrounds, and customs, and her citizens need to be tolerant of others who are different from themselves.

THE NATURALIZATION OATH OF ALLEGIANCE TO THE UNITED STATES OF AMERICA

I hereby declare, on oath, that I absolutely and entirely renounce and abjure all allegiance and fidelity to any foreign prince, potentate, state, or sovereignty, of whom or which I have heretofore been a subject or citizen; that I will support and defend the Constitution and laws of the United States of America against all enemies, foreign and domestic; that I will bear true faith and allegiance to the same; that I will bear arms on behalf of the United States when required by the law; that I will perform noncombatant service in the Armed Forces of the United States when required by the law; that I will perform work of national importance under civilian direction when required by the law; and that I take this obligation freely, without any mental reservation or purpose of evasion; so help me God.

OTHER USEFUL INFORMATION

NATIONAL LANGUAGE

Strangely, the United States doesn't have an official language, although English is the most commonly spoken, or *de facto*, language. Derived from the King's English, or the language spoken in Great Britain, Americans speak their own version called "American English." Attempts to make English the national language have failed in Congress many times due to constitutional challenges.

NATIONAL ANTHEM

"The Star Spangled Banner," written by Francis Scott Key in 1814:

> Oh, say can you see by the dawn's early light
> What so proudly we hailed at the twilight's last gleaming?
> Whose broad stripes and bright stars thru the perilous fight,
> O'er the ramparts we watched were so gallantly streaming?
> And the rocket's red glare, the bombs bursting in air,
> Gave proof through the night that our flag was still there.
> Oh, say does that star-spangled banner yet wave
> O'er the land of the free and the home of the brave?
>
> On the shore, dimly seen through the mists of the deep,
> Where the foe's haughty host in dread silence reposes,

What is that which the breeze, o'er the towering steep,
As it fitfully blows, half conceals, half discloses?
Now it catches the gleam of the morning's first beam,
In full glory reflected now shines in the stream:
'Tis the star-spangled banner! Oh long may it wave
O'er the land of the free and the home of the brave!

And where is that band who so vauntingly swore
That the havoc of war and the battle's confusion,
A home and a country should leave us no more!
Their blood has washed out their foul footsteps' pollution.
No refuge could save the hireling and slave
From the terror of flight, or the gloom of the grave:
And the star-spangled banner in triumph doth wave
O'er the land of the free and the home of the brave!

Oh! thus be it ever, when freemen shall stand
Between their loved home and the war's desolation!
Blest with victory and peace, may the Heav'n rescued land
Praise the Power that hath made and preserved us a nation!
Then conquer we must, when our cause it is just,
And this be our motto: "In God is our trust."
And the star-spangled banner in triumph shall wave
O'er the land of the free and the home of the brave!

NATIONAL SYMBOLS

- The U.S. Flag (50 stars on a field of blue; 13 stripes)
- The Great Seal of the United States
- The Bald Eagle
- The Liberty Bell
- The Statue of Liberty
- Mount Rushmore National Memorial
- The White House
- The U.S. Capitol
- The Lincoln Memorial

National Holidays

- New Year's Day: January 1
- Martin Luther King Day: Third Monday in January
- George Washington's and Abraham Lincoln's Birthday: Third Monday of February (celebrated together, although their birthdays are February 12 (Lincoln) and February 22 (Washington)
- Memorial Day: Last Monday of May
- Independence Day: July 4
- Labor Day: First Monday of September
- Columbus Day: Second Monday in October
- Veterans Day: November 11
- Thanksgiving Day: Fourth Thursday in November
- Christmas Day: December 25

Other Celebrations and Observances

While not federal holidays, the following observances are celebrated unofficially in the United States:

- Groundhog Day: February 2
- Valentine's Day: February 14
- Earth Day: April 22
- Arbor Day: Last Friday in April
- Mother's Day: Second Sunday of May
- Flag Day: June 14
- Father's Day: Third Sunday of June
- Patriot Day: September 11
- Halloween: October 31
- Pearl Harbor Day: December 7

To learn the meaning behind these holidays and other observances, go to usa.gov/citizens/holidays.shtml.

Ethnic and Religious Holidays

Various ethnic and religious groups in America celebrate days with special meaning to them, even though these are not national holidays. For example, Christians celebrate the resurrection of Jesus Christ on Easter Sunday; Jews observe their High Holy Days in September; Muslims celebrate Ramadan; and African Americans celebrate Kwanzaa. This is not a complete list; there are too many to list them all here.

CANADA

THE VALUE OF CITIZENSHIP

There are many benefits to becoming a Canadian citizen; chief among them is the fact that you will have many precious rights and freedoms. This may be one reason why the process to become Canadian is fairly rigorous. There are quite a few things you have to do and a lot you must know before you can take the citizenship test. But in the end, it will be worth the effort.

What unites many of the people who call Canada home is a personal history that includes immigration. Statistics Canada says that in a recent year, 81.5 percent of first-generation Canadians reported a single ethnic origin. The largest groups of immigrants in the country today include English, French, Scottish, Irish, and German; other groups that surpass one million people include Italians, Chinese, First Nations (North American Indians), Ukrainian, and East Indian, to name just a few.

RIGHTS AND BENEFITS OF CITIZENSHIP

According to Immigration and Citizenship Canada, Canadian citizens enjoy personal rights that date back nearly eight hundred years to the 1215 signing of the *Magna Carta*. This document, which is also known as the *Great Charter of Freedoms*, guarantees the following:

- Freedom of conscience and religion
- Freedom of thought, belief, opinion, and expression, including freedom of speech and of the press
- Freedom of peaceful assembly
- Freedom of association
- *Habeas corpus* (the right to challenge unlawful detention by the state)

The Canadian government gave these rights constitutional protection in 1982, when the *Canadian Charter of Rights and Freedoms* was added to the constitution. This document confirms that Canadians have the following:

- The right to live and work anywhere they choose in Canada
- The right to enter and leave the country freely
- Aboriginal peoples' rights (that the rights guaranteed in the Charter will not adversely affect any treaty or other rights or freedoms of Aboriginal people)
- Official language rights and minority language educational rights (English and French have equal status in Parliament and throughout the government)
- Multiculturalism (a fundamental characteristic of Canadian heritage and identity)
- Equality of women and men under the law

Source: Citizenship and Immigration Canada

In addition, Citizenship and Immigration Canada stresses that "Canada's openness and generosity do not extend to barbaric cultural practices that tolerate spousal abuse, 'honour killings,' female genital mutilation, forced marriage, or other gender-based violence. Those guilty of these crimes are severely punished under Canada's criminal laws."

RESPONSIBILITIES OF CITIZENSHIP

In Canada, rights come with responsibilities.

- **Obeying the law**: One of Canada's founding principles is the rule of law. Individuals and governments are regulated by laws and not by arbitrary actions. No person or group is above the law.
- **Taking responsibility for oneself and one's family**: Getting a job, taking care of your family, and working hard in keeping with your abilities are important Canadian values. Work contributes to personal dignity and self-respect, and to Canada's prosperity.
- **Serving on a jury**: When called to do so, Canadians are legally required to serve. Serving on a jury is a privilege that makes the justice system work as it depends on impartial juries made up of citizens.

- **Voting in elections:** The right to vote comes with a responsibility to vote in federal, provincial or territorial, and local elections.
- **Helping others in the community:** Millions of volunteers freely donate their time to help others without pay—assisting people in need, helping at your child's school, volunteering at a food bank or other charity, or encouraging newcomers to integrate. Volunteering is an excellent way to gain useful skills and to develop friends and contacts.
- **Protecting and enjoying our heritage and environment:** Every citizen has a role to play in avoiding waste and pollution while protecting Canada's natural, cultural, and architectural heritage for future generations.

Source: Citizenship and Immigration Canada

ELIGIBILITY REQUIREMENTS FOR ADULTS

According to Citizenship and Immigration Canada, individuals who wish to become Canadian citizens must qualify in six areas:

- Be 18 or older
- Have permanent resident status
- Have resided in Canada for at least 1,095 days (three years) in the four years before the date you sign your citizenship application
- Speak read and write basic English or French, the country's official languages
- Have basic, adequate knowledge of Canada and the responsibilities and privileges of citizenship
- Not be under a removal order (that is, the government has not ordered you to leave the country)

There also are criminal history prohibitions. A person who is charged with an indictable (criminal) offense or an offense under the Citizenship Act in the three years before applying may not become a citizen. In addition, those who are in prison, on parole, or on probation; are being investigated for, charged with, or convicted of a war crime or a crime against humanity; or have had their Canadian citizenship revoked in the previous five years are ineligible for Canadian citizenship.

Source: Citizenship and Immigration Canada.

Eligibility Requirements for Minors

Minors (children under the age of 18) may apply for citizenship provided they are permanent residents of Canada, they have at least one parent (including an adoptive parent) who already is or will become a citizen at the same time the children are naturalized; and they are not under a removal order by the government. In addition, a guardian may apply on behalf of a minor child provided the child has one parent who is a Canadian citizen.

Dual Citizenship

The Canadian government recognizes dual (multiple) citizenship, which means you may retain your previous citizenship and be a Canadian citizen at the same time. In addition to being a citizen of another country by birth, you might be a dual citizen because you're married to a foreign national, you lived for a long time in a foreign country, or your parent(s) or even grandparent(s) were born in another country.

Even if you're a dual citizen, once you've been naturalized you should always use your Canadian passport when you travel so you can obtain help at a Canadian consulate if you have any problems. The government also recommends always presenting yourself as a Canadian citizen when talking to local authorities.

There are advantages to dual citizenship, including having access to social programs and property ownership in another country. But there are disadvantages as well. You may have tax or military service obligations in the other country. You may also be subject to the other country's laws, and your marriage may not be recognized there.

The travel.gc.ca website (travel.gc.ca/travelling/publications/dual-citizenship) has stories about people with dual citizenship who were surprised to encounter problems when they traveled to a country where they also have ties. Those stories might be enough to convince you to renounce the other citizenship and be 100 percent Canadian.

Applying for Citizenship

Required Documents

• Form CIT 0002: Application for a Canadian Citizenship: Adults

- Photocopies of Record of Landing (IMM 1000) or Confirmation of Permanent Residence (IMM 5292)
- Copy of both sides of your Permanent Residence Card (PRC), if you have one
- Two pieces of identification, including one picture ID; acceptable ID includes a Canadian driver's license, Canadian health insurance card, and/or the page of your passport that contains your photo and personal information
- Two citizenship photos:
  (refer to Form CIT 0012 I Citizenship Photograph Specifications)
- Two copies of the receipt form showing the fee paid
- The document checklist (Form CIT 0462) found at cic.gc.ca/english/ pdf/kits/citizen/CIT0462E.pdf.
  Source: cic.gc.ca/ english/ pdf/ kits/ citizen/ CIT0462E.pdf

Mail your completed documents to:

Case Processing Centre, Sydney
Grant Adults
P.O. Box 7000
Sydney, NS B1P 6V69

THE CITIZENSHIP TEST

Every person aged between 18 and 54 who wishes to become a Canadian citizen must take the citizenship test, as well as meet the other requirements stated above. The test consists of twenty multiple choice questions. You must answer at least fifteen correctly to pass the test. According to Citizenship and Immigration Canada, the test covers

- The rights, freedoms, and responsibilities of Canadian citizens
- Canada's democracy and ways to take part in Canadian society
- Canadian political and military history (including the political system, monarchy, and branches of government)
- Canadian social and cultural history and symbols
- Canadian physical and political geography

The official test study guide is called *Discover Canada: The Rights and Responsibilities of Citizenship* and is available free from Citizenship and Immigration Canada at cic.gc.ca/english/resources/publications/discover/index.asp. The book is available in both English and French in multiple formats, including online; downloadable PDF, e-book, and mobile app formats (regular and large print); MP3; or as a hard copy. For sample study questions, go to cic.gc.ca/english/resources/publications/discover/questions.asp.

The test may be written or oral, depending on how proficient you are reading and writing in English or French. Oral tests are administered during an interview with a citizenship judge. Bring the original copies of the documents you submitted with your application for citizenship to the test site.

IF YOU DON'T PASS

If you don't pass the citizenship test but meet the other criteria to qualify for citizenship, you will be scheduled immediately to take the test a second time within about four to eight weeks. If your second effort is also unsuccessful, you must meet with a citizenship judge for an interview and assessment. The interview will take up to ninety minutes, during which the judge will ask you questions from the test to determine whether you meet the language and knowledge requirements. A failure on the third try requires you to start the citizenship process all over again.

EXCEPTIONS FROM ENGLISH LANGUAGE REQUIREMENT

Adult applicants fifty-five years of age and older are not bound by the English- or French-language requirement in order to become a Canadian citizen.

THE CITIZENSHIP CEREMONY

If you pass the citizenship test and fulfill all other requirements of citizenship, you'll receive an invitation to attend a citizenship ceremony, which usually takes place within six months of the completion of your test. All adults and children aged fourteen and up are required to attend this ceremony and take the oath of citizenship. Children under age fourteen are not required to appear, but are welcome and encouraged to do so.

In addition to bringing all your immigration documents to the ceremony, you must bring your permanent resident card. In addition, if you became a permanent resident prior to June 28, 2002, you must bring your Record of Landing (IMM 1000) as well.

At the ceremony, you will swear an oath of allegiance to the constitutional monarch of Canada, currently Queen Elizabeth the Second. You are welcome to swear the oath on the holy book used in your religion.

After taking the oath, you will receive a citizenship certificate, which will prove that you are a Canadian citizen. Make a few copies of the certificate and store the original in a safe place, like a safe deposit box.

THE OATH OF CITIZENSHIP

I swear (or affirm)
That I will be faithful
And bear true allegiance
to Her Majesty Queen Elizabeth the Second,
Queen of Canada,
Her Heirs and Successors,
And that I will faithfully observe
The laws of Canada
And fulfill my duties as a Canadian citizen.

OTHER USEFUL INFORMATION

OFFICIAL LANGUAGES OF CANADA

English and French

NATIONAL ANTHEM

"O Canada," written in French by Adolphe-Basile Routhier (words) and Calixa Lavallée (music) in 1880; officially adopted in 1980

O Canada! Our home and native land!
True patriot love in all thy sons command.
With glowing hearts we see thee rise,

The true North strong and free!
From far and wide,
O Canada, we stand on guard for thee.
God keep our land glorious and free!
O Canada, we stand on guard for thee.
O Canada, we stand on guard for thee.

Royal Anthem of Canada

A second anthem, the Royal Anthem of Canada , is called "God Save the Queen" (or "King") and is played in honor of the Sovereign.

God save our gracious Queen!
Long live our noble Queen!
God save the Queen!
Send her victorious,
Happy and glorious,
Long to reign over us,
God save the Queen!

National Symbols

The Canadian Flag of 1965
The Canadian Red Ensign—the national flag from 1868 to 1965
The Canadian Crown
The Maple Leaf
The Fleur-de-lis
The Royal Arms of Canada
The Beaver

National Holidays

New Year's Day: January 1
Sir John A. Macdonald Day: January 11
Good Friday: Friday immediately preceding Easter Sunday
Easter Monday: Monday immediately following Easter Sunday
Vimy Ridge Day: April 9
Victoria Day: Monday preceding May 25

Fête Nationale (Quebec): June 24 (Feast of St. John the Baptist)
Canada Day: July 1
Labour Day: First Monday of September
Thanksgiving: Second Monday of October
Remembrance Day: November 11
Sir Wilfrid Laurier Day: November 20
Christmas Day: December 25
Boxing Day: December 26

ATTA'S LESSONS

Next to the dream of making it to North America, the desire to become a citizen is every immigrant's goal. I remember getting great advice from a member of the church that sponsored me. He told me to work on becoming not just a citizen but a "great citizen"—someone who respects and obeys the laws/rules of his adopted country, gets engaged in the community, and lives up to his/her civic responsibilities and duties.

I took his advice to heart. I learned about U.S. history, the Constitution, the various branches of the government, voting, and various local and federal laws. This knowledge empowered me, and I became even more empowered when I became an American citizen.

I am a firm believer that it is every immigrant's job to take personal responsibility and proactively transform himself or herself into a productive member of society who makes a difference in others' lives. I hope you'll do this, too.

Chapter 5: Working in North America

While there are probably many reasons why you decided to emigrate to North America—from religious freedom to free speech—being able to earn a good living and create a better future for your family was probably at or near the top of your list. If so, then you've come to the right place. Both the United States and Canada offer many employment opportunities in numerous different fields for people who are honest and willing to work hard. While it's true that during economic downtimes, fewer jobs are available and it can be harder to find one, there generally is something you can do to "keep the home fires burning," as the saying goes, until something better comes along.

There's no denying, though, that most immigrant families arrive here with disadvantages—they may have only minimal education, poor proficiency in English, and a distrust of financial institutions and the government. They work hard in low-income jobs and still send a large portion of their earnings back home, making it difficult to get a foothold in what is called "the American Dream."

But while these disadvantages will not keep you from finding a job, they will limit your potential. Fortunately, North America is a land of opportunity, and many people before you have successfully made their way here. So in this chapter, you'll find advice and strategies that you can use to become gainfully employed or move into a better job if you're already working. But while you're seeking employment, please note that it's important to work on your English-speaking skills at the same time. There are laws in North America that protect people from discrimination on the basis of race, color, religion, gender, and ethnic and national origin. But let's face it: if you don't have basic English skills, it will be more difficult to find a job and harder to keep it when you land one. For this reason, then, you should sign up for adult education classes for students who speak English as a second language (ESL). Start with conversational English, then move on to more advanced classes that will teach you writing and public speaking skills. You'll find ESL classes in the adult education programs at high schools and community colleges, at community centers, and through some libraries and churches. Some communities even offer free literacy programs to help you hone your skills. Invest the time in yourself. It's worth it.

PERSONAL INVENTORY

Before you can find a job, you need to consider exactly what skills you can offer an employer. Maybe you have great organizational skills. Maybe you excel at strategic thinking. Or maybe you're a good plumber, caregiver, salesperson, writer, or any of a thousand other things. Figure out exactly what it is you can and are trained to do as a way to narrow your job search and improve your odds of finding a job for which you're qualified. Your educational background also will play a major role in your job search.

Employers generally want job candidates to have a certain set of skills, backed by a solid educational background. Yet job hunters commonly make the mistake of thinking that even though they're not 100 percent qualified for a job they're interested in, an employer will see the potential in them and hire them anyway. Unfortunately, it doesn't work that way, especially in this age of computers and resume databases. Employers typically scan or otherwise enter all the resumes they receive into a searchable database, and when they're looking for an employee for a particular job, they search the database for keywords that match the job description. So if your resume doesn't have those desirable keywords, which reflect your skills and capabilities, you'll never be called in for an interview.

So the first step in your employment search should be to create a personal inventory of skills and strengths. Make three columns on a sheet of paper or draw a three-column table using a computer program like Microsoft Word. Label one column "Skills," the second "Interests," and the third "Goals." Then list everything you can think of that you've done that relates to each category. This type of self-evaluation will help you to figure out exactly what you bring to the table and will help you decide what you'd like to do.

Armed with this information, start looking at the job market. You can approach this in various ways. The internet is the most common place to look for a job. There are numerous job-hunting websites, including Monster. com, Careerbuilder.com, Geebo.com, and Indeed.com, to name just a few. But these sites are not, by any means, the only places to job hunt, and, in fact, they're pretty oversaturated with job seekers. So, in addition to using job search engines, use the internet to identify companies you might be interested in working for, then go directly to their websites and apply there.

Applying in person can be a brilliant search strategy, because most people take the easy way out and apply over the internet. Stop by the human resources department of the companies you're interested in and ask to apply in person. It's possible that you'll be directed to a computer kiosk, or work station, to enter your information, but you could have an edge simply by showing up in person. In fact, sometimes it's even possible to get an immediate prequalification interview right on the spot.

Networking is another viable way to find a job. Think of everyone you know—friends and neighbors; people at church, your children's school, community organizations you belong to, and so on—and mention that you're looking for work. People genuinely like to help other people, and if they happen to be an employer themselves, they like to hire people they know. So it's worth a try.

Headhunters and placement agencies also can be sources of good jobs. A headhunter works with companies to identify good candidates for openings. Normally, a headhunter looks for the candidates directly, but you also can send your resume to a headhunter in the hopes of being matched with a job. Placement agencies, on the other hand, wait for you to come to them. They'll compare your qualifications against job openings in their database and will set up employment interviews for you. In both cases, the company that's seeking employees pays for the placement fee, but sometimes, the job seeker is responsible for the cost. Make sure you ask upfront if you use one of these employment professionals.

It's also quite possible that your community will host a job fair where you can meet a lot of employers all in the same place on the same day. Employers who take the time out of their busy schedule to attend job fairs usually have jobs they need to fill immediately, or they may have openings coming up in the near future. So this can be a very good way to land a job. Be sure to dress for success—that is, wear a suit and tie if possible if you're a man, or a conservative dress or skirt suit if you're a woman. The dress-for-success rule pertains even if you are applying for a blue-collar job, one that requires physical labor, like assembly work. Dressing professionally means you take your job seriously. Take at least twenty-five copies of your resume with you in a folder or briefcase to complete your look of professionalism, competency, and preparedness.

The telephone still works well as a job search tool. Making phone contact without an appointment is known as cold calling, and some employers will respond well to your effort to find out what types of jobs might be available at a company you're interested in. Frankly, employers today really don't expect job seekers to prospect this way, so taking a proactive approach like this could result in interviews. Also, it's a good way to help you learn how to deal with both rejections and objections.

During such a cold call, make note of anything a company employee says about you when you talk to him or her, and use that information when you try your next call. For example, someone might tell you that you just don't have enough experience at a certain task. This could be a red flag that indicates you're just not qualified for the job, but it also could be that you haven't prepared sufficiently to convince an employer that you are, indeed, the right person for the job. So take some time to think about what you could have said instead about your experience, and be prepared to offer up that information the next time someone raises the same objection.

A final way to find work is to go through the "help wanted" listings in your local newspaper's classified section. Printed help-wanted ads are actually on the wane, as more people use the internet to search for what they need. But there are still a surprising number of jobs that are placed there, especially entry-level and blue-collar positions, so be sure to look. If your reading skills aren't very strong yet, ask a more fluent friend or family member for help.

Other things to consider before applying for work are the hours you want to work, how far you are willing to drive to get to your job, whether you prefer to work for a large or small company, and, of course, how much you need to earn. You'll be more successful in your job hunt if you can be flexible in any of these areas.

WRITING A RESUME

Armed with this information about yourself and your skills, you can start assembling a resume that showcases your talents and experience. A resume is a document used to relay your accomplishments and qualifications to a potential employer, preferably on a single page. It shows, briefly and all in one place, everything you have done in your career so an employer can read through it quickly to see if you are a match for a position. In effect, it's a promotional piece about yourself, and you should use it to present yourself in the best possible light and prove that you can do the job.

Generally, a resume should be a one-page document on quality paper. (You can buy reasonably priced resume paper at an office supply store.) The document should be formatted with 1-inch margins around all four sides and should be printed in a standard typeface like Times New Roman in 12 point. Don't use a smaller typeface to squeeze more words on the page—it won't be as readable. Also avoid using italic type or a lot of bold text. Both can be distracting, as well as difficult to read when used extensively.

Other important formatting tips include the following:

- Spelling out all month names, since you can't abbreviate the shorter names (May, June, and July, for example).
- Using periods at the end of all complete sentences when writing bulleted lists; don't put periods at the end of sentence fragments. It's important to be consistent with this formatting throughout.
- Keeping the resume to a single page. Even the world's most successful corporate executives have one-page resumes. Edit out text if yours is too long.

If you've never written a resume before, you'll find it easier if you use a resume template to format it. A template is like a pattern that you fill with information. Microsoft Word has dozens of preloaded resumes from which to select. Pick the one that showcases your background best. For example, you'll find that some of the resume templates are better for job seekers with less experience because they have fewer fields to fill in and more white space. Using a template also assures that you include all the information a hiring manager is likely to need to make a decision about whether your qualifications match the job.

There are two types of resumes. A chronological resume lists your jobs in the order in which you worked them, although most resumes usually are in reverse chronological order, meaning that the most current job appears at the top of the list, followed by any other jobs you've held, from most recent to earliest. A functional resume focuses on the tasks you have handled rather than when you did them. A functional resume tends to be a little less detailed as a result and can be a good choice if you don't have much work experience or if you have gaps in your resume due to job losses like layoffs. This is not to say that you're trying to hide anything from an employer; rather, you're simply trying to present yourself in the most positive light.

A standard resume has eight different sections: the header, your objective, your qualifications, your experience, education, special skills, volunteer/pro bono (free) work, and keywords.

THE HEADER

- This is where you'll provide your contact information, including:
- Full name
- Complete address
- Home phone number
- Cell phone number
- Email address

If you wish to be contacted during the day while you're working for someone else, be sure to provide your cell phone number as your primary contact number so you can excuse yourself from a public room to take the call in privacy.

Contact information should appear at the top of the resume in a slightly larger typeface, say, 14 point, for better legibility. And here's one place where bold type definitely can be used. Put your name in bold to distinguish it from the rest of the type below it.

YOUR OBJECTIVE

This is where you'll indicate the type of job you want. Just be very careful that you focus on what you offer the employer, not what you want the employer to do for you.

For example, your resume will meet with a more positive reception if you use a "you-centered" objective like this: "A middle manager position in a progressive company where my experience and skills can help to advance the company's goals."

Avoid the following type of "me-centered" objective (even if it's true): "A full-time position in an environment that offers a greater challenge, increased benefits for my family, and the opportunity to advance rapidly."

Writing an objective can be tricky. So if you can't quite capture your needs in the objective without sounding needy or self-centered, write an objective that simply refers to the job without embellishment, as in: "A sales position with a medium-sized company."

Your Qualifications

This section is useful for showcasing special talents and skills you have. Mention accomplishments like special projects you've completed, sales goals you've achieved, and ways you've decreased costs or otherwise helped to build a company's bottom line. This is also a good place to list tasks you've done for more than one company. For example, if you have worked as a bookkeeper at several different companies, some of the responsibilities were probably the same. So you can mention them just once in the qualifications section rather than repeating yourself later when you list the name of each company you've worked for.

Your Experience

This section is compiled in reverse chronological order, which means your job history starts with the most recent job on top, then goes backward to the oldest job. This is done because employers usually are more interested in knowing what you've done most recently. Be sure to include the dates you were employed, the full name of the company, and its city/state or city/province location, and your title. Then include a few details about what you do on the job.

For example, here's how you could format information about a clerical job you currently hold:

> *2012-Present: Wayne's World Inc., San Bernardino, CA*
> *Clerk/typist*
> *Prepare monthly reports for two sales directors. Maintain and update a large electronic database. Type memos, letters, and reports; fill out forms.*

Here's an example of how a middle manager might format his experience, with supporting figures:

> *2007-Present: Sears Holdings Corp., Hoffman Estates, IL*
> *Hard Lines Merchandising Manager*
> *Purchased three new product lines that increased year-to-year bottom line by 20 percent. Merchandised key product placements in print and internet promotions that generated $3 million in new business.*

When compiling a list of job tasks, showcase only the ones that are closest to the qualifications of the job you're seeking. For example, if you're looking for an entry-level managerial job, but your first job out of school was as the office go-fer (that is, the person who goes for coffee and anything else the executives need), you definitely want to omit that from your list of duties.

Do include quantifiable information related to achievements like sales goals, cost-cutting measures, and other functions. For instance, maybe you increased production by 15 percent in one quarter, or you saved your employer $25,000 by streamlining operations, or you won an award for outstanding sales. Always include verifiable facts and figures like these, since they demonstrate your competence in and enthusiasm for your field.

If you have more than fifteen years of experience, you might want to consider leaving the older jobs off your resume. While age discrimination is illegal, it does exist; so if you have enough recent work experience to look attractive to an employer, it might be a good idea to focus on that experience and simply omit the older jobs.

Use action verbs when creating this section. Here's a list of strong verbs to pick from: analyze, arrange, assist, complete, conduct, control, coordinate, create, develop, direct, deliver, design, establish, generate, implement, improve, increase, lead, maintain, manage, organize, participate, organize, originate, oversee, perform, produce, promote, propose, recommend, setup, solve, supervise, support, write.

EDUCATION

This generally is the most important section of a resume. If you hold degrees from a college, university, or community college either here or abroad, list them at the top of this section, and include the city and state where the degree was earned. If you earned your degree outside North America, give the country name, too. Finally, if you attended more than one institution to get your degree, list only the terminal, or final, institution.

If your highest level of education is a high school diploma or its equivalent in your home country, use that instead. But anything older than that is ancient history as far as employers are concerned and won't help you in your job search, so leave it off. Likewise, if you have an academic degree, leave off any mention of high school altogether, even if you were a scholar or you earned academic awards. What matters is the degree.

If you attended and/or graduated from a trade school, this information also will be useful to a potential employer and should appear on your resume. This information is more important than a high school diploma, but less important than a college degree. In fact, here's the order educational information should appear in, from most significant to most basic:

- College/university information (name of the institution, dates attended, major/minor field of study)
- Trade school (again, with the name, dates, field of study)
- High school or foreign equivalent (only the name and city are necessary; plus the country name if outside North America)

Another important thing to note: if you have education that matches the job you're seeking, but your past experience is in other fields, you should move the education section above your experience section. This will help convince an employer that you could be right for the job even though you have done other types of work in the past.

Special Skills

Here's where you'll mention special knowledge you have, like computer software you know well, technical skills, clerical skills like word-processing speed, and languages you speak fluently. You don't have to put English on the language list because it's assumed that you speak it since you're applying for jobs in North America.

Volunteer/ Pro Bono (Free) Work

Donating your time for the good of others is a noble pursuit that employers will view favorably, especially if you have little job experience otherwise. If there's room, include a list of your volunteer activities at the bottom of your resume.

Keywords

Earlier you read that employers usually store resumes electronically in a database, or scan the paper copies they receive so the information can be added to the database. Since employers conduct candidate searches based on specific skills, you should include a list of keywords at the bottom of your resume that reflects the scope of your abilities. For example, here's a keyword list for a finance manager who has a bachelor's degree and three years of experience (apologies if you don't know what some of these financial terms mean): finance, financial, analyst, general ledger, due diligence, GAAP, capital financing, capital gains/losses, cash flow, collections, EBITDA, bachelor of science, three years' experience.

Here's a keyword list for a person with clerical skills: administrative assistance, clerical, screen calls, answer phones, receptionist, communication skills, record management, problem solving, scheduling, Microsoft Office.

Resumes that have more of the keywords the employer is seeking will rank higher in the search results, so include as many keywords as you can, up to about twenty, to improve your odds of making the cut for an interview.

Resume Don'ts

- *Don't include personal information like marital status, number of children, health status, age, and religious affiliation.* It's illegal for an employer to ask these types of questions, so don't offer the information.
- *Don't put your photograph on your resume.* Appearance isn't important; skills and talent are.
- *Don't list your references.* Put them on a separate sheet you can hand to the employer during an interview.
- *Don't mention hobbies.* They almost never have a bearing on the job (although some might argue that a good golf handicap might be helpful in some professions).
- *Don't include your Social Security number.* It's never needed until you've been hired, and only then so you can fill out employment paperwork.
- *Don't exaggerate or lie about your experience and other facts on the resume.* If you're hired and someone discovers you haven't been truthful, you could be fired on the spot.
- *Don't divulge your current salary.* Occasionally, a company will ask what your salary requirements are, but that information, if necessary, should be included in your cover letter (discussed in the next section).

The final step in the process is to proofread the document carefully to identify typos and grammatical errors. Employment experts say that a single typo can get a resume excluded from consideration, so use your spellcheck and grammar checks to identify errors, then proofread the resume manually. You may also wish to ask someone else to proofread it for you.

Examine the following for accuracy:

- Usage issues: Check for correct grammar, spelling, and punctuation.
- Capitalization: Only words at the start of a sentence or proper nouns are capitalized in English.
- Punctuation: Refer to a book like *The Gregg Reference Manual* or a website like the Purdue Online Writing Lab (owl.english.purdue.edu/owl/) for help.
- Dropped articles: Nouns in English almost always take an article (the, a, an) in front of them (the train, an apple, a quarter). Dropped articles are a sure sign of a non-native speaker.
- Run-on sentences: These are two separate sentences that are incorrectly stuck together without punctuation or conjunctions. For example: "I love traveling in California the weather is great there." Correct grammar would be "I love traveling in California. The weather is great there."
- Consistency: Be sure to use only one space after a period, always punctuate bulleted lists in the same way, and so on).

Finally, if your English grammar and/or writing skills are still under construction, consider having your resume written by a professional resume writer. Then you'll know it's letter-perfect and will represent you well in the job hunt.

The Cover Letter

A well-written, error-free cover letter personalized for the job you're seeking is a must in a job hunt. It might seem strange, but even companies that advertise online generally will require at least a brief cover letter to go with your online application.

Employment experts say that a cover letter can make or break your chances at getting an interview. That's because a cover letter reveals how good your communication skills really are, and if the letter contains typos or other errors, it reveals that you're not as careful about your image as you need to be.

The job description is like a roadmap: it leads you to the job you're seeking. For this reason, your cover letter should be tailored to fit the job description. Pick out words and phrases from the ad, and use them in your letter. Mention any skills you have that are a match for those in the job description. Also if you're proficient in or at least familiar with a particular software package or a particular program, mention that, too. Your goal here is to draw as many parallels between your experience and the job as you can.

But what if you are new in the job market or you don't have much experience? No problem. You can turn any job you've held into an asset by focusing on what you can do. Make a list of the skills you've acquired in the workplace, as well as your responsibilities, and tie them to the job you're seeking. Using this approach, even a retail sales or fast food job can be seen as an asset. After all, you've acquired useful skills in those jobs like money handling, managing people (if you have been in charge of a shift), and training (if you have been responsible for training employees).

Some people find writing about themselves in this way uncomfortable. But to get a job you have to provide good evidence that you're the right person to fill it, and that means talking about yourself, your skills, and your accomplishments. After all, the reader doesn't know you, so this is the only way to give him or her insight into who you are and what you can do. If you find it too difficult to praise yourself this way, consider having someone else draft the letter for you.

Other things to do in your cover letter include the following:

- Orienting the reader to the reason for writing in the opening statement: "I am interested in the marketing position you have open at XYZ Corporation."
- Using active verbs when describing your experience and capabilities ("directed, spearheaded, coordinated," and others described earlier in this chapter)
- Saying more than just what's on your resume (give more details or expand upon your experience)
- Providing your contact information—again—for easy access
- Asking directly for an interview

Format the letter in the same way that you formatted your resume, with 1-inch margins and 12-point Times New Roman type. Whenever possible, address the letter to a real person, not just "Dear Sir" or "To whom it may concern." You may have to call the company (if you know it) or go online to find the name of the right recipient.

Always include your return address at the top of the letter, as well as a section at the bottom where you can sign the letter (known as a complimentary close) before sending it. Of course, if you're applying online, you won't be able to sign the letter physically. Instead, simply type your name in capital letters after the goodwill line, like so:

Very truly yours,
ARUNA PALSANDRAM

If you'll be sending a resume and cover by email without the benefit of an online job search site, you should create what's known as an inline resume. In this type of document, all the type is moved to the left margin (known as "flush left"). In addition, decorative devices like centering, bold, and italic type are not used. You can, however, use a row of equals signs (======) if you wish to separate the different sections of the resume. And here's an important tip: always email a copy of your resume and cover letter to yourself first to check that the email journey won't scramble the text. Sometimes email programs can corrupt the format, skewing all the margins, adding weird line breaks, or double-spacing. Sending yourself a test document will help you identify any problems and correct them before you send a live copy to an employer who will have a critical or discerning eye.

If you're applying online, you may be invited to copy-and-paste your cover letter and resume into predetermined boxes on the screen. Alternatively, you may be able to attach these documents to the email. As a courtesy, save your documents as PDF files, if possible, because it's harder to transmit a virus attached to this type of file. You don't want a prospective employer to be talking about you because you sent a nasty virus to his or her mailbox.

Now that you have a functional resume and cover letter, you're ready for some effective job-hunting strategies. Turn to Chapter 6 to start the search.

Atta's Lessons

Watching my father work to provide for our family of twelve in a third-world country like Afghanistan taught me excellent lessons about hard work. So when I arrived in Germany after leaving Afghanistan, it was heartbreaking to learn that refugees were not allowed to enter the workforce for a number of years. Worse yet, I discovered that there were no real job preparation/readiness programs for most immigrants. Instead, they're confined to camps, which deprive them of the opportunity to become productive members of society.

But when I emigrated to the U.S., I was not only able to make a living; I was able to lead the productive life I wanted. The bottom line is: there are amazing opportunities here for immigrants to succeed as long as you embrace them.

Chapter 6: Finding and Keeping a Job

A job hunt is a methodical process; that is, it's conducted one step at a time. So here are some steps you can take to make your job hunt more successful.

Target Small to Medium-Sized Businesses

Smaller businesses are most likely to take a chance on someone less experienced or who has little or no advanced education. At the same time, though, they're likely to have smaller budgets and may take longer to hire. But you'll probably have more chance to flex your creative muscles while learning a lot.

Do Some Research

Always go to a job interview prepared with enough background information about the company so you can talk knowledgably about what it does and ask intelligent questions. This kind of preparation really impresses employers, because it shows that you have an interest in the company, not just in a paycheck. It's easy to find information online. Hoovers.com is a great place to learn about companies' backgrounds, investigate their financials, and learn about the industry they are in. A search of a company's website also will yield background information you can use.

Develop an All-Star Reference List

References are people who are willing to speak on your behalf about your skills, qualifications, and personality. So you need to compile a list of personal and professional references that you can share with interviewers. Keep in mind that interviewers will check your references, so make sure they're people who know you well. Also, as a courtesy, always ask the person if he or she is willing to be a reference. Most people will say yes, but some won't, and you want to find that out before you pass along that person's name and contact information to a potential employer.

Format your reference list on a sheet of paper separate from your resume and cover letter. It's a good practice to include one or two personal references (anyone except family members—friends, neighbors, and classmates are good choices) and two or three business references. If you have little or no job experience and, therefore, no references, you can ask the religious leader at your church (priest, pastor, imam, rabbi) to be a reference.

THE INTERVIEW PROCESS

Once you get that coveted call from someone to set up an interview, you have some important work to do. It helps to think of yourself as a salesperson going on a sales call. First, consider what you have to offer that particular employer, just like a salesperson would sell a product. Make a list of your skills and match them to the job description. If you don't know a lot about the job yet, go to the company's website. A detailed job description might be posted there.

Next, consider what you offer that makes you unique or different from the average job seeker. Maybe it's your foreign-language skills or your technical skills. Make a list of those things to crystallize them in your mind and help them spring out naturally when you're asked about them. Make sure you come up with examples to support your claims. For example, just saying you have strong organizational skills doesn't mean much until you back up that claim with evidence, such as describing a time when your organizational skills helped an employer (or your church or your family, if you have little job experience) do business better. Again, think of these traits and examples well in advance. When you're on an interview, you may be nervous and could forget important things you wanted to share.

Speaking of preparation, it's really important to prepare answers to two common interview questions that can trip you up if you're not prepared. Those questions are, "What are your strengths?" and "What are your weaknesses?" Think of strengths that make you seem confident and competent without being boastful. For example, you might say that your strength is courtesy and politeness, which would be helpful in customer service, or you have a knack for relaying technical information in language anyone can understand.

On the other hand, your weaknesses don't have to be terrible; they can just be something at which you don't excel. Think of something that doesn't come naturally to you, and use that as your weakness. For example, maybe you're not always especially organized. You could say that you have to work at being organized and rely on tools like phone apps and a daily planner to keep yourself organized.

Finally, practice making a "sales call." Practice introducing yourself and giving a rundown on your qualifications. Do this out loud, just as if you were talking to the employer. While it's true that you'll probably be asked a series of questions rather than just being given an opportunity to talk about yourself, practicing ahead of time still will help you deliver answers smoothly and confidently. You might even find it helpful to conduct a mock interview with a family member or friend acting as the manager. Have that person ask you questions about yourself and the job so you can get practice thinking on the spot and responding promptly.

THE DAY BEFORE THE INTERVIEW

You have worked very hard to get to this point—sending resumes, networking with peers, attending job fairs, and taking classes to make yourself more valuable to employers. So the day before the interview, put yourself in a success-driven frame of mind and…

Review your resume one last time. Make sure you're 100 percent comfortable with everything you've written.

Plan how you'll answer those tricky questions mentioned earlier (What are your strengths? What are your weaknesses?).

Go online. Check to see if there has been any late-breaking news on the company since you did your initial research, and check for information about corporate officers. If the company has posted its annual report, look at that, too.

Gather everything you'll need for the next day. This should include additional copies of your resume (four or five is a good number, for reasons you'll learn later), a good quality pen (no plastic stick pens), a pad for taking notes, and a folder or briefcase to put them into. If you have business cards, be sure to tuck a few into your briefcase. Also check your interview suit or other clothing to make sure everything is neat, clean, and well-pressed.

Then get a good night's sleep. If you're tired, your energy level will be low and you won't be able to impress the employer with your energy and enthusiasm for the job.

ON THE DAY OF THE INTERVIEW

It's show time—your opportunity to shine. You've prepared well already; now put that preparation into action. Some things to remember:

- Be on time . If you arrive late for any reason—even a legitimate one like a traffic jam—you send a message to the interviewer that you aren't serious about the job. The interviewer may also see your tardiness as a sign of disrespect, putting you at a disadvantage from the moment you arrive. Better still, arrive a little early—fifteeen minutes isn't too early—so you can observe people as they come and go. Watching the employees will give you some insight into the company culture.
- Shake the hand of your interviewer firmly and confidently. If the interviewer is a woman, be careful not to crush her hand accidentally.
- Maintain eye contact, both while you're talking and listening. People in North America generally prefer direct eye contact, which can be difficult if it's not common in your culture to look at people steadily. Just remember that it's not impolite to have good eye contact, no matter what's considered normal in your own culture.

AVOID SMALL TALK

Small talk is casual conversation; the type you might exchange at a party or over the fence with your next-door neighbor. But in an interview situation, always keep your conversation businesslike and on target. Don't comment on the interviewer's appearance, the things on his or her desk, his or her family, the view outside the window, and so on. It might seem friendly to exchange pleasantries, but in North America it's usually preferable at an interview to stick to business. This might be totally different from the way you'd interview in your home country, so be careful not to overstep your bounds.

POTENTIAL INTERVIEW QUESTIONS

While it's impossible to know exactly what you might be asked during an interview, there are some common questions (besides the two mentioned earlier) that you can expect and should prepare for in advance. They include the following:

- "What are some of your major accomplishments?" This is an opportunity to highlight professional milestones throughout your life. Two or three precise examples will suffice when delivered confidently. If you have quantifiable data—sales figures, awards, and so on—this would be the time to bring them up.
- "What experience do you have in this field?" Speak about specifics that relate to the position you are applying for. If you do not have specific experience, get as close as you can.
- "Why did you leave your last job?" You need to respond positively, no matter what the conditions actually were. Never talk poorly about previous management, supervisors, or other employees. It will make you look bad.
- "Where do you see yourself in five years? Ten?" The interviewer wants to know whether you'll be committed to the company, not whether you want to be CEO someday. Prepare a reasonable answer like, "I see myself with more responsibilities that will allow me to make a bigger contribution to the company's bottom line."
- "What salary are you looking for?" This is a tricky one. You don't want to ask for too much and put yourself out of contention for the job, or ask for too little and look as though you don't value your own abilities. It's usually best to say that the salary is negotiable (meaning it's open for discussion) or to give a range. Better still, check a website like salary.com or payscale.com to find out what the average salary is for the job in your area so you know how much to ask. Then turn that figure into a range so there's room to negotiate.

Ask Questions

You're likely to have a chance to ask questions, too, usually at the end of the interview. This is the time to make use of the information you gathered through research before you went to the interview. Ask about company goals, sales forecasts, or other business information. Do *not* ask about the salary, the benefits, the vacation policy, or anything else that makes it looks as though you're only concerned with the benefits you'll gain. Instead, if you demonstrate a real interest in the company, the interviewer is likely to have a similar interest in you later.

MORE HELPFUL INTERVIEW TIPS

There are a few more things you can do to gain an edge over your competition both before and after the interview. First, try to schedule your interview early in the day. This will allow you to see the office and its employees when they're busiest, which will give you some insight into the corporate culture. Next, converse for a few minutes with the receptionist when you arrive. It's not uncommon for interviewers to ask the receptionist for his or her first and overall impression of a candidate. Also, if you're offered a tour of the facility, always accept politely. This will give you additional insight into how well the office runs and whether you think it might be a place you'd like to work.

During the interview, stay focused. Turn off your technology so you won't be interrupted by a ringing phone (*very* bad form), and don't let your mind wander. If you have to keep asking for questions to be repeated, it will be a signal that you're not paying close enough attention, and the interviewer will not be pleased. Focusing all your attention on the interviewer also will help if he or she says something you don't quite understand or don't quite catch. If this happens, politely ask the interviewer to repeat what was said. It's also okay to admit that you don't understand one of the words that were used and ask for an explanation. A gracious interviewer will define the word and move on.

After an interview, be sure to send a brief thank you note to the interviewer. This can be sent by mail or email. Since email addresses can be difficult to obtain, ask the interviewer before you leave whether you can email if you have any questions, then write down the address you're given. Be sure to send the thank you note no more than a day or two after the interview so you can be sure the interviewer still remembers you.

PANEL INTERVIEWS

Most interviews are conducted one-on-one; that is, with just you and the interviewer in the room. But a trend has developed over the past decade toward panel or group interviews. This is generally done so anyone you might work with, from decision-makers to co-workers, will have a chance to size you up all at the same time. But it can be intimidating having questions tossed at you by several grim, unsmiling people all at once.

A lot of times, you won't even know you're going into a panel interview until you arrive, at which time your anxiety level is likely to climb. But if you've done your homework and have investigated the company and its executive team, you should be able to speak confidently and handle all questions.

Pay particular attention when the interviewers are introducing themselves. You'll want to send a thank you note to each of these people after you leave, so you need to know who was present. If you miss a name, call the human resources department right after you leave and ask for the names of the panel participants and their correct spellings. In this case, you'll probably have to send a note by mail, since a human resources representative might be cagey about giving out email addresses.

Earlier in this chapter you were advised to bring four or five copies of your resume. Here's when you'll use them. Before the interview starts, give a copy to each person at the table. Then when you're asked a question, speak to each member of the panel. Keep your eye contact steady, and slowly move your eyes from one person to the other. Avoid jerky, fast, or sidelong glances, because that will make you seem nervous.

At the conclusion of the interview, ask for the job. This isn't being too pushy—it merely shows that you're excited about the opportunity and want to be part of the team. Then shake hands with each participant before you leave.

It's acceptable to phone a few days after your interview to ask whether the interviewers have any additional questions and whether a hiring decision will be made soon. If the time drags on and you don't hear anything, you can feel free to call again a week or so later.

Stay Upbeat

Naturally, you won't land every job for which you interview. So if you have to keep looking, because a job you wanted doesn't pan out, make sure you keep your resume updated and stay confident. Even when the economy is depressed, there are far more people working than not, so something will come up for you, if not today, then eventually.

JOB SEARCH MISTAKES

Employment experts say that it's always better to have a job already when you're looking for a new opportunity. So if you're unhappy with your job, you need a position that pays more, or you want to change career paths, sit tight in your current position until you actually land that new job.

When you change jobs, you should do many of the same things you did before you landed your present job, from researching the market and the field the prospective employer is in, to investigating the companies that interest you. But one thing not to do is to change jobs only to make more money. You could end up accepting a job you really hate, and the money won't necessarily make it better. It's preferable to wait a little longer to find a job you will enjoy doing, than to jump just for a bigger paycheck.

By the same token, if you want to change careers, make sure you have adequate training and preparation for the new field. A person with a degree in history is not going to be successful as a financial analyst or logistics coordinator if he or she doesn't get the appropriate education first. Some companies do offer on-the-job training, but if the job you're seeking is too different from what you've done before, there's no incentive for the employer to even consider you.

Finally, don't bad mouth (criticize) your current or previous employer, either during a job interview or while you're at your new job. It's not professional to do so, plus you never know when you will encounter someone from the previous job, either in public or at another company where you wish to work. There's an expression in English that you shouldn't "burn your bridges"—this is a good example of when you should keep your lighter in your pocket.

UNEMPLOYMENT

As you probably know, a lot of people get away with bad behavior without consequences. (You'll find some examples in Chapter 5.) But you might not be so lucky. One day you could find yourself out of a job. Or sometimes, even if you're doing a good job, you could lose your job due to a downturn in the economy, a lost client, or other factors.

Unemployment can be devastating, especially if you're the sole support for your family. Unemployed people often feel hopeless, become depressed, and feel sorry for themselves in the aftermath of a firing or layoff. This can crush their motivation to look for a new job. But sitting around and doing nothing is the worst thing to do. Instead, it's important to start looking for a new job right away using the same techniques described earlier.

As soon as you find yourself separated from your job, you should apply for unemployment benefits. Such benefits are awarded at the state level in the United States, and on the federal level in Canada, where it's called employment insurance (EI). In the case of EI, you must have paid into a special fund while employed to be able to collect benefits when you are no longer employed.

While many people are eligible to receive benefits after losing a job, there are restrictions. Generally, you must be employed at the job for at least a year in the United States or a specific number of insurable hours in Canada in the previous fifty-two weeks. In both countries, you must not have been fired for misconduct, and if you quit your job, you're definitely not eligible for benefits. Check with your state's unemployment office or Service Canada to determine whether you're eligible.

While receiving benefits, you must be ready, willing, and able to work. The United States and Canada both require you to be actively seeking work while collecting benefits, and you'll be asked to provide proof, usually by providing a list of the places where you've applied. Contact your state unemployment office or Service Canada for more details.

It may be possible to work a certain number of hours every week and still receive unemployment benefits. For this reason, you may wish to find a temporary job to supplement your benefits. Try applying at an employment agency, which will have a list of available jobs. There's usually no charge for the job seeker; rather, the employer pays the finder's fee.

During your period of unemployment, review and revise your resume, and update your skills. There are many free resources available on the internet, including tutorials, e-books, and how-to videos. If you're financially able, this is also a good time to take courses to improve your business skills and make yourself more valuable to a future employer. Community colleges and high schools, adult education centers, and even libraries usually offer adult education courses at reasonable rates. Taking courses like this will demonstrate to a new employer that you're serious about your work and that the layoff or termination was only a minor roadblock on the road to success.

By the way, if you're unemployed long enough, you'll end up with a gap in your job experience. These days, it's not uncommon for people to be unemployed for a while, but it's quite likely that a prospective employer will ask why you're not working. The best policy is honesty. If you were laid off, there's no stigma attached. But if you were fired, that sends up a red flag for an employer. Be honest, but in a way that doesn't put you in a really bad light.

Saying something like, "The corporate culture wasn't right for me" or "I had a disagreement over policy with my previous employer" is specific enough to reassure the employer without ruining your chances to get a new job.

It's really important to find a new job as soon as possible. Even though it's a discriminatory practice, the trend in business today is to not hire people who have been unemployed for a long time. Working hard to find a new job right away will help you avoid that problem.

Volunteer While You're Unemployed

Volunteerism is not just a noble act; it's one of the pillars that America was built on. But during a time of unemployment, volunteering also is a great way to keep busy, network, and fill any gaps on your resume that might result from an extended period of unemployment.

Choose an organization that can benefit from your particular skills. For example, if you're an accountant or bookkeeper, find an organization that could use some pro bono (free) assistance filing its taxes. Or if you're a fundraiser, offer to help an organization promote its fundraising efforts. Volunteering also shows good character and integrity, two traits employers seek in their employees.

Start Your Own Business

If you have ever had a desire to start you own business, this could be the time to do it. Self-employment is a wonderful thing. You can do whatever you want, whenever you want to do it, all without a boss looking over your shoulder. However, self-employment does come with risks, many of them financial. But if you need to support your family right away (and who doesn't?), and you have a marketable skill, it makes sense to consider starting a business of your own.

Self-employment has another benefit. If you ever decide to work again for someone else, you'll have that pesky hole in your resume filled, plus most employers will applaud your efforts to be proactive and productive.

Be aware that you may need some training in areas you're not proficient in, if you're going to be your own boss. For example, if you have never created a marketing plan, or you are not proficient at recordkeeping, you will either need to take a class to get the knowledge you need or hire another professional to step in for you. For example, if you're not a computer wizard, hire a consultant who can come in and keep your equipment running well and virus-free. When you're self-employed, it's more important to spend your time on the things you do well rather than trying to figure out the activities that don't come naturally to you. You'll find more information on starting your own business in Chapter 8.

Stay Informed

Spend some time every day reading the local and national news in the paper and on the internet to see which industries are hot at any given time. Jobs could open up when you least expect it, and if you're following particular industries and businesses, you'll be ready to apply when the opportunity arises.

Build Connections

Networking is a phenomenal way to make new business contacts that could turn out to be good sources of job leads. If you don't already belong to a professional association, sign up now. You also should consider joining civic groups like the Rotary Club (rotary.org) or Soroptimist (soroptimist.org). If you start a business, you definitely need to join your local chamber of commerce, which exists in part specifically to foster networking opportunities.

But don't stop there with your networking efforts. Let friends, acquaintances, and people where you worship know you're in the job market. Go to an office supply store like Office Max and have simple business cards printed up with your contact information so you can make it easier for people to contact you later or pass along your information to someone who might be hiring. If you distribute enough cards, you're bound to get some leads eventually.

OTHER GOVERNMENT SUPPORT PROGRAMS

PUBLIC ASSISTANCE

In a tough job market, it can take a while to find a new job. If that job search lasts longer than a year or so and you have little or no savings, you may find yourself without any means to support your family. If that happens, you may be able to obtain public assistance from the government.

Known variously as general assistance (GA), public assistance, or welfare in the United States; or by names like social assistance or hardship assistance in Canada, these programs are not meant to support a person for life. Rather, they offer a hand up in times of need, rather than just a handout. GA or income-assistance recipients may also be eligible for food stamps, medical care, and other benefits. Contact your state's human services department or go to CanadaBenefits.gc.ca in Canada for information about whether you qualify and how to apply.

In the United States, individuals who are permanently disabled and/or older than age sixty-two are eligible for Social Security benefits or Supplemental Security Insurance (SSI) through the Social Security Administration rather than general assistance. Information on how to apply is available in sixteen languages besides English, including American Sign Language, Arabic, Armenian, Chinese, Farsi, French, Greek, Haitian Creole, Italian, Korean, Polish, Portuguese, Russian, Spanish, Tagalog, and Vietnamese at ssa.gov.

Canada takes care of its senior citizens through a program known as Old Age Security. It's available to people sixty-five years old and up who meet residency and legal status requirements. You may also be eligible for other benefits, including guaranteed income support. In addition, persons aged between sixty and sixty-four whose spouses are receiving guaranteed-income support may be eligible for an allowance, while those who are between sixty- and sixty-four-years old and are widowed could be eligible for a survivor's benefit. Materials are available in English and French. Contact Service Canada if any of these situations apply to you.

Additionally, assistance is available in Canada for people with disabilities, war veterans, and others through the provincial and territorial governments. You can start exploring the options at CanadaBenefits.gc.ca.

You'll find more information about these retirement benefits in Chapter 22. If you'd like more information now, go to ssa.gov (U.S.), where you can use a retirement calculator tool, view documents and webinars, and listen to podcasts; or to Service Canada (servicecanada.gc.ca) for similar online resources.

Child Care Assistance

Additional financial assistance may be available through your state if you have children (who are minors) and have become unemployed, disabled, or otherwise incapacitated (unable to live normally). The amount is based on various factors like income, number of hours worked, and so on, and funds may be used to pay for day care and other child-rearing expenses, such as when a relative cares for your kids while you're working. The age threshold for minors varies by state, although the benefits are generally reserved for children under twelve or thirteen years old. For more information, contact the child care services department in your state government.

The Canada Child Care Tax Benefit is available to eligible families with children up to the age of eight. It is a tax-free benefit paid by the Canada Revenue Agency. You must be a Canadian citizen, a permanent or temporary resident, or a protected person (such as a refugee) to qualify for these tax-free payments. Other criteria may apply. Again, Service Canada is the place to go for information (servicecanada.gc.ca)

ATTA'S LESSONS

Upon my arrival in the United States in late December 1981, I set a goal to find a job within a month. I was determined to take advantage of my adequate English knowledge, and I remember wrapping up blisters and wiping blood off my feet for quite a few days as I walked the streets of San Francisco in search of a job.

I met my goal: I landed a bank teller job within two weeks, thanks in part to my personal role models. My parents and friends taught me that hard work and determination will take me far. I parlayed that teller job into a successful banking career that lasted twenty-eight years, culminating in a position as a senior vice president regional manager.

During my career, I met many other successful immigrants who have made amazing strides and progress despite many challenges. For that reason, I am firm believer in hard work, dedication, and the realization that the sky is indeed the limit.

Chapter 7: The 9-to-5 Life

You did it—you've landed a job that will help you take care of your family and build a nest egg for the future. So in this chapter, you'll read about what to expect in the workplace when you start your new job, as well as how to be a model employee.

EMPLOYEE ORIENTATION

Most companies, even small ones, will expect you to attend an employee orientation on your first day at work. The orientation may be very simple and brief—perhaps nothing more than a short meeting with your supervisor or someone from the human resources department who will welcome you to the company, tell you about office expectations like starting and quitting times, and explain the benefits the company offers.

Larger companies tend to make the orientation process more detailed. It's not uncommon for employees at these companies to spend a whole morning or even a full day in an orientation session. Furthermore, depending on the type of job you land, you may even find yourself sent out for training that can last a week or more. It all depends on the company culture and the nature of the work you're doing. Typically, the employee orientation covers the following.

Introduction of Key Executives

In a larger company, especially when there are a lot of new hires starting on the same day, people like the chief executive officer (CEO), president, and other key executives may actually come in to introduce themselves and address new employees. In a smaller company, you may just get a handshake and good luck wishes from the top guy or gal.

Review of Company Regulations

You'll learn things like the company's starting and ending times, how to enter and leave the grounds and building, where to park, and so on. The typical workweek for full-time workers in both the United States and Canada is 35 to 40 hours, which generally includes unpaid time for lunch breaks. You're also entitled to two 15-minute breaks during the day in the United States (per the U.S. Department of Labor); in Canada, breaks must be provided after every five hours of work and may be paid or unpaid at the discretion of the company.

The business workday in North America typically runs from 8 a.m. to 4:30 p.m., or 9 a.m. to 5 p.m., but there are many variations depending on the company and the type of work it does. For example, hospitals, manufacturers, and law enforcement organizations work in shifts, meaning that employees cover all hours of the 24-hour day in rotating groups. A typical 24-hour shift runs from 7 a.m. to 3 p.m.; 3 p.m. to 11 p.m.; and 11 p.m. to 7 a.m. You could also have a job that has ten-hour days, so you'll work four days, then have one day off.

You may also be asked—or possibly be required—to work overtime hours, which is time worked beyond your basic workweek. Overtime is paid at the rate of 1½ to 2 times your regular rate of pay, if you are an hourly worker. If you're a salaried worker, you're out of luck; there's no additional pay for overtime.

Your new company may require you to have an identification badge, which probably will have a stripe on the back encoded with your personal information and the access you have to various areas of the business. You'll use it to enter the building and secure areas inside, and possibly to enter and leave a secured parking area. You'll be photographed for this badge on your first day on the job. If your religion requires you to wear a head or face covering, you'll be required to show your face when the photo is taken.

Your company also may have a no-smoking policy in its building(s) and even its parking areas. Smoking regulations are very strictly observed and could be grounds for dismissal if you smoke anyway and are caught. Many—but not all—companies provide a sheltered place outside where smokers can take a break. Make sure you ask about this if you're a smoker so you don't break any rules.

Review of Employee Expectations

This may cover everything from behavior on the job (code of conduct), to onsite uses of technology like social media and smartphones, the company's sexual harassment policy, and annual performance evaluations. You'll probably receive an employee handbook or a link to an online version that details these expectations. You should read or skim through the handbook so you have a good idea of what is expected of you while on the job.

It's quite common for employers to have a probationary period for new hires. This period can be as short as thirty days to as long as six months or even a year. During the probationary period, the intent isn't to get you to do something that can get you fired; rather, it's meant to be a time for you to learn and grow on the job. Occasionally, an employee will not make it through the probationary period and will be dismissed, but more often than not, you'll sail through without any problems.

You won't get a certificate or other recognition at the end of the probationary period; more likely, you'll just continue to go about your job and no one will ever bring it up again.

Discussion of Benefits (*aka* "Perks" or "Fringe Benefits")

Your benefits will probably include paid vacation time after a certain period of service (often a year); paid holidays (including nine paid holidays for U.S. federal workers, and eight statutory holidays for Canadian federal workers; nonfederal workers get a few less); personal days (a day or two off with pay for conducting personal business); medical insurance; flexible spending accounts; retirement plans; and more. Health insurance and retirement plans are discussed below. Also, please note that depending on the type and size of the company, you may not receive all these benefits.

Working from Home

Some employers will allow you to work offsite in your home office. This is known as telecommuting, and employers like it because it saves them money in their operating budget.

While working at home may sound like a dream job, there are drawbacks. First, you need to be very disciplined, since you must stay at your desk during office hours. Second, you have to set ground rules for your family so they know you're not available to play catch, go to the grocery store, or fold the laundry. Finally, you'll need a physical space in which to work.

Still, if you have an up-to-date computer system, a good phone, and some office furniture, this can be a good option. You'll save on the cost of commuting to the office, a business wardrobe, lunch money, and so on.

Not all jobs lend themselves to telecommuting, and new employees generally don't get this perk. But if you're interested, ask the human resources department about telecommuting after you've been on the job for a while.

EMPLOYEE PAPERWORK

Paperwork you'll be required to fill out will include tax, benefit (insurance) enrollment, retirement, and other forms. (You'll learn more about these issues later and in Chapter 6.) You'll also fill out a personal information document for your personnel file that will ask for information like who should be called in case of an emergency.

FACILITY/OFFICE TOUR

If the building where you're working is very large, you may be taken on a tour to familiarize you with where everything is located, including important departments like human resources and occupational health (where you'll go if you're injured on the job), the company cafeteria, the restrooms, and other key sites.

Health Care Insurance (United States)

Larger companies (more than fifty employees) usually offer some kind of a medical benefits package for you and possibly your dependents. Benefits usually include health, dental, and vision coverage. Companies with fewer than fifty employees are not required to offer insurance, which means you'll have to buy your own coverage.

Most companies pay only a percentage of the cost of the medical insurance, which means you'll have to pay the rest. The cost of the monthly premium you're required to pay will be deducted from your paycheck, which is still likely to be much less than if you purchased your own insurance.

New employees like you usually have a month or so to sign up for these benefits. Make sure you don't miss the deadline, because you'll have to wait until the next open enrollment period. That could be nearly a year away, depending on when you were hired.

Also, if your company covers spouses and dependents and your spouse is already covered, or if you're covered by your parents' insurance policy, it's possible that your employer will give you a small stipend because it doesn't have to pay for your insurance. It usually doesn't amount to much, but it helps.

Health Care Insurance (Canada)

Canadian employers usually offer health insurance as part of their employment benefits package. The insurance usually covers medical, dental, and vision. If your company doesn't offer insurance, you can buy private insurance instead. You also can rely on Canada's publicly funded health-care system, but it covers just basic services. You'll have to pay for things like corrective lenses, medications, and home care out-of-pocket.

Other Types of Insurance (United States)

Some companies offer various other types of insurance you may find helpful as an additional way to protect your family. They include life insurance (sometimes up to the full amount of your annual salary, plus you may be able to extend coverage to your spouse and children), accidental death/

dismemberment insurance, short- and long-term-disability insurance (which replaces part of your income if you're too ill or injured to work), and long-term-care insurance. You generally have to pay premiums to get this coverage, but often, the rates you'll pay are lower than what you'd pay if you bought the policies on your own. You'll have the option of paying with pre- or after-tax funds. Be sure to weigh the tax consequences carefully before you make a decision.

OTHER TYPES OF INSURANCE (CANADA)

Depending on the employer, you may be eligible for a variety of insurance plans other than medical, including insurance to cover accidental death and dismemberment; critical illnesses; short- and long-term disability; extended health care; and group life. What's available varies from one employer to the next, and larger companies are more likely to offer the additional coverage.

FLEXIBLE SPENDING ACCOUNT (UNITED STATES)

A flexible spending account (FSA) is a type of voluntary savings account set up by your employer that will help you save money on your income taxes. Each pay period, you can contribute the dollar amount you specify from your paycheck into the FSA. These funds can then be used to pay for qualified expenses like medical or dependent care costs. Because the funds are deducted from your pay before taxes, in essence you're getting a tax deduction on your medical costs. It's a great plan, but it does have a catch: if you don't spend all the money before December 31, you'll lose it. So if you decide to contribute to an FSA, make sure you calculate the amount of money you think you'll use every year very carefully, then divide that amount by the number of paychecks you'll get in the next year. Have that amount withheld from your paycheck.

HEALTH SPENDING ACCOUNT (CANADA)

An increasing number of employers in Canada are offering a health-care spending account (HSA) as part of their employment packages. Its purpose is to give employees a way to set aside pretax funds to pay for medical expenses not covered by health insurance. So in essence, you're getting tax-free health-care dollars.

If your employer doesn't offer an HSA, you can set one up yourself and deposit funds into it on your own. However, be careful how much money you deposit because this is a "use it or lose it" account. Unused funds you deposit one year do carry over to the next plan year, but after that, you forfeit them.

Employer-Sponsored Retirement Plans (United States)

Larger companies generally offer tax-deferred retirement savings plans to help you save for retirement. A 401(k) plan, or defined-contribution benefit account, is the most common type of retirement plan; a 403(b) plan is for people in public education, health professions, and the ministry. Some companies will contribute to or match the amount of money you contribute to your account, which helps your savings grow faster. For more details about these plans, see Chapter 22.

Employer-Sponsored Pension Plans (Canada)

The two most common types of employer-sponsored pension plans are the defined contribution plan (DCP) and the defined benefit plan (DBP). Under a DCP, both you and your employer contribute funds to the account. Your contribution is a percentage of your paycheck, and you should try to contribute as much as possible, especially if your employer is matching the amount. That will build your balance more quickly. Returns are based on investment performance and are not guaranteed. With a DBP, only the employer contributes to the plan, and you'll have a guaranteed pension. However, you have no control over how or where the money is invested. In addition, the employer decides which type of plan to offer. You don't have a choice in the matter.

Legal Services

Almost everyone needs the services of a lawyer once in a while, for instance to set up a trust, review legal documents, or even change one's name to simplify its spelling. (Immigrants do that all the time to fit into their new country better.) So if your employer offers a legal services plan, you might want to sign up. The per-pay cost is usually fairly low.

Health Club Discounts

Some companies offer free or discounted health-care memberships to encourage their employees to get fit and healthy. If you think you'll use it, it's usually a great deal.

Employee Stock Purchase Plan (ESPP)

This is another type of savings plan offered by public companies that allows workers to buy stocks or shares in the company at a discount and without brokerage fees. Purchases are made with payroll deductions in after-tax dollars. Furthermore, you don't have to pay taxes on the stock until you sell it, at which time you'll pay capital gains taxes.

YOUR FIRST PAYCHECK

Getting your first paycheck at a new job can be an exciting experience, but one look at the many deductions against the gross (before taxes) amount can be a bit of a letdown. In addition to deductions taken to pay for the various benefits and savings accounts just mentioned, you'll have inescapable tax deductions as well. The payroll taxes are deducted out of every paycheck and include federal and state or provincial taxes based on your income tax bracket. These taxes include the following.

Payroll Taxes (United States)

Employers are required to withhold a portion of each paycheck to pay state and federal income tax on your behalf. The federal taxes are paid to the Internal Revenue Service (IRS) and are based on your income bracket tax rate, which can be 10 percent, 15 percent, 25 percent, or more. The state taxes are sent to your state's treasury. On the federal side, you'll also pay FICA (a Social Security tax under the *Federal Insurance Contributions Act*) and a Medicare tax.

Income Taxes (Canada)

Employment income taxes are paid quarterly to the Canada Revenue Agency (CRA). You must make income tax installment payments if your annual net tax earnings will be more than $3,000 ($1,800 in Quebec). Sometimes employers are not required to withhold income tax from employees' paychecks, which means that you have to be diligent about sending in the tax payments yourself and on time. Income taxes are due in full on April 30 of every year.

However, you may have employment income tax withheld by your employer by giving the payroll department a completed Form TD1 (Personal Tax Credits Return). In Quebec, you must file both a TD1 form and a provincial Form TP1015.3-V (Source Deductions Return).

Alternately, you can make installment payments yourself through CRA's "My Account for Individuals" (go to cra.gc.ca/mypayment) service, where you'll use one of the agency's official "sign-in partners" to send your payments. The participating financial institutions include BMO Financial Group, Choice Rewards MasterCard, ING Direct, Scotiabank, and TD Canada Trust. You also can use the online banking system offered by your own bank to send in your payments.

Payments are also accepted in person at a financial institution or by mail using a check or money order. You must submit your payment with a CRA remittance voucher. The voucher may be obtained online at cra-arc.gc.ca/esrvc-srvce/tx/ndvdls/myccnt/menu-eng.html or by phone at (800) 959-828. The CRA will personalize the vouchers and mail them to you. Be sure to use only the vouchers issued to you, or your payments may not be credited correctly. Always write your Social Insurance Number (SIN) and tax year on your check.

Things You Should Never Say to Your Boss

Following are some things you should *not* say to your boss because they could cause trouble for you and disrupt the work environment:

"I'm in this for the money." You can imagine how well that would go over. Even though it's probably true, don't say it out loud.

"I need this job because I'm broke / I'm bankrupt / my spouse is taking all my money." That's no one's business but your own. Keep such information private.

"I'm only here until I buy a house / car / motorcycle / etc." This essentially gives your boss the go-ahead to find your replacement.

"I'm so exhausted. I was up partying all night." Don't share this kind of information—you're supposed to be alert and ready to work. The boss might think you're trouble waiting to happen.

"This job is so boring." To which the boss may respond, "Then go work somewhere else."

"I can't get along with / don't like Bob (or Sudheer or Anya)." You can't pick the people you work with, unless you're the boss. Get over it and do your job.

"It's not my job." Yes, it is.

"The old way works better than the way we're doing things now." Resisting change just makes things worse and makes you look like a complainer.

Add in nonverbal language like sighs, grimaces, eye rolls, or retching sounds when making any of these comments and your opinion becomes very clear—and it's not very flattering. Such behavior is likely to offend or upset the boss and make him or her less confident in your abilities. If you want to keep your job, even if it's just until you find something better, avoid these behaviors.

BAD HABITS TO AVOID AT WORK

Now that you've landed your new job, it's important to present a professional demeanor to those with whom you work. That means treating others with courtesy and respect, coming to work on time every day, remaining until the end of the day, and carrying out your duties competently and willingly. In addition, be sure to avoid the following bad habits, which can create bad feelings among your coworkers:

- *Being unprepared for meetings and not meeting deadlines.* This makes you look bad and shows a lack of respect for both your boss and your coworkers.
- *Being "me-focused" instead of "you-focused."* There's an expression in English that there's no "I" in "team." If you're not a team player, your value to the company is greatly diminished.
- *Not being self-sufficient.* You need to be able to solve problems on your own, not rely on your boss or coworkers to do the work for you. When you have a problem you need to discuss with the boss, always go in with possible solutions. Don't just dump the problem on the boss and expect him or her to take the lead.
- *Eating foods with strong odors, especially in crowded lunchrooms.* Ethnic foods like curry can be very pungent and may offend others who are trying to eat their own lunch in peace. Likewise, try to avoid eating such foods when you know you'll be in close contact with other people, like during meetings.
- *Talking too loudly on the phone.* Many immigrants come from cultures where it's acceptable—and maybe even necessary—to speak loudly. But in North America, where people work in tight quarters, loud conversations are disruptive and annoying to others. Not to mention, be careful in general about what you discuss on the phone in the office. Your private business should remain just that: private.
- *Taking or making too many personal calls.* You were hired to work when you're at work. It's okay to make the occasional personal call, but limit those calls. In general, you should turn your phone off while you're working. If you need to keep an eye on your kids, consider signing up for a home monitoring system like Comcast Home Control, which allows you to see what's going on at home right from your computer. It's an easy way to monitor your kids' or other family members' activities without being on the phone with them constantly.
- *Going to work when you're sick.* Your dedication to your job is admirable, but if you're sick, you run the risk of making everyone around you sick, too. No one is so important that he or she can't stay home to rest and recover.

BEHAVIORS TO AVOID IN THE WORKPLACE

Your personality makes you who you are. But if you have personality traits that make you hard to get along with, your relationships in the workplace will be strained and unpleasant. Worse yet, if your behavior is disruptive enough, you could end up being dismissed from your job.

It's not easy changing your basic makeup, but there are behaviors you can try to temper in the interest of having a more peaceful workplace. For instance, being moody and unpredictable can really be disruptive to others, while sudden outbursts can make people uncomfortable to the point that they won't want to work with you. This doesn't foster a team atmosphere.

Likewise, the opposite behavior—acting aloof—can make you seem like you're uninvolved with or disinterested in others. Since it's not uncommon for people to spend more time with the people they work with than with their own families, it doesn't make for a pleasant workplace if you are withdrawn and uncommunicative. Make an effort to get to know the people you work with and you'll seem more approachable and likeable.

Following are other traits to avoid or reduce:

- *Indecisiveness:* If you can't make a decision because you're afraid of making a mistake, you can't help the team. It's better to take a chance and make a mistake than never to try.
- *Distrustfulness:* Being suspicious of everyone and everything hurts your ability to contribute to the team in a meaningful way.
- *Undermining others:* Acting as though you're cooperating with people while privately opposing and undermining them causes trouble.
- *Arrogance:* Believing that you're better than everyone else causes resentment and anger among your coworkers.
- *Misbehaving:* Testing limits by "acting out" and deliberately "pushing someone's buttons" (irritating him or her) to cause trouble is both childish and immature.
- *Acting flaky:* Exhibiting odd or unusual behavior (being "flaky") makes others suspicious of you and is disruptive to the work environment.
- *Seeking attention:* Being overly dramatic is a way to get attention, but in a bad way.

- *Toadying:* Trying to make everyone happy to avoid conflict while compromising your own values or the policies of the company is dishonest and never ends well.

ATTA'S LESSONS

One thing I have always been grateful for is the range of benefits offered by American employers. I will say, though, that they can be a confusing for immigrants with limited language skills. In some respects, understanding benefits can be like navigating the ocean in a small sailboat. You know where you want to go, but it's hard to get there.

I learned about long-term disability the hard way, when I saw my young supervisor at the bank collapse right in front my eyes just a few months after I started my job. He had a stroke and was never able to walk again. But he survived, thanks to excellent health-care coverage and long-term-disability benefits. Until then, I didn't know about the amazing short- and long-term benefits my employer offered, benefits I could get at a very low monthly cost.

As for payroll taxes, even as a banker, it took me a good ten years to figure out the various payroll tax benefits and advantages, during which time I literally lost thousands of dollars. Don't let this happen to you—seek professional advice so you understand your options, then share your knowledge with your entire family and your friends.

CHAPTER 8:
ENTREPRENEURSHIP

As you know from Chapter 6, North America offers many employment opportunities to the people who step up to grab them—even those who are
newly landed here or are immigrant residents. But among those people are
individuals who dream big. They want to control their own destiny. They
aspire to creating a livelihood that is fulfilling and satisfying. And they do
this by starting their own business.

These people are entrepreneurs, or what the *Merriam-Webster* dictionary
defines as people who "start a business and [are] willing to risk loss in order
to make money." Historically, there have been many American and Canadian
immigrants who were willing to take the risk and found great success. For
example, Nicolai Tesla, an inventor, engineer, and physicist, was a Serbian
immigrant. Sergey Brin, a native of Russia and cofounder of Google, the internet search engine, was six when his family fled his homeland for America.
Maxwell Kohl, the founder of Kohl's department stores, is from Poland;
he grew his successful retailing chain out of a single grocery store. Robert
Herjavec, who you might know from the TV reality show *Shark Tank*, is a
Croatian-born entrepreneur who founded two successful internet security
software companies. And the list goes on.

In fact, immigrants have had an impressive record of success in North
America for decades. According to an article in *Forbes* magazine, 40 percent
of Fortune 500 businesses, which are the largest companies in America based
on revenue, were founded by immigrants or their children. That's an amazing
statistic—and something that should inspire you.

The successes of the people just mentioned didn't happen overnight, of
course. Every one of these people—and the tens of thousands of others
who start small businesses—started out exactly like you would today: with a
dream, a little cash, and a lot of determination. Keep in mind, though, that
people who own their own small business tend to work harder and longer
hours than they would if they were employed in a conventional 9-to-5 job.
But the satisfaction that comes with owning a business that you created out
of your own hard work and innovation and provides the means to take care
of your family well is indescribable.

There's another important reason besides personal satisfaction that drives immigrants to start their own business. It's a sad but well-known fact that even the most educated immigrants often find that their background and training are lacking in the eyes of North American employers. This is not an insult; rather, the educational systems in other countries differ significantly from those in North America, and the two don't always mesh well. This is particularly a problem for highly educated professionals like physicians, lawyers, and even university professors. It's not uncommon to find an immigrant who has a doctorate degree in his homeland, working in a minimum-wage job like janitorial services after coming to North America, just so he can make a living. Owning your own small business will help you circumvent this type of distressing situation.

More Benefits of Owning Your Own Business

- You are in control of the entire operation.
- You can hire and work with the employees you choose.
- You control the level of rewards, from salaries and bonuses to time off.
- You control the financial risks, taking on only what you're comfortable with.
- You can follow your own instincts without fear of reprisal.
- You can establish a direct connection with your customers.
- You can reach out to and serve your community.
- You can create a work/life balance that allows you to enjoy life while attending to the needs of your family.
- You'll have pride in your accomplishments while building a legacy for your children.

So no matter whether you're one of those professionals who suddenly finds his or her credentials aren't strong enough for North American employers, you want to manufacture something, or you simply want to provide necessary services like tailoring or catering, you *can* be an entrepreneur and grab your piece of what is known as the American dream (with apologies to Canada).

Read on for some ideas on how to make that dream come true.

Laying the Groundwork

As with any other important venture, it's important to make some plans be-fore attempting to launch your own business. Start by making a personal in-ventory, as discussed in Chapter 5. You need to identify your skills, strengths, and weaknesses, and recognize the areas that need to be strengthened and developed before you can confidently start a business. Your strengths may be your education, your previous record of success, or even just your confidence and enthusiasm. Your weaknesses might include low-to-no startup funds and sketchy English-speaking skills.

As mentioned in Chapter 5, the best thing to do about the communication gap is to take conversational English classes. But it takes time to acquire fluency. So here's another option in the meantime: sell products and ser-vices to people from your homeland. For example, you could specialize in selling products that are used back home but are not readily available in North America, either in a store or through a mail order company. (The internet makes such products easier to obtain these days, of course, but not everyone is computer-savvy or has access to a computer.) Just consider: were there products that you really missed when you relocated to North America? Become a supplier. Are there services you could provide—say, financial, insurance-related, and so on—that immigrants may not have because they don't understand English well enough to acquire them?

This approach has two advantages. First, you'll forge a successful company that has the potential to provide you and your family with a good income. (It does take time though; be patient.) Second, you'll help other immigrants who may have struggled to find the products and services they need. It's a win-win situation, meaning both sides win.

As for the financial side of the equation, not all businesses have huge startup costs. For example, let's say you want to be a hotel services consultant (like the guy on TV who goes around showing how hotel owners can im-prove their operations) or a wedding planner. The most you'll need when you start out—besides clients and conversational English—will be a computer, a phone, some business cards, and a place to make the magic happen. That place can be right in your own home, which saves you the huge expense of leasing a commercial office space. If you plan to manufacture something—say, dog sweaters, or smartphone covers, or some innovative thing that everyone will want—you'll need more startup cash, which you may not have unless you can find investors or a silent partner (more about that later).

And here's another suggestion: how about starting an eBay or Amazon business and selling to people all around the world? Millions of people do just that. However, you will need startup funds for inventory, plus it's advisable to have your ad copy written by someone fluent in the English language.

To determine exactly what the possibilities are, do a financial inventory. Do you have enough money in the bank to purchase initial store inventory or establish an eBay storefront? Would you be able to survive for a while without earning much money in your new venture? (Not many people can.) Is there another person in the family who could cover the monthly expenses until you start making money? If so, you'd be freed up to pursue your new venture without fear of foreclosure or losing your lease.

In addition, you'll need what is known as "a nest egg," or a certain amount of cash set aside that can be used to pay household and other living expenses, until the business actually starts making money. Optimally, that nest egg should be equal to a *minimum* of six months' worth of expenses. A full year of money for expenses is even better; three years is optimal. The Small Business Administration (SBA) says that it can take a small business up to three years to show a profit, and you wouldn't want to give up your dream of being a successful small business owner because you ran out of cash.

So here are the options. First, start your small business as a part-time or side venture and keep your day job (if you have one) so you can meet your monthly expenses while the business is growing. When the day comes that your small business is paying enough to cover those expenses, you'll be ready to quit your regular job. But make no mistake: it's difficult to juggle a job, a small business, and family obligations. But it can be done if you're determined.

Second, find someone who might be willing to invest in your small business and provide startup and ongoing funds. You could structure this as a loan or an arrangement where the investor receives a percentage of business revenues once the company is profitable. Banks are notoriously reluctant to back new small business owners, so try approaching a successful entrepreneur in your community instead. Better still, identify and approach a successful person who comes from your homeland. That person, being an immigrant himself or herself, is likely to be sympathetic to your cause.

Third, find a business partner. This option works only if you have some money in the bank and can share expenses. The business split doesn't have to be equal—if you can fund only 30 percent of the business, for example, your partner would be the majority shareholder by providing 70 percent of the funds. However, this means you will be giving up control of the company you've established and you will be subject to the whims of your partner. If you do go this route and you eventually want to be the majority shareholder—or the only owner—at some point, be sure to work out a legal arrangement in advance in which you are able to buy out the other person's share. You'll learn more about partnerships and other types of business structures later in this chapter.

Setting Up a Monthly Budget

When figuring out your financial needs, don't forget to include everything you currently pay in your household budget: food, medical expenses, utility payments, child care costs, home and auto insurance, car loans, and any other bills you receive on a monthly basis. If you don't have enough money to cover these expenses for six months to a year, you run the risk of having to close the business before it ever really gets started, because you've run out of money to cover those day-to-day expenses.

Of course, if you're working a low-paid job now and you're sending money home to help the people you left behind in "the old country," you may have very little money left over to save for the future, let alone to build a nest egg for a business startup. But this doesn't mean that your dreams of self-employment must be abandoned. Rather, you'll need to keep your business expenses as low as possible every month, something that might actually cramp your business development if you need to travel for business, for example. If you don't have the funds, you'll simply have to postpone that particular plan or find another way to float it.

And incidentally, many small businesses are home-based, which saves a lot of money every month. If the space in your home is limited, try to find a quiet corner for a table, chair, computer, and phone, at the very least. But, if at all possible, designate a room in your home—maybe what is now the den or a spare bedroom—and use it solely to run your business. Part of the reason is so you actually feel like you're going to work when you sit down at your desk for the day. The other reason is so others in the family respect that you are working. If you're sitting at the kitchen table trying to make deals while the family is preparing dinner around you or giving the dog a bath, you won't feel very professional—and worse yet, the client on the other end of the line won't think you are, either.

Business Ownership Structures

Once you've identified your skills and nailed down your finances, it's time to move on to creating the business structure. Forming a business in the United States and Canada is much simpler than it is in many other countries. You literally can decide to start a business today and begin operating immediately. But as discussed earlier, it's a better idea to put some thought into the process first.

The type of business you form will dictate the type of business taxes you pay and the amount of risk you'll assume, so choose your business structure carefully. There are four legal forms of business available in both the United States and Canada: sole proprietorship, partnership, corporation, and limited liability company.

Sole Proprietorship

This is the easiest, simplest, and least expensive business structure. The business is considered an extension of the owner (sole proprietor), who usually operates it under his or her own name. There is little paperwork involved in a sole proprietorship. Basically, all a U.S.-based sole proprietor must do at tax time is file Schedule C, Profit or Loss from Business, with his or her personal income taxes (Form 1040), as well as a few other tax forms related to home-business deductions, if any, and estimated tax payments. (As a small business owner, you'll have to send in quarterly tax payments on annual earnings of $600 or more, both to the IRS and your state treasury.) A Canadian sole proprietor files Form T2125, Statement of Business or Professional Activities, along with his or her personal taxes (Form T1 General).

Now for the downside: a sole proprietor is responsible for all business debt, and both personal and business assets may be seized to pay any outstanding debts.

PARTNERSHIP

As discussed earlier, a partnership is a business alliance formed with another person or persons. This type of legal entity usually is formed to pool the funds, skills, and talents of one or more individuals, and ownership can be equal or unequal. Whoever has the majority share is the primary decision maker, so think carefully before giving away control of the company. Each partner also shares the risk inherent in the partnership, as well as the profits and expenses. As with a sole proprietorship, partnership income and expenses are reported on each partner's individual tax return, and business risk is shared. Because personality conflicts, workloads, and even honesty can be issues in a partnership, be sure to have a legal partnership agreement drawn up if you choose to take on a partner or two.

CORPORATION

Business liability is considered to be separate from the individual who forms a corporation, so this can be beneficial if your tolerance for risk is low. Forming a corporation is more expensive, and you must have articles of incorporation (a legal document), elected officers, and an annual meeting (even if you hold it in your living room).

In the U.S., there are two types of corporations: S corp and C corp. The S corp is usually better for small business owners, because it's taxed at the partnership rate, but profits and losses are reported on the owner's personal income tax form. However, you have to qualify for S corp status. C corps require more paperwork and are taxed at a higher rate, because income is first taxed at the corporate level, then at the individual level, resulting in double taxation, which is not advantageous for a small business owner.

In Canada, there is only one type of corporation, which operates as a legal entity separate from its owners. It files articles of incorporation at the federal, provincial, or territorial levels, and must also file its own corporate tax return separate from the corporation's directors. Issues relating to the directors' liability are complex. Refer to Information Circular IC89-2R2 at cra-arc. gc.ca/E/pub/tp/ic89-2r2/ for more information.

Limited Liability Company

There's one final type of legal structure of note that's available only in the United States. A limited liability company (LLC) can be owned by a single individual (similar to a sole proprietorship) or multiple owners (similar to a partnership). As the name implies, the owner's liability is limited, and the owner receives the tax benefits of a sole proprietorship or partnership. An LLC is a great choice for someone who wants to reduce risk while maximizing profits.

As you can see, selecting a legal entity can be a complex and confusing process. Most small business owners do fine with a sole proprietorship when they start out, so you might want to go that route, too. You can always convert to another legal business form as your company and profits grow. When that time comes, you'll want to consult with a lawyer who specializes in taxation to ensure you make the best choice for your situation.

Franchise Businesses

Before leaving this discussion of small business ownership, there's one more type of business opportunity you might want to consider. A franchise operates under a license granted by the franchise holder ("franchisor") to market its products or services, but you actually own your location and make all the business decisions. With a franchise, you have what is known as a turnkey operation—that is, a business based on a proven business model in which everything is provided to you to run it, from the building, to the inventory and the advertising/promotional materials. You also get the benefit of the franchise's recognized brand name, which is extremely valuable for a new business startup. Examples of well-known franchises are McDonald's, Hampton Hotels, and Supercuts. Some famous Canadian franchises include Shoppers Drug Mart, Second Cup, and Canadian Tire.

A franchise might sound like your business dream come true, but there are some drawbacks. First, a franchise license for one of the best-known businesses can cost *big* bucks. For example, the cost to open a Subway restaurant franchise, which is one of the fastest-growing franchises in the world, ranges from $116,000 to $262,000, while the initial investment for a Tim Horton's franchise in Canada is a staggering $430,000 to $480,000 CDN. Makes you wonder how people do it, doesn't it?

One way they do it is by pooling resources. For example, an entire family could sink their life savings into a franchise license, and as long as the franchise is successful, they could end up earning a good living for everyone. You also could take on a partner or two—or ten—to make the financials work.

Let's say you *can* make it work financially. Some other things to think about before signing on the dotted line include the following questions.

Are the Financials Overly Optimistic?

Remember that a franchisor is in the business of making the franchise look irresistible to aspiring franchise owners and may paint a much rosier picture of potential and profits than is necessarily true. Also, historical data and sales do not always translate to future profits. So if you're interested in acquiring a franchise operation, make sure you analyze its financials and record of success very carefully. Naturally, a well-known operation like Burger King or 7-Eleven won't be as risky to buy into, which is why their initial investment cost is so high.

Can You Expect Many Out-of-Pocket Costs?

Some franchises will let you buy in for a modest initial cost, then will sock you with additional fees after you've committed yourself. To forestall this, speak to current and former franchise owners outside your target market area about their experience and ongoing costs. If they would buy another franchise location, it's a pretty good bet that the franchisor is treating them well.

Does the Franchise Have a Proven Business Model?

Let's face it: while it might be exciting to sign on with a startup franchise because there's the potential to make a lot of money, it's a pretty risky venture that could cost you the business and your entire initial investment if it doesn't work out. Generally, it's best to go with a proven company that has a history of success. Of course, you will pay more for that privilege, but it's the best way to make sure you'll come out ahead in the long run.

ATTA'S LESSONS

While working as a senior regional manager in banking, I decided to pursue my dream of business ownership: in 2006, I invested in a restaurant operation. Not only did the resulting business venture not get off to a good start, but it also nearly cost me my twenty-eight-year banking career because of a lack of proper planning, forethought, adequate research, and experience. I ultimately lost my entire investment in the partnership, as well as thousands of dollars in out-of-pocket costs.

Learn from my experience. Ask yourself the following questions before deciding to start your own business.

Are you emotionally and financially prepared to leave your job?

- Have you tallied up all potential business costs? Do you know how you'll cover them?
- Do you have adequate back-up funds to run the business without any profits for at least two to three years?
- Have you compiled a full list of personal expenses and examined how you would cover them each month?
- Do you have adequate funds in savings to pay for all your personal and household expenses for at least two years?
- Do you have adequate health care coverage and/or benefits through another member of the family?
- Are you able to purchase and replace all current employee benefits for yourself and members of your family?
- Have you thought about how you'll replace employer-sponsored life- and long-term-disability insurance?
- Have you considered how you'll manage your current employer-sponsored retirement funds?
- Do you have adequate reserves to pay for and finance all your costs for the potential business?
- Do you have adequate knowledge and understanding of taxation and insurance requirements for the potential business, or do you have a trusted advisor?

If you can answer "yes" to most of these questions, you should be in a good position to start your own business. But if you answered "no" too many times, postpone your new business venture until you can settle your personal affairs and come up with enough cash to fund the business.

Chapter 9: Transportation

Unless you have emigrated from an enormous country like Russia or China, you probably have never seen anything like the vast, open spaces of North America. Even if you have only been exposed to America's and Canada's major cities, you know that North America is quite unlike Europe and many other parts of the world.

This sprawling vastness is why North Americans tend to own their own transportation rather than rely on public transportation. While it's true that some urban centers—like New York City, San Francisco, and Philadelphia—have busy subway, cable car, and bus systems, respectively, if you're a North American resident, you're much more likely to drive yourself around in your own vehicle.

As an immigrant or other newcomer, it's important to understand your transportation options and to know how to navigate the roadways. This will protect not only yourself, but your family and others around you. Statistics show that new drivers are involved in the most accidents across North America, and not surprisingly, young drivers, especially those aged between sixteen and nineteen years of age, have higher traffic accident rates than any other group. Inexperience is a big part of the problem among this age group, but recklessness and alcohol also figure significantly into the statistics. So it's no surprise that both new and younger drivers pay more in auto insurance premiums. (Insurance is discussed in detail in Chapter 20.)

Despite the fact that so many people drive their own vehicles in North America, if you're an inexperienced driver it's usually best if you start out using public transportation before buying a car. Granted, there are certain urban areas where it can be very challenging to find reliable public transportation (Detroit, among them), but if there's a way to get around town by having someone else drive, it's highly recommended.

SIGNAGE AND STREETS

Even if you're used to driving on the same side of the road in your home country as drivers do in North America, you'll still find it challenging to get around in North America. To begin with, signage here tends to be wordier than the traffic signs you're used to seeing in other countries. While you will see some of the standard passenger/pedestrian symbols used around the world on North American signs—symbols like an airplane to signify an airport or a railcar to indicate a nearby railroad station—you're just as likely to see "Sea-Tac Airport" or "Grand Central Station" and a bunch of accompanying information on a sign instead of the symbol. This can be confusing if you're trying to drive and read the signs as you navigate your way around.

In addition, in some parts of the United States, signs are in both English and Spanish, while in Quebec, Canada, you'll find English and French sharing space. If you don't know either one or you have only a passable vocabulary, you can get a real dose of culture shock when you try to drive anywhere, which can make you nervous behind the wheel.

Then there are the street names posted on relatively small green or blue signs about ten feet above the roadways. It can be hard to catch the names if you're traveling at a high rate of speed or you're not in the lane closest to the sign. Not to mention, some cities and states have very colorful and confusing street names. Just try to find Kuilei Street in Honolulu, Hawaii, for example, when all the streets around it are named Kahoaloha, Kapaakea, Kapiolani, Kaipuu, Kaaha, and Kamoku. Or try navigating the streets of Miami, where SE 1st Street intersects SE 1st Avenue. If you're planning to drive in an unfamiliar city where the names are confusing, always study a map before you set off or get driving directions from your local auto club, MapQuest.com, MapQuest.ca, or maps.google.com.

ROAD CONSTRUCTION

Residents of northern U.S. states who have a sense of humor believe that there are only two seasons: winter and construction. The fact is, though, that you may find orange construction barrels blocking off the lanes of large and small highways alike at any time of the year. Driving around barrels while trying to figure out where you're going can be challenging, especially during rush hour when the weather is bad. Listen to the local radio traffic report before you set off so you can find an alternate route, or check the local auto club website or a national traffic condition website like fhwa.dot.gov/trafficinfo, which has links to the websites of every U.S. state's transportation website through the "National Traffic and Road Closure Information" link. For Canadian road condition information, go to th.gov.bc.ca/drivebc_supp/ Canada_map.html.

TRANSPORTATION OPTIONS
Automobiles, Trucks, and SUVs

If there's one thing that defines America, it's the car culture. America is the birthplace of the modern auto industry—Henry Ford built his first automobiles in Detroit, *aka* the "Motor City"— and people *love* their cars. They show them off at car shows and during car "cruises." They take road trips down legendary highways like Route 66 and the Skyline Drive in Shenandoah National Park. They also pamper their cars, buy them gifts (really—just take a look at the aisles in any auto parts store), and practically love them to death. Literally. Some car buffs have been buried in their cars.

There are numerous motor vehicle companies in North America. The largest domestic companies in both the United States and Canada include General Motors, Ford, and Chrysler, while the biggest foreign car companies are Toyota, Honda, Volkswagen, and Kia. But this is by no means a complete list of the manufacturers—British, Swedish, and Korean automakers, among others, all have a market presence here.

The car companies build passenger cars, trucks (both for city and rural use), minivans, and sport utility vehicles (known as SUVs). The type of vehicle you buy will depend on how many people will ride in it and the purpose for which it's used. For example, if you're commuting to work around those construction barrels mentioned earlier, you may prefer a sedan. If you will be carrying a lot of cargo, a truck may be a better choice. If you have a large family and need many seats, a minivan or SUV could be your best choice.

New Vehicles

If you're in the market for your first vehicle in North America, you have numerous purchase options. A new car dealer usually has the biggest car lot in town, filled with all types of shiny vehicles in brilliant colors. (New car dealers usually carry cars, minivans, and SUVs; trucks are generally sold at their own dedicated dealerships.) You'll pay the most for a new vehicle, of course, but it can be worth the money, because you get to select the vehicle options you really want, and you'll get a new car warranty that usually runs for a few years or a certain number of miles. This type of basic warranty is known as bumper-to-bumper coverage, meaning that major components in the electrical, fuel, air conditioning, and audio systems, as well as the vehicle sensors, are covered. You may also get powertrain coverage for the engine and transmission. A powertrain warranty typically runs ten years or 100,000 miles, whichever comes first.

You're also likely to be offered an extended warranty at an additional cost. This is a supplemental warranty contract that begins at the end of the basic warranty included with your new vehicle. The warranty usually runs several years and has a deductible. Coverage varies from one automaker to another, so be sure to ask specific questions about what's covered. The extended warranty can be expensive, but since it's transferable to a new owner when you sell the vehicle, so it becomes a positive selling point when you're ready to part with your "ride."

Auto dealers offer their own financing, but you can choose to finance through your own bank or credit union instead. You'll find information about financing in Chapter 13. And, of course, cash is also gladly accepted when you buy your vehicle.

It's worth noting that American automakers have worked hard to catch up to imports in terms of quality and durability. For example, North American vehicles have finishes that resist rust and parts that are engineered to last a long time. So you can buy a domestic vehicle with confidence.

Used Vehicles

Used vehicles represent some of the best values for your money. A new vehicle automatically depreciates, or loses value, as soon as you drive it off the lot. That can amount to big bucks. According to Bankrate.com, the basic rule is that a vehicle loses 10 to 20 percent of its value each year. But when you purchase a used vehicle, the previous owner has absorbed some significant depreciation already, which means you get a better deal. In fact, CNNMoney.com estimates that if you purchase a three-year-old vehicle, you could save as much as 30 to 40 percent over the cost of a new one.

You can buy a used vehicle from many sources, including used-car dealerships (which typically have the *second* largest car lot in town). While most used-car dealerships are independently owned, chain dealerships do exist.

One national chain to investigate is CarMax Inc (CarMax.com).

When you buy from an established used-car dealer, you can be assured that the vehicle has been inspected and cleaned thoroughly, especially if the dealer sells "certified" used cars. Dealers that are backed by vehicle manufacturers sell newer used-cars (usually less than three years old) that have passed a series of inspections before being certified. Once a car passes, the manufacturer adds a new warranty of up to twelve months or more. Furthermore, these used vehicles can be financed.

One way to check whether the vehicle you've chosen is sound and reliable before you sign on the dotted line is to order a Carfax or AutoCheck vehicle history report. The reports start at $29.99 and will tell you things like whether the car has ever been in an accident or sustained other major damage like from flood waters or hail. These reports also will tell you whether the vehicle has a "lemon history," which means there are indications that the vehicle has problems too severe for it to operate properly. These reports also verify the last reported mileage and estimate how many miles the vehicle has been driven annually, which will give you an idea of how much wear and tear there has been on the engine and other components. According to the website CNNMoney.com, about one in ten of the cars in the Carfax and AutoCheck databases has had some kind of service problem, so it's a good idea to order a report before you buy. Make sure you have the Vehicle Identification Number (VIN), which is usually listed on a metal plate just inside the windshield, before you go to carfax.com or autochek.com to get your report.

OTHER USED CAR SOURCES

Naturally, an established used-car dealer has overhead and has to pass on those costs to its customers. So if you're really looking for a bargain on a used car, consider one of these sellers instead:

- *Private seller:* This is a person who is selling his or her own vehicle. If you ever see a lone car or other vehicle sitting in a parking lot with a "for sale" sign in the window, then you know you're dealing with a private seller. Vehicles of all kinds are also sold by private sellers through newspaper classified sections and on Craigslist (craigslist.com).
- *Online sellers:* Dealers commonly use online resources like AutoTrader. com and Cars.com to spread the word about their inventories to a wider

market. Just enter your ZIP code on either site, and you'll get a selection of cars within ten miles or more of your home. These sites are just like classified ad sections in the newspaper, but you'll get a lot more details about the vehicle there than you will in the newspaper.

- *eBay Motors:* While private sellers sell their cars through eBay Motors (ebay.com/motors and ebay.ca/motors), you're somewhat more likely to encounter used-car dealers in this online marketplace. There is some risk purchasing something this expensive sight-unseen, plus you have to make your own arrangements to pick up the vehicle you've won. Even so, you can get some serious deals.

BUYER BEWARE

Not sure if the price the seller is asking is fair? Then check Edmunds.com and Kelley Blue Book (KBB.com). Your bank or credit union will also have a copy of the blue book. These free services will tell you the going price for vehicles of nearly almost every make, model, and year, both new and used. It's a good way to make sure you're not paying too much for the car or other vehicle of your dreams.

Once you find the used vehicle you want, have a mechanic inspect it before you buy it. Used cars and other vehicles are sold "as is," meaning what you see is what you get. If you accept a vehicle without checking it out, and later find out it has major problems, you're stuck, because there are no refunds or adjustments with an "as is" purchase. You can expect to pay about $100 for an inspection.

You have a little more protection if you buy your used vehicle from eBay Motors. It offers purchase protection on every vehicle, which covers odometer-rollback problems, missing titles, and other issues. eBay Motors also has paired with SGS Automotive, a national inspection and testing company, to offer independent third-party vehicle inspections for just $100. For more information about vehicle protection, go to ebay.com/motors and look for the Vehicle Purchase Protection link.

A word of warning: if a private seller refuses to allow you to have the vehicle inspected, walk away. It's possible that the seller is hiding something—maybe shoddy repairs, evidence of significant damage from a crash, odometer rollback, or some other safety hazard. It's also possible to plug radiator or oil leaks temporarily, conceal body damage with a putty product known as "bondo," or otherwise hide things the seller doesn't want you to see until you've handed over the cash and it's too late to complain. And incidentally, used-car/vehicle dealers won't allow you to have an independent inspection, but that's not because they're hiding something. Dealers generally have their own in-house inspection and repair teams, so if the dealership has a good reputation and/or sells certified used cars, you should be able to trust its integrity. But there's no reason why you can't bring your own mechanic with you when you buy the vehicle to give it a quick once-over.

Driving Tips

Before you get behind the wheel of that new (or used) vehicle, don't forget there are some things you must do to be a good citizen.

Take a Driver's Training Class

Even if you've driven in your home country, the rules in North America are different from what you're used to. Look for an instructor-led driver's training class at the local high school or community college, or sign up at a driving school to learn the rules of the road.

Get Licensed

Every state and province requires drivers to be licensed to drive a passenger vehicle. If you were licensed in your homeland, you probably will be able to drive in the United States or Canada on that license for a limited period of time (usually six months to a year). But to continue driving, you need a U.S. or Canadian driver's license.

In the United States, you'll apply at the department of motor vehicles, secretary of state, or other state agency. Generally speaking, you must be sixteen years old to operate a motor vehicle and must have a certain number of hours of training and behind-the-wheel experience, but that may differ by state. Unfortunately, there is not a central office or website you can access to find out your state's regulations. Instead, you must contact your state's transportation department or website for specific information.

Canada's driver's license agencies also have varying names. For instance, you might apply at a DriveTest Centre (Ontario), Access PEI office (Prince

Edward Island, *aka* PEI), or Driver and Vehicle Licensing Office (Nunavut). See Service Canada at servicecanada.gc.ca/eng/subjects/cards/drivers_li-cence.shtml for specific information. Likewise, the licenses have different names in each province. For example, Ontario issues a G-class license, while PEI issues a Class 5 license for operators of passenger vehicles.

If you're a permanent resident in Canada, you'll probably need to show your permanent resident card, record of landing (IMM 1000), confirmation of permanent residence (IMM 5292), and provincial photo card to apply for a license, although this, too, can vary by province.

To become licensed for the first time, you'll have a vision screening, then will take a written test. If your written English skills aren't very strong yet, ask if you can take the test in your native language. You will also have to take a road test, so make sure you practice driving with a licensed driver in the car before you apply for your driver's license.

Avoid Distracted Driving

According to the National Highway Traffic Safety Administration, crashes caused by distracted driving killed 3,300 people and injured 387,000 people in a recent year. Distracted driving includes doing things behind the wheel besides driving, including talking on a cell phone, texting, eating and drinking, putting on makeup, shaving, reading a map, adjusting the radio, programming a GPS device, and many other things. Whenever you drive, concentrate on driving only. Pull over to make a phone call or send a text, and do your grooming at home. It's the best way to stay safe on the road and protect others around you, too.

Local Bus System

Most large cities in North America have their own local bus system to take you everywhere from shopping centers to church. These buses stop frequently—possibly as often as every few blocks—to get you as close to your destination as possible. Bus systems tend to offer extended hours daily, as well as shortened schedules on weekends and holidays. The best thing about local bus service is that it's fairly inexpensive. The bad thing is that in some major cities where crime is a problem, the buses may not be as safe as you would like. Avoid wearing flashy jewelry or clothing, or using expensive electronic devices (including iPhones) while waiting for and on board a bus. If you are aware of your surroundings at all times, you should be fine.

You'll need exact change, a bus token, or a bus pass to ride on a bus. You can buy tokens (which are usually discounted) and bus passes at a bus transit center, an automated vending machine, online, or possibly at other designated locations like libraries and grocery stores. If you need to transfer from one bus to another to get to your destination, you'll need to purchase a transfer when you board the first bus.

Buses often have designated seating at the front of the vehicle for senior citizens and people with disabilities. Please be courteous and give up your seat if a senior or disabled person comes aboard.

Commuter Bus System

Commuter buses carry business people and other workers who live in the suburbs to big-city jobs quickly and affordably. They usually travel longer distances without stopping, so you get to your destination faster. These buses usually run Monday through Saturday during peak rush-hour times (typically 5 a.m. to 10 a.m. and 3 p.m. to 8 p.m.), although some cities have extended service from 5 a.m. to midnight. Riders usually leave their personal vehicle at a Park and Ride location, then catch the bus for the trip to the city.

Commuter buses usually accept cash and bus passes. You can usually get a good discount if you buy a monthly pass, although you'll also get a discount on a daily or weekly bus pass. As with local bus systems, you can buy passes at the bus station, online, or from other designated ticket sellers.

Subway (Rapid Transit)

Subways (*aka* metro systems, rapid transit, or skytrains) aren't as prevalent in North America as they are in Europe and on other continents, but if you have a subway nearby, it's a great way to get around. Major cities like New York, Chicago, Washington, DC, Los Angeles, Toronto, and Vancouver have their own rapid-transit systems, and the trains run frequently every day of the year. As with local buses, it's important to be vigilant when you're riding them to avoid trouble. You can purchase subway fares or passes right at the subway station.

Rail

North Americans don't travel by rail as much as people do in the rest of the world, but the rail system is there if you need it. The U.S. passenger rail line is called Amtrak; in Canada, it's VIA Rail Canada. Both offer high-speed intercity rail service and cross-country travel, and especially in Canada, service to remote areas. Amtrak services thirty-nine states and the District of Columbia, and some of its long-distance trains travel 2,400 miles. VIA Rail runs from coast-to-coast year-round and in all weather. Its northernmost point is Churchill, Manitoba, on Hudson Bay.

Rail trips are a great way to see North America, and both Amtrak and VIA Rail Canada offer vacation packages. Talk to a travel agent, use one of the online travel companies like Hotwire.com, Expedia.com, and Expedia.ca, or go to the rail websites at Amtrak.com or Viarail.ca.

Light Rail

Trains that travel along city streets on fixed tracks are known as light rail. Light rail trains are also variously called streetcars, cable cars, and trams, and can be found in large cities like Minneapolis, San Francisco, and Boston, as well as in Canada in Ottawa, Calgary, Edmonton, and Toronto. There are actually more light rail systems in the United States than there are subways.

Fares are usually based on the distance traveled across different zones. As with buses and subways, you can purchase discounted frequent-traveler fares online or at the rail station.

Carpooling

A great way to get around cost effectively while doing something to save the planet is by carpooling. Also known as ride sharing, carpooling is a way for two or more people to travel together to work or other destinations. This saves gas, parking costs, tolls, and wear and tear on personal vehicles—and your nerves. Carpooling is also environmentally friendly; carbon emissions that can harm Mother Earth are reduced when the number of vehicles on the road goes down.

Carpooling works best when the participants live close to each other or can get to a central meeting place, and if they all work at the same place or close by. If each person in the pool takes his or her turn driving, then that person handles the expenses. If one person prefers to do all the driving, the other carpoolers should contribute an agreed-upon amount of money to offset the cost of gas and other expenses.

Car Sharing

There are several car-sharing companies within larger cities throughout the United States and Canada. Car sharing provides 24/7 access to a car when you need it, without having the responsibilities or cost of car ownership. To use these programs, you usually join a membership online, reserve a car nearby through the car-sharing company's website or phone number, find the car and unlock it, and drive. Car sharing is affordable because you pay by the minute, hour, or day, depending on how long you need it. Car sharing is a simple, convenient, and environmentally friendly option of urban transportation. For more information on car sharing options in the United States, you may visit Zipcar.com and Carsharing.net. In Canada, visit Autoshare.com and Car2go.ca.

Taxicab

If you need a lift unexpectedly or other transportation isn't available, try a taxicab. In cities with dense populations like New York and Toronto, you'll find cabs trolling the streets, looking for fares. Otherwise, you'll have to call for a ride. Cab companies are easy to find using your smartphone or the Yellow Pages.

Other Ways to Get Around

Bicycling

Depending on where you live, you may find that your city has bike paths you can use to get around town safely. Word of caution: buy a bicycle lock and chain or a U-lock to deter theft when you leave your bike unattended.

'WALKING'

Though not strictly a form of transportation, walking is a viable way to get around. It's true that because America and Canada are both so large, and the U.S. is so car crazy, not a lot of people choose this healthy and cost-effective way to get where they're going. But major urban centers—New York, Chicago, Seattle, Boston, and Toronto, for instance—are laid out to walk around comfortably. Just be sure to have the price of a bus ticket or taxicab fare in your pocket in case the going gets tough due to weather or fatigue.

ATTA'S LESSONS

When I was a child in Afghanistan, I walked four miles to and from school. So it was a happy day in my junior year of high school when my father bought me a bicycle. This taught me the value of public transportation, which is why I relied on it for several years after arriving in the United States. I'll admit, though, I was tempted—just like millions of other immigrants are—to buy a fancy car. But I was determined to not fall into debt and, three years after arriving in the United States, I finally settled for an old Ford Maverick, which cost me $700.

Over the years, I have seen many people spend money on fancy cars and pay thousands of dollars in interest charges on those purchases when they could have used public transportation instead. It's your choice, but think about it. You can save a lot of money taking the bus, train, or subway; or by walking or riding a bike—and the physical activity is good for your health. If that's not possible, at least consider buying a used rather than new vehicle, and make sure it's a fuel-efficient model. By avoiding the competition trap, you'll save money.

Vehicle Identification & Registration Information

Vehicle	Make/Model	Model Year	VIN	Registration Exp. Date
Vehicle 1				
Vehicle 2				
Vehicle 3				
Vehicle 4				
License Plates	License Plate #			
Vehicle 1				
Vehicle 2				
Vehicle 3				
Vehicle 4				

Chapter 10: Shopping

No matter whether you just shop for the necessities you need from day-to-day, or you love to shop-'til-you-drop, you'll find the variety of merchandise and stores where you can buy things is breathtaking virtually anywhere you go in North America. Even states and provinces with sparse populations—like Wyoming or Nunavut—have an impressive selection of whatever you need. In this chapter, you'll read about the various places you can spend your hard-earned dollars, from brick-and-mortar stores to online storefronts, as well as the various ways you can pay for those purchases.

WHERE TO SHOP

If you've lived in North America for any length of time, you probably are well aware that bigger is better here. We have big cars, bigger houses, enormous parks, and humungous packages of cereal purchased from huge grocery stores. So you might find it hard to believe that North Americans also like smaller shopping venues that probably resemble the types of small businesses you shopped in back in your home country. Here's a look at the various types of stores from which you can choose.

Mom-and-Pop Shops

This type of business is very small and is usually run by the owner and possibly a helper or two. A mom-and-pop shop can be as small as an outdoor roadside stand that sells vegetables in the summer to a small store that shares space with other small businesses in a bricks-and-mortar building. Because they're so small, they usually don't have their own building. Also, they're not just run by moms and dads; that's just a colorful name for them.

Mom-and-pop stores can sell anything from produce to jewelry. They're fun to shop in, because they're run by the owner who may be willing to negotiate a better price. It never hurts to ask.

BOUTIQUES

This type of store is also usually quite small and specializes in fashionable, one-of-a-kind, and often expensive items like wedding gowns, designer clothing, and jewelry. There are even food boutiques that sell upscale items like caviar and fine wine. You may find a boutique inside a high-end store (like Nordstrom's or Saks Fifth Avenue) or sharing space with other pricey boutiques, like in a resort town. And those stores you find at the airport, like the duty-free shop? They're a type of boutique, too.

Of course, not all boutiques are high-end. Rather, what makes a boutique unique and fun to explore is its specialty merchandise, which may include everything from handmade beaded jewelry to trendy or funky clothing and shoes, handbags, and even bed linens.

Small businesses like the mom-and-pop stores and boutiques have their own promotional day: Small Business Saturday, which falls on the Saturday after Thanksgiving Day, which you may know is the busiest weekend of the year in retailing.

CHAIN STORES

A store that can be found in numerous cities or states/provinces and sells the same type of merchandise in each location is known as a chain store. Dollar stores are chain stores and can be found everywhere from Walla Walla, Washington, in the Pacific Northwest, to Orlando, Florida, in the southeast. This is handy when you move from city to city—you always know what the store will carry, no matter where you are. Chain stores usually have their own building and are located in a retail area next to other stores. Target, Kohl's, and Macy's are all chain stores.

Chain stores tend to be department stores—that is, they have numerous departments selling a wide variety of merchandise, all under the same roof. For example, at Target, you can shop for clothing, handbags, sporting goods, electrical items, furnishings, and food, all in the same store.

BIG BOX STORES

This type of store usually is a chain store, too. But it differs from department stores in that big box stores normally are *huge*. They often specialize in a certain type of merchandise, like electronics (Best Buy) or building supplies (Home Depot). The name "big box" refers to the interior of the building—it's usually wide open with no frills, just like a big box. For this reason, you'll usually need a shopping cart to carry your purchases from one end of the building to the other.

SUPERMARKETS

Basically, a supermarket is a big-box store for food and household products, organized into product aisles. Most products are self-serve, meaning you pick them up off the shelves yourself and take them to the checkout counter. Exceptions may include the meat counter, where a clerk will package the fresh, prime cut of meat or fish you choose, or will slice and package luncheon meat and cheese; and the bakery department, which generally stores the fresh cakes, bagels, and other products in a display counter. Of course, you can also choose prepackaged meat, fish, cheese, and other products right out of the refrigerated cases, so you don't have to wait in line. In addition, supermarkets often have nonfood departments, like a pharmacy and a florist, and some even have bank branches, post office locations, and coffee shops, as well as a gas station in the parking lot.

Supermarkets tend to be regionally based. The largest U.S. supermarket chain is Kroger, with more than 2,400 stores in thirty-one states. You might know this chain by other names, like Ralph's in Southern California or Fred Meyer in the Pacific Northwest and Alaska. Other major supermarket chains include Piggly Wiggly in the southeast United States, and Loblaws and Sobeys in Canada.

After you've made your selection, you take your cart or basket to a checkout lane, where a clerk will scan your items and collect your money. However, many supermarkets also have self-checkout lanes where you can play cashier yourself.

Not all supermarkets are big-box stores—smaller supermarkets abound, too. These stores have a smaller selection of merchandise, which is handy if you only need a few things or you don't like shopping in a huge store.

Membership Warehouse/Wholesale Clubs

Speaking of big stores, the largest retail stores around are known as warehouse or wholesale clubs. These types of big-box stores usually look just like a warehouse, with shelves of merchandise stacked as high as the very high ceiling, and giant bins of fresh produce, meat, fish, and whatever else you need. These types of stores are no-frills, meaning they're very basic. Although warehouse stores do tend to sell more than just food, you won't find specialty shops like a florist inside—although you might find bunches of flowers in a bucket on the floor. Also, you have to buy a *lot* of whatever you're shopping for. Everything is sold in multiples—for example, you might have to buy ten boxes of macaroni and cheese in a single package, five jars of spaghetti sauce, or twenty-five rolls of paper towels. Items are sold this way to keep the prices down, since purchasing a higher quantity leads to bigger savings. If the packages are too large for your family—or your pantry—consider splitting the package and the cost with other family members or friends.

Warehouse clubs you may have heard of include Sam's Club, Costco, and BJ's Wholesale Club.

You have to be a member to shop in one of these stores. Besides paying an annual membership fee, you'll pay an extra percentage on the total bill when you check out. Even so, you can save a lot of money shopping at warehouse clubs. Just be sure you have enough room to store all your discounted treasures.

Convenience Stores

At the other end of the shopping spectrum—that is, the small end—is the convenience store. Like the name says, they're a convenient place to shop when you just need a few things. Stores like 7-Eleven and Circle K, and drug stores like CVS and Shoppers Drug Mart are convenience stores. In some cases, you can do a lot of your grocery shopping at a convenience store, since they generally have everything a grocery store carries except fresh meat, fish, fruit, and vegetables. But beware: you'll pay extra—and sometimes a *lot* extra—for that convenience. But if you're in a hurry, convenience stores are great places to shop.

Strip Malls

Speaking of convenience, if you're looking for a smaller shopping venue where you can buy a variety of items, then a strip mall may be the place for you. Strip malls usually are in well-populated areas, and consist of a bunch of stores connected to each other in a line, or strip. The stores tend to be one-of-a-kind or smaller chain stores, although it's possible to find a strip mall that is anchored by a larger retailer, like Sears or J.C. Penney'. Typical strip malls include businesses like clothing stores, a hair and/or nail salon, a cellular service company, a package delivery company (like UPS), and possibly a restaurant.

Because strip mall stores are smaller, they tend to charge higher prices. But like convenience stores, strip malls allow you to get in a store, make your purchase, and get out fast, which can make the extra cost worth it.

Malls

Another variation on the many-stores-in-one-place theme is the shopping mall. While some malls have outdoor access to their various tenants, most malls are enclosed. Inside, all the stores open into a main arcade, which makes shopping and browsing easier, as well as warm (or cool) and dry. Malls generally are anchored by large department stores, such as J.C. Penney, Macy's, and Dilliard's in the United States; and The Bay, Marks & Spencer (or "Marks & Sparks," as the locals call it), and Zellers in Canada. In addition to the department stores, malls will have a lot of other stores under their roof, including shoe stores, music stores, bookstores, and more.

Many malls have tenants with reasonably priced or discounted goods. But some malls, especially in cities like Houston, Los Angeles, Scottsdale, and Miami, to name just a few, have tenants with extremely expensive merchandise. You can get a reasonable idea about how expensive the retailers are by the mix of stores. If the mall is anchored by Eaton's, J.C. Penney, or T.J. Maxx, the prices will be appealing to the average person. But a mall that features Neiman Marcus, Saks Fifth Avenue, and Bloomingdale's will be much more upscale and expensive.

OFF-PRICE STORES

So what do you do if you're on a budget or you're a bargain hunter? You certainly can get deals in traditional stores by shopping sales and clearance events. But for everyday off-price shopping, you might want to try the following shopping venues:

- Farmers' markets: Generally run by the people who grow the vegetables or raise the animals whose meat they sell, farmers' markets offer fresh food at reasonable prices. They can do this because they don't have the overhead of big grocery stores. Depending on the climate, many farmers' markets are open air, or they might have a canopy or roof over them.
- Orchards and vegetable patches: If you're willing to pick your own apples off a tree or harvest ears of corn right from the field, then these pick-your-own-produce farms are a great source of extremely fresh and reasonably priced food.
- Roadside stands: Wherever you see fruit and vegetables growing, you're likely to see a roadside stand, which usually is just a table or small covered stand at the side of the road. Bring your own bag and cash if you want to shop there.
- Outlet malls: If you're looking for good quality, brand-name merchandise, chances are there's an outlet mall in your area that sells at discounted prices. The merchandise in an outlet mall often consists of past-season items, products that are flawed in some way, factory overruns (caused when a factory makes more items than can be sold), and so on. Many outlet malls sell low- to mid-priced items, but some sell designer clothing and upscale products. For example, the stores at Birch Run Premium Outlets in Birch Run, Michigan, include Coach, BCBG Max Azria, Tommy Hilfiger, Longaberger, Lancôme, and Bose, to name just a few of its nearly 150 stores. It's a good idea to do some comparison shopping and take your iPhone or other Wi-Fi-enabled device with you when you shop the outlet stores. Sometimes, the prices aren't much better than what you'd pay in a regular retail store, and you might be getting a factory second (imperfect) item rather than something of the highest quality.
- Pawn shops: This type of business offers secured short-term loans to people who wish to pawn, or temporarily sell, an item. Often, people pawn "big-ticket items," or merchandise that originally cost a lot of

money, such as diamond jewelry, big screen TVs, fur coats, and even luxury automobiles. The pawn shop holds the item for a certain length of time, like ninety days, and the seller can return during that period to "buy back" his or her item by paying back the loan plus interest. If an item isn't picked up, then it goes on the shelf in the pawn shop for anyone to purchase. You often can get very good bargains on expensive items, so it's worth a look.

- Thrift stores: If you're in the mood for some outrageously discounted retail therapy, head for a thrift store. Thrift stores often are run by charitable organizations, like the Salvation Army or Purple Heart, and sell new and used merchandise that has been donated by caring individuals. Thrift stores have clothing, shoes, knick-knacks, books, furnishings, and tons of other stuff. Going to a thrift store is like going on a treasure hunt—you never know what you'll find, and what you do find usually is priced way below retail price.

- Flea markets/swap meets: You won't find any fleas at a flea market—hopefully—but what you will find is a crazy mix of new and used stuff in every product category. Looking for a steel coil ox for the 1913 Ford Model T you're restoring? You'll probably find one there. Or how about a steamer trunk you can use as a coffee table? Start looking. In fact, you usually have to do a *lot* of looking to find what you want or need. But for people who love flea markets, that's part of the fun.
  Here's something else you might like about flea markets: it's usually possible to negotiate a better price with the seller, much like you might do in your home country. People in North America call this "haggling," and not everyone will do it. But it never hurts to ask.

- Garage sales: These are like flea markets on a tiny scale. A person cleans out his or her garage, house, car, and so on, puts a sign in the yard or an ad on Craigslist (discussed a little later), sets up a table, and starts selling. Garage sale items sell for just a fraction of their original cost, and you often can find brand-new and perfectly good used items. You'll need cash to shop a garage sale. No credit cards accepted.

CABLE TV SHOPPING

A revolution in shopping via cable TV began with the debut of QVC in 1986. The network adopted its current 24/7 broadcasting schedule in 1987, and other shopping networks have followed suit.

QVC and other shopping networks like Home Shopping Network (HSN) and The Shopping Channel (TSC) in Canada sell a little of everything. Product lines include clothing, jewelry, upscale handbags and shoes, beauty items, kitchen and food items, electronics, and much more. Purchases are paid for with credit cards or by using the company's payment plan on certain items.

ONLINE SHOPPING

Of course, these days you don't have to turn on cable TV or show up in person at a bricks-and-mortar store or other physical site to buy whatever you need. You can shop online twenty-four hours a day, seven days a week, on the internet (also known as the "web"). Online shopping is also known as electronic commerce (or e-commerce), and stores that exist on the internet are called online or virtual stores. Following are a sampling of your online shopping choices.

ONLINE STORES

Most of the stores you like are probably on the Web, from Nordstrom's and Target, to Pizza Hut and Dollar Tree, and Coach and Payless. (The cable TV shopping networks also have online stores.) One of the largest internet stores is Amazon.com (Amazon.ca in Canada), where you can buy pretty much anything you want. One of the good things about Amazon is that if you buy $25 worth of qualifying merchandise, the order will ship free to your home or office. That might encourage you to spend more than you should, which is why you might want to use Amazon's online shopping cart system, where you can virtually "park" items you want until you're ready to buy them. Just wait until you have $25 in qualifying merchandise before you place an order to save the shipping costs.

Other huge online marketplaces include Overstock.com, Walmart.com, Costco.com, and Samsclub.com (although as noted earlier in this chapter, you have to be a member of these warehouse clubs).

Online Marketplaces

- eBay: This is probably the world's most famous online marketplace. eBay is a place where anyone can sell virtually anything. But it's not just companies that are selling—it's also average people like you, who sell both new and used merchandise. EBay is an auction site, meaning you have to bid on what you want and hope no one bids higher than you. You'll also find many "Buy It Now" auctions on eBay so you can lock in your price immediately instead of waiting for an auction to close. Whatever you win or buy outright is mailed or shipped directly to your door, but you have to pay the cost to get it there. It's actually a lot of fun to look at the offerings on eBay, even if you're not buying. Go to eBay.com and eBay.ca.
- Craigslist: This is an online classified ads website. Classified ads are brief notices describing items for sale by their owners. Most items on Craigslist are used, which means you can get some great bargains. Check them out at Craigslist.com, then type in the name of the largest city near you. That's important because the private sellers on Craigslist generally won't mail items to buyers. You have to make arrangements to pick up your new treasures.

HOW TO PAY

Depending on the type of shopping you're doing, you may have several options when paying for your purchase. Generally, here's what you can expect (although circumstances may differ by location): Chart on the next page...

Venue	Cash	Credit Card	Pre-Paid Card	Debit Card	Personal Cheque	Electronic Cheque	Paypal/Bill Later	Money Order
Big box store	X	X	X	X	X			
Boutique	X	X	X	X	X			
Cable TV	X	X	X	X	X	X	**	
Chain store	X	X	X	X	X			
Convenience store	X	X	X	X				
Craigslist	X							**
Dept store	X	X	X	X	X			
eBay		X	X	X		X	X	X
Farmer's market	X							
Flea market	X							
Garage sale	X							
Mall*	X	X	X	X	X			
Membership Warehouse club	X	X	X	X	X			
Mom & Pop store	X	X	X	X				
Online store		X		X			**	
Outlet mall	X	X	X	X	X			
Pawn shop	X			X				
Roadside stand	X							
Strip mall store*	X	X	X	X	X			
Supermarket	X	X	X	X	X			
Thrift store	X	X	X	X	X			

*May vary by tenant

**Possibly may accept

You'll find a discussion about each of these payment methods in Chapter 13.

SHOPPING TIPS

Whether you love it or hate it, shopping is one of life's necessary chores. You need to buy food for the family, pick up new clothes for school and work, and buy other day-to-day necessities.

But while most people shop only for life's necessities, other see shopping as a fun recreational activity that in some cases can become an addiction. There's even an English word for people who shop for fun: "shopaholic."

The companies that sell us everything from toothpaste to luxury automobiles are very smart marketers. They know what to say and how to show it off to tempt us into buying things we may not need or can't afford. This can especially be a problem for people who are not native-English speakers, since they may not always understand exactly what they're getting into. So here are some tips to help you avoid making costly shopping mistakes and make the best use of your money and time:

- Establish a budget before you shop, and make sure you don't exceed that amount.
- Be disciplined and pay off whatever you buy on credit within the credit card's thirty-day grace period.
- Buy only what you really need; don't just stroll around a store to kill time. You'll be tempted to buy things you don't need or haven't budgeted for.
- Compare prices carefully. Just because something is on sale doesn't mean it's cheaper at that store—it just means the retailer has discounted the item. You might find the same item cheaper elsewhere.
- Go for the best quality you can afford. Paying a little more for an item that will last longer is the wisest choice. This is particularly important when it comes to big-ticket items like appliances and furniture.
- Watch out for "bait-and-switch" techniques, in which a retailer lures you into a store with an advertised "low" price, then tries to sell you a higher-priced product instead.
- Avoid paying with a credit card. A Dun & Bradstreet study showed that people spend up to 18 percent more when using a credit card instead of cash.
- Carry just one credit card with you when you shop. You won't be tempted to buy more stuff just because you could spread the total cost over more than one card.

- Don't shop when you're in a bad mood, or if you're angry, hungry, or tired. You may be tempted to buy something to make yourself feel better.
- Bring a family member or a trusted friend along when you're purchasing a big-ticket item, like a wide-screen TV or a car. A companion can help you avoid making a bad purchase and remind you to stick to your budget.
- Ignore "limited time" deals, which often are just a trick to get you into a store and aren't really limited. Worse yet, the "deal" may actually cost more.
- Shop at the end of each season, when retailers clear out items to make room for new merchandise. You often can get a great deal during clearance sales.
- Want a bargain? Some of the best bargains are found at garage sales, pawnshops, flea markets, auctions, liquidation centers, and thrift shops, as well as in the classified section of the newspaper or on Craigslist.
- Use coupons and read grocery store circulars to find weekly specials that can help you stay within your budget.

You can save a lot of money using the strategies in this chapter. To figure out what to do with all that extra cash, be sure to check out Chapter 13, which focuses on finances.

ATTA'S LESSONS

Shopping is addictive, especially for immigrants. It's easy for them to be dazzled by the range and availability of merchandise to buy, especially if they didn't own much in their homeland. It's also easy to fall into the trap of wanting to have more than your neighbors and friends, because you want to show off. The expression for this in English is "keeping up with the Joneses."

That happened to me, too, when I first came to the United States. I spent way more on shopping than I put aside in savings. Eventually, I realized that buying things instead of saving was having a huge impact on my well-being and on those close to me.

I recommend that you stop competing with others and stop acting rich by buying a lot of stuff. It's more important to build a solid financial life so you'll be self-sufficient and won't have to rely on anyone else or the government to come your rescue. You're in the driver's seat—and hopefully, that seat is in a used and affordable car.

Chapter 11: The North American Educational System

Education is one of the most precious things you can earn, and it remains part of who you are for a lifetime. It opens the doors to greater job opportunities, which can increase income. It boosts economic growth and business opportunities, which can improve the standard of living for the populace and reduce poverty. It can even foster peace, since education helps people develop a broader world view, introspection, and more tolerance, characteristics that are necessary to develop peaceful relations among people.

This chapter covers the educational systems in North America. The systems in the United States and Canada actually share a number of similarities. But to make it easier for you to differentiate between the two countries (since it's assumed you're interested in just one or the other), their educational systems are discussed separately.

United States

Education is compulsory (required) for children in the United States. The age at which students can end their studies by choice varies by state, but is usually sixteen or seventeen years old. Early departure is discouraged, because it can greatly impact a child's social development and future earnings potential. For this reason, traditional school ends around seventeen to eighteen.

Public School System (K-12)

Public education is tax-subsidized, meaning it's provided at no charge to American students. School systems are funded by property and school taxes that are levied by each state. The American public school system, known as the K-12 system, consists of the following levels:

PRESCHOOL

Nursery school or preschool is for children as young as six weeks old. Often, parents elect to enroll their child in nursery school because both are employed, so the school acts as a type of day care. But the overriding goal of nursery school is to socialize their small charges. Naturally, at the earliest ages, infants and babies benefit more from cuddling and early developmental activities, but as soon as they are ready, play-based education helps them develop both mentally and physically. Nursery school is not usually considered part of the K-12 educational system.

KINDERGARTEN

Kindergarten is for children aged four to five; it's the "K" in "K-12." The focus is on play-based activities, as well as arts and crafts, singing, and other activities that develop intellectual, creative, and social skills, as well as develop their self-esteem, cultural identity, independence, and individual strengths. Children's time in kindergarten also will include outside activities (weather permitting), story time, snacks (no doubt the reason why adults universally look forward to lunch while on the job), and naptime to recharge them for the next task. They'll learn their letters and numbers, start learning how to read and use a computer (if they haven't used one at home already), and learn how to speak better.

ELEMENTARY (PRIMARY) SCHOOL

Elementary school is for children ages six to twelve. Elementary school runs from first through fifth or sixth grade and focuses on subjects like math, reading, language arts (writing), science, history, and social studies. Students are often introduced to foreign languages like Spanish in elementary school (particularly in the southwest United States), and art and music may also be part of the curriculum. The educational mix varies from one school district to the next. Students usually earn a diploma upon successful completion of their studies.

Junior High (Secondary) School

Also known as middle school, students are aged twelve to fourteen and work their way up from either grade 6 or 7 to grade 8. Students continue the studies begun in elementary school, but at a more advanced level. They're also likely to take computer, art, drama, and physical education classes. Students who graduate earn a diploma.

High School

Students at this level are aged fourteen to eighteen and progress from grades 9 to 12. The high school curriculum is the most rigorous in the public school system and often is seen as preparation for college. Honors classes and college prep classes are specifically for this purpose. Most subjects are taken for the entire four years of high school and include a range of subjects:

- language arts/writing
- math (usually a sequence that includes algebra, geometry, algebra II, trigonometry or calculus, and statistics)
- science (biology, chemistry, physics, and earth/space science)
- social studies (U.S. history and government, economics, world history, geography)

Many of these classes are available as advanced placement classes meant to help students excel on college application tests. In addition, many high schools in the United States require students to take at least one year of foreign language instruction (most often Spanish, French, or German), as well as a year of computer applications. Physical education and the arts generally round out the curriculum.

Gifted students typically take advanced placement courses and may actually graduate in three years rather than four. All students earn a diploma at the end of their high school studies.

Students who enter high school but drop out before completing their four years of schooling can earn a GED (general educational development), which is a high school equivalency credential. They must take a test to demonstrate their proficiency in reading, writing, math, science, and social studies. These students may also have to take high-school-level classes to prepare themselves to take and pass the exam.

Receiving Grades in Public Education

The grading scale differs depending on the educational level. Children in kindergarten usually aren't graded, per se, while children in grades 1 and 2 typically receive grades of S (satisfactory; i.e., "meets the grade level requirement"), P (progressing; "making progress that doesn't quite meet grade-level standards"), or U (unsatisfactory; "not making progress nor meeting grade-level standards").

From grade 3 and beyond, the academic grading scale usually is A (excellent), B (above average), C (satisfactory), D (below average), and F (unsatisfactory, or failing). Some school districts, as well as many universities and colleges, use a plus/minus system to make grades even more representative of achievement. For example, an excellent grade might be expressed as A+, A, or A-. An unsatisfactory grade of F is always expressed simply as F (no F+ or F-).

Some schools, including the Montessori schools mentioned below, don't award letter grades at all, preferring instead to provide written and oral narratives documenting a child's success, supported with a portfolio of his or her work. Whether or not grades are awarded depends on the school's educational philosophy.

Finally, colleges and universities may express grades as a percentage rather than a letter. They typically have two other grades as well: I, or incomplete, meaning the student must complete certain course requirements to receive a grade; and W, indicating that the student has withdrawn from a class (no grade).

ALTERNATIVES TO PUBLIC K-12 EDUCATION

Not everyone chooses to go the traditional public school route. Following are other options:

Charter School: This type of public school (for ages fourteen to eighteen) is similar to a private school. Incoming students are selected by lottery, because there are only so many available spots each year, and they pay tuition if they're fortunate enough to be selected. Charter schools tend to have more rigorous standards, and use more innovative teaching methods than public schools.

International Baccalaureate (IB) School: For children aged three to nineteen, this type of school "help[s] develop the intellectual, personal, emotional, and social skills to live, learn, and work in a rapidly globalizing world," according to the International Baccalaureate website (ibo.org). Classes are student-led, with teachers acting more like mentors than educators. The theory is that students learn more when they're immersed in the learning process. IB programs also emphasize critical thinking, writing, and group activities, and require students to participate in various community service activities. There are only about 1,400 IB schools in the United States, plus some public schools have their own IB programs as part of their standard curriculum.

Parochial Schools: These are private primary and secondary schools (no kindergarten) that are supported by religious organizations. Most of the parochial schools in the United States are affiliated with Roman Catholic parishes, but other religions, including evangelical Protestant, Lutheran, Muslim, Orthodox Jew, and Seventh-Day Adventist also have parochial schools. Parochial schools charge students tuition to attend.

Private Schools: These grade 1-12 schools are independent of state and local jurisdictions and are funded by tuition rather than public taxation. As a result, enrollment is selective. Day schools and boarding schools are examples of private schools.

Montessori School: Montessori is a type of public school that operates independently of local and state jurisdiction and charges tuition. The Montessori method calls for students to work in mixed-age classrooms in three- to six-year age groups (for example, ages 0-3; 3-6, and so on), through to age eighteen. They work and learn in uninterrupted three-hour blocks of time. In addition to academic pursuits, Montessori schools focus on character education to encourage students to become self-sufficient, polite, considerate, and helpful.

Homeschooling can be a great way to educate your kids, especially if you have any concerns about the curriculum or the safety of the local school district. Keep in mind, though, that homeschooling can be as much or more work for you as it is for your kids. You'll be responsible for devising the curriculum, researching and buying educational materials, organizing educational field trips, and keeping your already rambunctious kids in line and motivated. For these reasons, some parents choose to employ a tutor instead to do the deed. Homeschooling is legal in every state. Read about the laws in your state at the Home School Legal Defense Association (HSLDA) website at hslda. org/laws. For more information about homeschooling, see Appendix A.

Adult Education: Many school districts offer reasonably priced, introductory-level classes to motivated adults through their community adult-education program. Classes run the gamut from business pursuits (accounting, marketing, and so on) to leisure time activities like watercolor painting and low-impact aerobics. Adult education classes are a great place to learn computer and internet skills.

HIGHER EDUCATION (UNIVERSITY OR COLLEGE EDUCATION)

Beyond twelfth grade, students must choose either to go directly into the job market or continue with their schooling and get a college or vocational degree.

COMMUNITY COLLEGE

This two-year post-secondary institution offers an associate degree to people in a particular geographic location (often a city or county), as well as to those who live outside the immediate area. Also known as a junior college, these institutions offer curricula that focus on liberal arts and the sciences, as well as vocational training (such as law enforcement) and technical education that allows them to enter the workforce right after graduation. Some people attend community college where the tuition is less expensive, and then transfer their credits to a four-year institution, where they earn a bachelor's degree.

Community colleges also generally offer noncredit courses for adults through continuing education programs, or industry-specific training that doesn't lead to a degree. A high school diploma or GED is necessary to attend; otherwise, admission requirements are minimal.

UNIVERSITY

These institutions of higher learning offer four-year, undergraduate bachelor of arts and science degrees. Admission to most universities is very competitive. Applicants must have a certain high-school grade-point average upon application, meet expectations on a standardized college admission test, such as the SAT, and submit letters of recommendation, and an admission essay.

Those who qualify and are admitted may come from any locale but will pay higher tuition (known as out-state tuition) than those in its immediate market area. Because many people come from outside the area, universities usually offer on-campus, dormitory-style housing; however, they may have a high percentage of students who commute as well.

Many universities also offer graduate-level (post-bachelor) degrees, including master of arts and science degrees; and doctorate degrees (including doctor of philosophy, or PhD; and doctor of education, or EdD). It can take an additional two to three years of full-time study to earn a master's degree after earning a bachelor's degree; and three to five years full time, depending on the field of study, to earn a doctorate. Medical degrees (MD, DO, DDS, and others), which are equivalent to doctorates, take four years or more of full-time post-bachelor education, while a law degree (Juris Doctor, or JD) generally requires three years of post-bachelor education.

Online/Distance Education

Many colleges and universities, including some of the nation's most prestigious, offer online courses that allow students to complete many or all of their degree requirements in a virtual environment rather than in person, and with the same course load and schedule as in a face-to-face class. This is a great time-saver for students, especially those who are pros at using technology to manage their time. But working from the comfort of home robs students of the college experience—absorbing course material in real time in the classroom, interacting and bantering with other students and professors, and soaking up the rarified feel of higher education. Still, it's a viable option for those who are motivated to complete the coursework as assigned.

Trade or Vocational School

Vocational schools offer coursework specific only to the trade or vocation, and never or rarely provide instruction in liberal arts and other core fields found in colleges. Trade school curricula prepare students for careers as computer-aided designers and drafters, automotive technicians, electricians, machinists, commercial truck drivers, among others. They also generally assist graduates with finding employment. It takes as little as a few months to earn a diploma, and students pay tuition to attend.

Paying for It All

Between tuition and fees, books and living expenses, college is a very expensive proposition. But the good news is financial assistance may be available to help you put your child through college. Gifted children may be eligible for scholarships, while others may be able to secure low-interest federal loans that come due after a grace period at the end of the loan (typically six to nine months). Other forms of financial aid, like grants, also may be available, but you have to go looking for them early enough to secure them when you need them. Banks and lending companies are the top places to go for financial aid like loans, but other reliable sources include private organizations, such as clubs and religious groups, state governments, and the colleges and universities themselves.

Start the search for financial aid by filling out the Free Application for Federal Student Aid (FAFSA) from the Office of Federal Student Aid. All requests for financial aid in the United States start with this form, which you can find online at the FAFSA website at fafsa.ed.gov. The form must be filled out before the deadline imposed by the school you're applying for, so be sure to fill it out and submit it early.

Federal loan programs you or your child may be eligible for include the William D. Ford Federal Direct Loan, the Perkins Loan Program, and the Stafford Loan Program. For more information about federal loans, see studentaid.ed.gov/types/loans.

Savings Plans

In addition to securing loans and scholarships, you'll still need to set aside funds if you wish to make college a reality for your child. Optimally, you should start saving for college as soon as you bring your little one home from the hospital. Many states have college funds that grow as your child grows, and with a little planning, will yield enough cash for him or her to enjoy the college experience without the threat of tens of thousands of dollars in debt hanging over his or her head in student loans.

The United States has a tax-advantaged savings plan just for saving money for college. Called the 529 plan, or qualified tuition plan, this savings vehicle gives you a safe and reliable way to save. All fifty states and the District of Columbia have at least one 529 plan; state agencies and educational institutions also offer the plan.

Yet another vehicle for saving for college is the prepaid tuition plan. Usually sponsored by state governments, this type of plan allows you to purchase "credits" toward future tuition costs, and possibly room and board expenses. It's also possible that the educational institution you're interested in may offer a prepaid plan.

For more information about the 529 plan and prepaid plans, visit the U.S. Securities and Exchange Commission website at sec.gov/investor/pubs/intro529.htm.

PERSONAL GUIDANCE

All the activities necessary to get into college can be a lot to take in, especially when you or your child is just embarking on the college application process or your English-speaking skills are basic. So it may make sense to hire a college consultant to steer you in the right direction and help you make the right course corrections along the way. These specialists are well-versed in both the application process and the financial side of college, and can help you and your student figure out what needs to be done and when. Typically, a college consultant starts working with a client and his or her parents around the ninth grade. That gives the family plenty of time to identify promising colleges, write the college essay, and steer the student toward courses, and high school and extracurricular activities (like volunteering) that can help your student look motivated, mature, and civic-minded.

College consultants don't come cheaply. Generally speaking, you can expect to pay a minimum of $3,000 for a consulting package, which includes consultations on the college essay, high school activities, applications, and so forth. But the amount charged will vary by geographical region, and $3,000 is by no means set in stone. Some consultants charge—and get—much more. This might seem like a lot of money when you're also trying to save for college tuition. But college consultants—the good ones, anyway—have a knack for matching students up with the college where they'll thrive and excel, and that can make the expense worthwhile.

To find a college consultant, go to the Independent Educational Consultants Association website at iecaonline.com. Alternately, you can ask the parents of college-aged children if they can recommend a reputable consultant.

Education Best Practices for Students

- Don't procrastinate. Finishing your homework should be your number-one priority. TV and other electronic devices should be accessed only after all homework assignments are completed.
- Organize your school gear. The number-one problem for failing students is a lack of organization (forgetting homework/books and notes at home, and so on). Always pack your school bag in advance so you can grab it and go in the morning.
- Ask for help when you need it. It's okay if you don't understand an assignment, need help getting it done, or don't know what to do about a personal situation. Your teachers are always willing to help with schoolwork; your parent, siblings, and other family members understand and will support you in other matters.
- Prepare for college. With the help of your counselor, create a four-year development plan for your years in high school. This will help you set short-term goals for future college success.
- Get involved in school clubs so you can learn how to lead, network, and interact with others.
- Start investigating colleges in junior year; take the SAT (sat.collegeboard.org) or ACT tests (act.org) to assess your readiness.
- Have fun!

CANADA

Education in Canada is managed separately by each provincial government, and the various levels (especially in Quebec) tend to have different names. Generally speaking, the levels of education that follow have descriptions that are very similar to the U.S. levels discussed earlier in the chapter. So please refer to those earlier descriptions for details. There is one significant difference between the two countries: Canadians learn British English, while Americans learn American English.

School attendance in Canada is mandatory (required) until the age of sixteen in all provinces and territories, except Manitoba, New Brunswick, and Ontario, where students must stay in school until the age of eighteen. There are some exceptions; consult your provincial or territorial government's education department for information.

The grading scale varies by province and territory. Typically, students in Canadian high schools, colleges, and universities are graded on a combined letter-percentage grade scale. The following grade scale is an example from British Columbia. Other provinces' grade scales vary slightly, but follow this same pattern:

Grade	Percent
A+	90-100%
A	85-89%
A-	80-84%
B+	76-79%
B	72-75%
B-	68-71%
C+	64-67%
C	60-63%
C-	50-59%
F	0-49%
I	Incomplete
W	Withdrawal

Elementary schools may or may not use the same grading scale. In addition, colleges and universities typically have two other grades: I, or incomplete, meaning the student must complete certain course requirements to receive a grade; and W, indicating that the student has withdrawn from a class (no grade). Finally, some schools, like the Montessori schools mentioned below, don't award letter grades at all. They may instead provide narratives, either in writing or orally, documenting a child's level of success. The educational philosophy of the school dictates whether or not the traditional grading scale is used.

Primary and Secondary Education

The Canadian primary and secondary educational levels everywhere, except in Quebec, include the following:

• Junior kindergarten; pre-kindergarten (Ontario only): for children ages three to five

- Grade primary or kindergarten: for ages five to six
- Elementary education: grades 1-6, for children ages six to twelve
- Junior high/middle school: for ages twelve to fifteen
- High school: for ages fifteen to eighteen; and grade 12+ (Ontario only, for ages eighteen and older)
- Elementary and secondary education is government-sponsored and free.

Higher Education

Following are the options for higher education:

College

This term refers to community colleges, as well as technical, applied arts, and applied sciences schools. Among the degrees granted are diplomas of college studies (DCSs) in Quebec, associate degrees, and bachelor's degrees.

University:

'Undergraduate'

To be admitted into any Canadian university, students must meet minimum academic qualifications, which vary between provinces, but are outlined on each university's admission requirements websites. Most undergraduate programs require three years of study or four years for degrees in engineering, education, medicine, and law.

'Graduate (aka Postgraduate)'

These programs require one or two years of additional study for a master's degree and three or more years for a doctoral degree.

Primary and Secondary Education: Quebec
Quebec follows a different system for primary and secondary grades:

- *Préscolaire* (preschool): for children under age five
- *Maternelle* (kindergarten): for ages five to six

- *École primaire* (primary or elementary school): grades 1-6, for ages six to twelve
- *École secondaire* (high school): includes grade 7 (known as secondary 1, for ages twelve to thirteen); grade 8 (secondary 2, for ages thirteen to fourteen); grade 9 (secondary 3, for ages fourteen to fifteen); grade 10 (secondary 4; for ages fifteen to sixteen); and grade 11 (secondary 5; for ages sixteen to seventeen)

Higher Education: Quebec

The Quebec system is different for higher education levels as well:

College *(collège d'enseignement général et professionnel [CÉGEP])*: This is a government-run institution with pre-university programs of two years. Typical courses of study include the arts, social sciences, and natural sciences. Professional programs like paralegal, dental hygienist, nursing, and so on require an additional year of study. Graduates earn a *diplôme d'études collégiales (DEC)*.

University *(collège d'enseignement général et professionnel [CÉGEP])*: This is a public institution with subsidized tuition. Quebec controls tuition costs at the non-public universities.

'Undergraduate'

A student must have a diploma of college study (DCS), a *diplôme d'études collégiales* (DEC), or the equivalent to enroll at a university. Like other Canadian universities, most Quebec undergraduate programs require three years of study, or an additional fourth year for degrees in engineering, education, medicine, and law.

'Graduate (aka Postgraduate)'

Graduate students are awarded a master's degree after one to two years of study or a doctoral degree with an additional three or more years.

ONLINE AND DISTANCE EDUCATION

The internet has made education outside the classroom both easy and rewarding. Universities, colleges, and schools in virtually every province and territory now offer distance-learning opportunities, which are great for people who work nontraditional hours, who are too far away from a bricks-and-mortar classroom, or who prefer to work at their own pace. See the Canadian Information Centre for International Credentials (cicic.ca/419/Online-and-Distance-Education.canada) for more insight and information on why this might be a good choice for you or your children.

Alternatives to Public Education

As in the United States, there are alternatives to the traditional public education path:

- *Charter schools:* This is a type of publicly funded school in Alberta. According to Alberta Education, charter schools "provide innovative or enhanced education programs that improve the acquisition of student skills, attitudes, and knowledge in some measurable way." There are charter schools for gifted students as well as schools that focus on science or the arts. For more information, go to The Association of Alberta Public Charter Schools at taapcs.ca.
- *International baccalaureate (IB) schools:* The IB philosophy is the same in Canada as it is in the United States. There are only about 325 IB schools in Canada, and classes tend to be advanced, fast-paced, and challenging. Students do pay tuition, and scholarships may be available. For more information about the IB concept, see ibo.org.
- *Parochial school:* In Canada, the term "parochial school" refers only to Catholic schools, which can be found in Alberta, British Columbia, Newfoundland, Nova Scotia, Ontario, Quebec, and Saskatchewan. Catholic schools focus on faith, values, and community service, while inspiring students to greater levels of achievement. Although Catholic schools are faith-based schools, anyone of any faith can attend. Unlike public education in Canada, a Catholic school education is not free. The regulations and rules concerning tuition are set by each province. To find a Catholic school near you, go to catholiclinks.org/colegios-canada.htm.

- *Separate Schools:* This term refers to publicly funded Roman Catholic and Protestant elementary schools (up to grade 8) in Alberta, Northwest Territories, Nunavut, Ontario, Saskatchewan, and Yukon. They're actually a little controversial because of the public funding they receive.

- *Montessori School:* This type of schooling features mixed age, student-led classrooms, three-hour blocks of uninterrupted study, and instruction offered through working with materials rather than listening to lectures. Classes usually consist of children aged 0-3, 3-6, 6-12, and 12-18. Montessori education is said to focus on psychological, physical, and social development, while encouraging creativity. For more information about this unique educational model, visit Association Montessori Internationale at ami-global.org.

- *Homeschooling:* Homeschooling is legal in every Canadian province and territory with varying degrees of regulation. It can be a wonderful way to control what your children learn and when they learn it. It also will help you bond more deeply with your children, while allowing you to share your enthusiasm about learning. But keep in mind that homeschooling means that you'll basically be with your children 24/7, which limits their exposure to other children, other adults, and other learning opportunities. You'll also find that homeschooling is a lot of work. You'll have to plan lessons, grade papers, lead field trips, and handle a myriad of other tasks. Still, it can be very rewarding. For general information about homeschooling and ideas you can use, visit homeschoolcanada.ca; while information about provincial and territorial homeschooling laws may be viewed at homeschoolcanada.ca/canadian-homeschool-laws/.

- *Vocational Schools/Technical College:* These post-secondary schools focus on teaching the skills related to a particular trade rather than prepping students for a traditional degree based on a liberal arts curriculum. There are trade schools across Canada offering classes on everything from carpentry and plumbing to automotive service, game design, network systems administration, and much more. They're a great place to learn skills you can use immediately to earn a living and support a family. Explore your options by visiting the Trade Schools, Colleges, and Universities website at trade-schools.ca.

PAYING FOR IT ALL

Contrary to popular belief, higher education in Canada is not free the way other public education is. But all is not lost—the Canadian government offers many monetary resources and financial assistance plans to students who wish to pursue education beyond a high school diploma. Chief among them are the Canada Student Loans Program, which offers assistance to full- and part-time post-secondary students in all provinces and territories, except Quebec, the Northwest Territories, and Nunavut. These jurisdictions have their own programs.

A number of grants, which do not have to be paid back, are also available. For a list and links to further information, go to hrsdc.gc.ca/eng/jobs/student/loans_grants/index.shtml or the National Student Loans Service Centre at csnpe-nslsc.cibletudes-canlearn.ca/eng/Default.aspx.

FINAL WORDS

No matter which educational route you pursue, from a high school diploma to a doctoral degree, the most important thing to remember is that you should always be eager about and open to learning new things. Education doesn't happen only in the classroom; if you open your mind, you can learn from everyone and everything around you. Begin with the things you're passionate about. Then observe the world around you and let your curiosity drive you to learn about other things.

The internet is a rich source of information that can feed your curiosity. But beware: anyone and everyone can post information to the internet, and what they post is not necessarily true. When you seek information, look for websites written by reputable people and organizations. For example, if you're looking for information on treatments for prostate cancer, go to the American Cancer Society website rather than visiting the "Bob's Cancer Journey" website. Bob might have a lot of insightful things to say about his brave fight against cancer, but he's not an expert. But the American Cancer Society will give you well-researched facts and insight.

The internet is also a great place to go to keep in touch with the happenings in your homeland. You can even search the internet in your own language using Google. The North American Google addresses are Google.com and Google.ca; change the suffix to the one for your language to get translated pages. For example, Google.de (for *Deutschland*) will give you pages in German; Google.af will take you to pages in Afghani. You can find a list of country domain extensions (the letters after the website name) at domainit.com/domains/country-domains.mhtml.

Never Stop Learning

Your local library is a great place to continue your own education, even if you've been out of school for years. This free resource is packed with printed books, books on tape, e-books, newspapers, and magazines. If the library is large enough, it may even have books in your native language. But now that you're a North American resident, it's a good idea to work on your English- or French-language (if you're in Canada) skills. Pick up materials written at a level just slightly more difficult than you can read now. That will challenge you to work harder. Or try reading books written for middle school or high school students. The writing style will be less complicated, and the vocabulary will be easier.

Be sure to ask about literacy classes that may be available in your community. These classes focus on improving students' English (or French) reading, speaking, and writing skills. There's usually no charge for these classes.

Alternately, you may be able to take a low-cost class through the continuing education department of your local community college. And don't forget to look for ESL (English as a second language) websites on the internet, which have exercises, reading materials, and quizzes to help you improve your skills.

ATTA'S LESSONS

I feel extremely lucky that I had a very disciplined and diverse education in my early years. But when I came to the United States, I found myself completely overwhelmed by the system, and at first couldn't figure out how to use my skills and education. To combat this, I enrolled in various classes and training courses to improve my skills.

I believe this happens to most immigrants who enter the United States. They are overwhelmed by the job market and are upset to find that the education and credentials acquired in their homeland may not be accepted here. So instead of trying to fix that, they sit back and go through their lives without trying.

This is a sad and costly fact within many immigrant communities. But this doesn't have to happen to you. Look for ways to enhance your knowledge and expand your expertise. There are many online courses and other education programs that make it easy to update your skills. Start now.

College Preparation Guide

Following are the steps to take to prepare for college, along with the recommended timing.

During Middle School

- It is best to take the most challenging classes.
- Develop goals, actions, and practice sessions with the help of parents and teachers.
- Volunteer in your community.
- Try various skill-assessment tests in your areas of interest.
- Engage with counselors and parents about careers that interest you.
- Organize classroom plans.
- Sign up for summer-school enrichment programs.

Freshman/Sophomore Years in High School

- Retake various skill-assessment tests to establish potential career options.
- Discuss options and education required for desired careers with school counselor(s).
- Review college expense options and plans with parents.
- Research and find out your school's requirement/program for SAT/ACT preparation.

- Participate in extracurricular activities.
- Sign up for challenging classes to improve knowledge and skills.
- Sign up for college credit classes.

Junior Year
- Attend college and financial-aid events/programs.
- Seek help from mentors.
- Mentor others.
- Take the PSAT during fall in preparation for the SAT.
- Explore future career options; investigate the type of education needed.
- Research university/college websites; request materials and information.
- Visit schools that interest you.
- Participate in as many extracurricular activities as possible.
- Ask for financial-aid and admissions forms.
- Sign up for classes that provide college credits.
- Take the ACT or SAT.
- Enroll in available enrichment programs.
- Save money for college by working a part-time job.
- Look for paid internship programs.
- Continue to research and learn about various private scholarship options.

Senior Year: Fall
- Take the most difficult and challenging classes.
- Narrow down potential career choices by taking career-interest assessment tests.
- Participate in extracurricular activities.
- Volunteer in various community activities.
- Create a resume of your academic, athletic activities, and achievements.
- Visit the campuses of schools you're interested in. Narrow down the list of potential colleges.
- Explore various facilities to get a good feel for what college life will be like.
- Check out school facilities, equipment, etc.
- Sit in on a college class or two.
- Talk to students and a couple of instructors.
- Meet with an admission counselor and financial-aid counselor.

Senior Year: December–February

- Apply to apply to colleges of interest. Be sure to retain copies of applications.
- Review your college payment plan and financial-aid options.
- Apply for scholarships offered by colleges that you are applying to.
- Apply for financial aid right after January. Be sure to make the previous year's income tax information available.

Senior Year: March–May

- Follow up to make sure your school transcript was sent to the college that has accepted you.
- Notify any colleges that have accepted you that you will be going elsewhere.
- Send required fees to the college of your choice.

Summer Following Senior Year

- Get a job; save as much money as possible.
- Review all college-orientation material thoroughly.
- Familiarize yourself with college living conditions.
- Find a roommate (if one is not assigned).
- Establish communication with your future roommate. Meet in person to get to know each other.

Your First Semester at the University

- Study hard and make your parents proud!

Chapter 12: Navigating the Health Care System

While the United States and Canada have similarities when it comes to daily life, the health-care system is one place where they differ significantly. The United States' health-care system is unique among industrialized nations in that it is entirely free-market based; that is, while government regulations require insurers to adhere to certain minimum standards, health-care insurers can set their own prices without government intervention. In addition, it's a direct-pay system, meaning that either an insurance company (on behalf of subscribers) or the health-care consumer pays for services. When the consumer pays, the cost usually comes directly out-of-pocket, although supplemental insurance and federally subsidized plans can help reduce the cost.

Canada has a state-funded health-care program that is almost entirely paid for by tax dollars. All citizens and permanent residents have access to free, quality health care throughout the country. As a result, it is considered to be one of the primary benefits of citizenship/residency in Canada. The few services that are not covered (discussed later in this chapter) may be covered with supplemental insurance to reduce out-of-pocket expenses for consumers.

This overview of the two North American health-care systems should answer many of your questions about access to health-care services for both you and your family. However, the health-care system in the United States, in particular, is rather complex. So you'll find many websites listed throughout the chapter where you can go for more information. In addition, this chapter covers only the health-care system in each country. Health insurance is covered in detail in Chapter 20.

UNITED STATES

The United States spends more on health care than any other nation and has the most plan choices. While it might sound great to have many choices, the reality is it makes the system complicated and difficult to navigate. Add in the requirements and ramifications of the *Affordable Care Act* (ACA) passed by the Obama administration, and things become even more confusing.

'THE AFFORDABLE CARE ACT'

Implemented in 2014, the *Affordable Care Act* mandates that all Americans must have health insurance. This insurance can be employer-provided, privately bought, or purchased through a state health insurance exchange (HIX). People who can't afford health insurance usually qualify for Medicare, Medicaid, or CHIP assistance. Since these are insurance matters, they're discussed in detail in Chapter 20.

WHERE TO OBTAIN HEALTH SERVICES

The United States has many clinics and other facilities where you can get medical treatment. The primary place is the office of a primary care physician (PCP). PCPs are generalists; they take care of a person's medical needs from infancy to old age. They also are diagnosticians; that is, they diagnose illnesses and injuries, treat those they are qualified to, and refer to specialists who have additional knowledge and training beyond their expertise. For example, a PCP can treat you for an upper respiratory infection or manage your diabetes care. But if your PCP diagnoses skin cancer that is too advanced to treat in the office, he or she will refer you to a cancer specialist.

Specialists are on the next rung of the health-care ladder. Surgeons fall into this category, as do specialists like internal medicine practitioners, endocrinologists, podiatrists, psychiatrists, and any other physician whose practice focuses on a particular illness or condition. Like PCPs, specialists have their own offices where they see patients.

It's also possible to obtain care at medical clinics, which are usually staffed by physicians who work on a rotating basis. There are clinics for general care, as well as for indigent care, which is care provided at no charge to extremely poor people. You can even find small clinics right inside drug stores. They are usually operated by a nurse practitioner and/or physician assistant who can care for minor medical conditions like sinus infections. They're also qualified to administer flu shots and give sports physicals, among other things. Finally, these practitioners can write prescriptions, which you can pick up right in the store.

For more critical care, you may need to visit an urgent care facility. These medical offices are open only certain hours of the day, generally after the regular office hours of a PCP. Common hours of operation are 7 p.m. to midnight or 7 p.m. to 7 a.m. Their main purpose is to provide care to people who can't wait for their regular medical office to open. For instance, if you have a severe sore throat, a urinary tract infection, or an eye irritation (including pink eye), you may wish to be treated at an urgent care facility so you'll start to recuperate faster. However, urgent care is not a substitute for emergency treatment. If you have severe chest pain, uncontrollable bleeding, trouble breathing, a gunshot wound, or pregnancy-related problems, among others, you should head for the emergency department at a hospital instead.

Hospitals provide emergency care, as just discussed, as well as outpatient treatments and procedures (that is, treatments that allow you to go home the same day), and inpatient surgical care (which requires an overnight or longer stay). An example of an outpatient procedure is a colonoscopy, which is a test for colon cancer that requires sedation; an example of an inpatient procedure is coronary artery bypass grafting (CABG), which treats blocked coronary (heart) arteries. Hospitals also generally offer wellness services, health education classes, and seminars to help improve the quality of your life.

Mental health facilities may be inpatient or outpatient, and treat disorders of the mind. Psychiatrists are medical doctors who are skilled in the diagnosis and treatment of mental illnesses, including mood disorders like bipolar disorder, anxiety disorders like obsessive-compulsive disorder, and psychotic disorders like schizophrenia. They also treat eating disorders (anorexia and bulimia), as well as other mental illnesses.

> ### Health Care Best Practices
>
> Here are some easy ways to save on health-care costs without sacrificing quality:
>
> Use company-sponsored health-care resources like smoking-cessation programs, fitness memberships, and health assessments. Some companies even offer a cash incentive to employees who complete annual health screenings or can demonstrate that they're tobacco-free.
>
> Use an urgent care facility rather than the emergency department when you need after-hours medical care. Even if you have insurance that covers an emergency department visit, the cost will be up to ten times higher than you'd pay for urgent care.
>
> Do what your doctor tells you. Studies indicate that up to 20 percent of people don't follow their physician's orders, don't take medication prescribed for them, and they end up right back in the doctor's office. That wastes both money and time.
>
> Ask your physician to prescribe generic rather than brand-name drugs. Generic drugs have the same active ingredients as their higher-priced prescription counterparts, so they're safe and effective.
>
> Request ninety-day prescriptions from your physician rather than thirty-day supplies. Pharmacies often offer a small discount for ninety-day prescriptions, plus you'll save time, because you won't have to go to the pharmacy as often.

LOOK BEYOND THE BORDERS

The United States may have one of the best health-care systems in the world, but let's face it: it's expensive to obtain care here. For this reason, there may be times when you might like to seek medical care outside the country. For example, let's say you need surgery for a particular condition, and your insurance company tells you the copay (copayment) in your high-deductible insurance plan will be $30,000. So you search the internet and find out you can have the same procedure done in Panama for $12,000. If you can verify the surgeon's skills and the safety of the hospital, it might be worth considering having the surgery there. There's even a term for going elsewhere to acquire medical care: "medical tourism." Just be very, very careful that you'll receive quality care. Certain countries are notorious for providing cheap care with questionable results. Your health and well-being are worth much more than saving a few bucks.

In addition, some prescription medications are available at a lower cost from reputable Canadian companies. The U.S. government prohibits cross-border mailing of prescription medications to U.S. citizens, because it claims there's no way to assure product purity and quality. However, Canadian citizens living in the United States may have their medications mailed, as long as a photocopy of the original prescription and proof of Canadian citizenship are affixed to the outside of the package in a plastic pouch. That way, the documents can be inspected by customs officers. This applies to all medications, except controlled drugs and narcotics, which cannot be mailed under any circumstances.

If you're an American citizen or resident living near a Canadian border and would like to buy your medication from a Canadian pharmacy, you can do so. Technically, it's prohibited by U.S. law, but as long as you bring back no more than a ninety-day supply of a drug that is not a narcotic or other controlled substance, and it's for personal use, border agents generally won't stop you.

A final word of warning: it's usually best to avoid prescriptions obtained from any country other than Canada, especially drugs purchased over the internet. You never know what substance you're actually getting in those capsule and tablets. Just remember the Chinese milk and pet-food poisonings of 2008 and 2013, respectively, to understand why.

CANADA

Canada has a publicly funded health-care system known as Medicare (*assurance-maladie* in French), universal coverage, or socialized care. Canadian citizens and permanent residents are entitled to insured services like preventative care and medical treatment from primary care physicians, as well as hospital care, dental surgery, and other necessary medical care. (Room and board is not included; that's discussed later in this chapter.) The system is almost entirely free, although technically, it really isn't free. Rather, it is a covered benefit paid for by the income taxes the Canadian government collects from your paycheck. You just don't have to pay when you receive services. The exceptions are British Columbia, Alberta, and Ontario, which do require health-care premiums for services. Check with the provincial health ministry for more information. In addition, with just a few exceptions, you can't be denied care, no matter what your previous medical history is, what pre-existing conditions you may have, or how much you earn.

There isn't a single health-care system in Canada. Rather, health insurance is administered by each province and territory individually and differs from one location to another. When you immigrate to a province or territory, you must apply to receive health coverage. The application form is available at doctors' offices, hospitals, pharmacies, and immigrant service organizations. The form is also available online through your provincial or territorial ministry of health. When you apply, you'll need to show personal identification like your passport, permanent resident card, or confirmation of permanent residence (IMM 5292).

Under the aegis of Service Canada, all provinces and territories, except Manitoba, issue a health insurance card to each family member. (In Manitoba, only adults receive health insurance cards.) This card, known as the Care Card, has a ten-digit personal identification number that is unique to you and can't be shared with another person. Always carry it with you, because you must present the card when you go to a physician's office, clinic, or hospital for health services. See Service Canada's website at servicecanada.gc.ca/eng/subjects/cards/health_card.shtml for more information.

There is a waiting period of up to ninety days in most provinces and territories before public health insurance begins. Citizenship and Immigration Canada says you must apply for temporary private health-care coverage insurance within five days of arriving in your new province or territory, or insurers may not provide coverage for you. You'll find more information on private insurance later in this chapter.

TEMPORARY HEALTH-CARE COVERAGE FOR REFUGEES

If you're a resettled refugee or a government-assisted or privately assisted refugee, you may be eligible for temporary limited health-care coverage through the Interim Federal Health Program. You can check your eligibility at cic.gc.ca/english/refugees/outside/summary-ifhp.asp.

Insurance Portability

Another advantage of Canada's health-care system is that if you're already a citizen or a permanent resident and you want to move from one province or territory to another, your coverage will follow you—at least temporarily. Under the *Canada Health Act*, insurance is portable, meaning if you move, your previous provincial or territorial coverage moves with you temporarily through the minimum waiting period (usually no more than ninety days). For this reason, it's very important to apply for health coverage immediately after you move.

In addition, because coverage varies from one province/territory to another, always check your coverage before you travel. If your coverage isn't compatible with that province or territory's coverage, you may need to purchase temporary private health insurance.

Supplemental Health Benefits (Private Insurance)

While the public health-care system covers most of the doctors' visits and medical services you need, not everything is covered. For this reason, you may need supplemental or private health insurance. Some non-covered health-care costs include private hospital rooms, prescription drugs, dental care, and prescription eyeglasses. Your employer may offer you the option of paying for any additional health insurance you may need through payroll deduction. If your employer doesn't offer this benefit or you're unemployed, you must cover these costs out-of-pocket instead.

For more information on the Canadian private health-care system, including links to provincial and territorial ministries of health, and links to provincial/territorial-specific health-care insurance information, go to hc-sc.gc.ca/hcs-sss/delivery-prestation/ptrole/index-eng.php. You can also download free pamphlets from Health Canada (hc-sc.gc.ca/index-eng.php), or pick them up at doctors' offices and pharmacies.

Where to Obtain Health Services

In Canada, where the emphasis is on prevention, the main providers of health-care services are the primary care physicians (PCPs *aka* family doctors), nurse, or other health professionals. In addition, some primary care is provided through phone contacts or computer-based service providers.

When a condition is serious enough that it can't be treated entirely by a PCP or other licensed medical practitioner, or surgery is required, a patient will be referred to a hospital or similar long-term-care facility. Under the *Canada Health Act*, the health-care services provided at such facilities are paid for by the provincial/territorial governments. However, certain costs, like meals, assistance devices like crutches and wheelchairs, in-room TV service, and outpatient medications) are not covered. Also, the cost of private and semi-private rooms is an out-of-pocket expense. Always check your coverage in any supplemental policies you have so you're not surprised when you get the bill.

Other places you can receive care include medical clinics and emergency departments (for critical urgent care). Finally, some care can be delivered in-home, including specialized nursing care, adult day care, and midwifery (for uncomplicated births).

In addition, certain groups of people, including senior citizens, children, and recipients of social assistance, may be eligible to receive supplemental benefits that normally are not covered under the public health plan. These benefits may include prescription drugs, dental care, vision care, and medical equipment and appliances (such as artificial limbs and wheelchairs). The services of allied health professionals (such as podiatrists and chiropractors) may also be covered for this population. For more information, visit the Health Canada website at hc-sc.gc.ca/index-eng.php.

Finally, First Nations people and Inuit are eligible for additional benefits. If you fall into one of these groups, see the First Nations and Inuit pages on Health Canada's website (hc-sc.gc.ca/fniah-spnia/nihb-ssna/index-eng.php) for more information.

ATTA'S LESSONS

Shortly after my arrival in the United States in 1981, I met a close friend and co-worker from Afghanistan who had gained weight since I had seen him a couple of years before in Germany. He immediately told me that I would gain weight, too, and be much heavier in a couple of years. So I vowed that I would never put on more than a couple of pounds for the rest of my life. To seal the deal, my friend brought a scale from the bathroom so I could weigh myself. At the time, I was 175 pounds. Today, I am 168 pounds, and I remind him about that all the time. I also happily inform him that I only have to visit my doctor's office once a year for an annual check-up. I walk ten to twelve miles a week and I stick to a daily diet that consists of one banana, one apple, and various nuts and green vegetables. That's all I need—that, and the love of family members and friends.

Chapter 13: Finance Basics

There's an old song that says, "Money makes the world go 'round." If you have money, you know just how true that statement is. On the other hand, if you don't have money, the truth is just as apparent. The difference is that without money you have to watch the world go 'round from the sidelines.

As much as we'd like to think we're not ruled by material things, money really does impact virtually every aspect of our lives. It makes it possible to give our families a comfortable lifestyle. It allows us to buy things that make our lives easier. Basically, it puts us in the driver's seat of our own lives, so to speak, just as much as it can put us in the driver's seat of our own car. When the bills are taken care of and we have things—even simple things—that bring us comfort, we are happier and possibly even more productive.

This chapter discusses money management and the financial tools you need to keep your life on track. And if you happen to use this advice to buy nice things for your family and yourself, go ahead—you deserve it.

THE NORTH AMERICAN BANKING SYSTEM

The banking systems in the United States and Canada share many similarities. Both are considered to be among the safest and soundest financial systems in the world, and they offer similar personal banking products and financial business services. The systems are, in fact, so compatible that some Canadian banks offer the option of conducting day-to-day banking transactions in U.S. dollars.

The top banks in the United States in terms of assets are JPMorgan Chase & Co., Bank of America, Citigroup, Wells Fargo, and Goldman Sachs. In Canada, the top five banks are the Royal Bank of Canada, Toronto Dominion Bank, Bank of Nova Scotia, Bank of Montreal, and Canadian Imperial Bank of Commerce. But these are by no means the only places to bank: each state and province/territory has plenty of smaller banks from which you can choose. Since banks are so competitive and tend to offer the same range of services, your main reason for choosing one over another probably will be driven by its location more than anything else.

Banks are also into convenience and try to serve people no matter where they are. That's why it's common to find mini bank branches in airports, department stores like Walmart, and even casinos. These small branches are not full service, meaning the number of services they offer is limited, but they can still be convenient for cashing checks, making deposits, paying bills, and other basic services.

Another type of financial institution is the credit union. Credit unions are nonprofit, member-owned and operated financial cooperatives. They generally offer the same products and services as banks, but they usually have fewer and lower fees than banks.

In most cases, you have to qualify to be a member of a credit union. Credit unions serve different groups of people—for instance, teachers, auto workers, universities, Catholics, to name just a few—so you probably can find a credit union where you'd qualify for membership. A downside to credit unions is that they have far fewer branches than your friendly neighborhood bank, and they may also have shorter hours. But a lot of people love their credit union—and, in fact, more than a third of the population in Canada belongs to one or more credit union. So they must be doing something right.

Both banks and credit unions have two main functions. First, they serve as a place for people, called depositors, to keep their money safe while earning money, or interest, on deposited funds. (More on that later.) Second, financial institutions are in the business of making money for themselves. They take the money you deposit, pay you a small amount of money (interest), expressed as a percentage, for the privilege of using your money, then make their own investments as a way to grow that money further. Banks are thought to be rich and powerful, but that's not always the case. Especially in the years from 2001-10, some very large banks failed, which put them out of business. To some extent, this happened because banks wrote a lot of what are called sub-par (undesirable) mortgages for people who couldn't afford to make the payments, which left the banks liable for the money the mortgagees didn't have.

Fortunately, in the United States, an organization called the Federal Deposit Insurance Corporation, or FDIC, protects depositors' accounts of up to $250,000, so if a bank fails, depositors don't lose their money (see fdic. gov for more information). But if one day you have more than $250,000 to your name, remember that you should put it in more than one bank so you're assured of getting all your money back if that bank fails.

Canada has a similar organization called the Canada Deposit Insurance Corporation (CDIC), which protects depositors' money up to $100,000 CDN. See cdic.ca for more information.

BANK PRODUCTS

Even though credit unions offer most if not all the same products and services as banks, for simplicity's sake, this chapter uses the term "bank" from here on to refer to all financial institutions and their products. Among the products banks offer are the following:

SAVINGS ACCOUNT

This type of account is at the heart of the banking system. People like you entrust their paychecks, inheritance money, lemonade-stand money, and other funds to banks, and in return, receive a small percentage of that money as a "reward," so to speak. That payment, called interest, is paid quarterly and is deposited right into your savings account. If you leave both your principal (the original deposit) and the interest in your account, you'll receive interest on both amounts when the next quarter rolls around. This is a process known as compounding, and over time, you can accumulate a fair amount of money.

In the United States, most interest paid on your account is taxable under the IRS code. At the beginning of a new tax year, you'll receive a 1099-INT form from the bank stating how much interest you earned in the previous year. This amount must be reported to the IRS when you file your income tax forms.

Likewise, in Canada all interest income is taxable and is reported on a T5 slip from the bank. However, banks generally don't send out T5 slips for interest amounts under $50, even though you still have to report that interest on your tax return. You'll have to refer to your bank statements and calculate the amount you earned yourself.

There are numerous types of savings accounts. The most common are the regular savings account, which is the most basic account (as previously described); and the money market savings account, which pays a higher interest rate but may require a higher balance. Most money market accounts allow you to access your funds at any time, but there may be restrictions. Be sure to read the account disclosure carefully to maximize your savings potential.

Regular savings accounts usually can be started with very small deposits, although you may have to pay a fee if the balance remains low (fees as discussed later in this chapter). However, there are no limits on deposits or withdrawals. You can access your account in several ways:

- *Visit a bank branch and have a teller handle your transaction(s).* This can be done inside the bank or at a drive-thru window outside the bank.
- *Use an ATM (automatic teller machine) or an ABM (automated banking machine) for simple transactions* like making deposits and withdrawals.
- *Use the bank's internet banking service.* The service is free, but it must be set up in advance through the bank and is accessed by using your account number and a personal identification number, or PIN, assigned to you by the bank.
- *Use the bank's pay-by-phone system,* which allows you to phone the bank, input your account number and PIN, and do most common banking transactions.

Financial Best Practices

- Grow your savings faster by setting up automatic deposits into your savings account. You usually can authorize either your employer or your bank to make automatic biweekly (every two weeks) or monthly transfers right into your savings account.
- Increase the amount of money direct-deposited as your earnings grow, as well as when you get a raise at work, or when you get a large income tax refund.
- Try not to use the funds in your savings account for ordinary purposes. Instead, treat the account as an emergency fund, as well as a way to save for retirement.
- Minimize the amount of cash you withdraw from your account on payday and leave the rest in your savings account to maximize your earnings.
- Maintain a detailed record of your deposits and withdrawals. If your bank doesn't issue you a passbook (and few do these days), create your own record on a spreadsheet or use a phone app to track deposits and withdrawals. But never put your account number or password into the app. Hackers have figured out how to break into phone apps and could subsequently break into your accounts.
- Review the monthly statements sent by your bank for accuracy. If you aren't receiving statements now (electronically or in the mail), contact the bank.
- Sign up to use your bank's online banking system. That way, you can access your accounts 24/7 to check balances, transfer money between accounts, pay bills electronically, and more.

Personal Checking Account

This is a type of account that allows you to make payments to other people or companies using a paper document called a check. The check has spaces for the name of the payee (the person or company being paid), the amount of the check (written in words; for example, "eight hundred fifty-six and 77/100 dollars"), and your signature. Your name, address, account number, and bank routing number (the nine digits across the bottom of the check that identifies the bank) are printed on the face of the check, and you must sign the check to make it legal tender (that is, an official form of payment).

Checking account holders are typically charged a monthly maintenance fee, especially if the account balance is below a certain amount. Talk to your bank to see how much you must keep on deposit to avoid monthly services fees, or find a bank that offers free checking. Incidentally, credit unions usually offer free checking. Since it's a simple matter to send direct-deposited payroll funds to numerous financial institutions, you might want to think about joining a credit union and establishing a checking account there even if you have the rest of your paycheck going to a bank.

When you open a checking account at a bank, you'll be issued a set of starter checks, which are generic checks with little else except the bank's identifying information printed on them. Most businesses won't accept starter checks, so be sure to order a set of official checks right away. You can order them at the bank when you open your account, which tends to be expensive, or you can order them online from reputable companies like Deluxe (deluxe. com), which is the industry leader and has been in business for nearly a hundred years; Checks in the Mail (checksinthemail.com); and the Bradford Exchange (bradfordexchangechecks.com). Even Walmart (walmartchecks. com) and Costco (costcochecks.com) offer affordable checks.

Checks are numbered sequentially in the upper right corner, usually starting at number 101. Since some companies are reluctant to accept low-numbered checks, you might ask your check printer to start your checks at 301 instead. Businesses know about this trick, of course, but it still can save you some hassle when writing checks in person.

When arranging for the printing of your checks, never have your driver's license number, Social Security Number, or phone number printed on your checks. That's like issuing an invitation to a dishonest person to steal your identity and everything you've worked so hard for. If a store or other business insists on having this information before it will accept your check, write the number on the check yourself.

Once you open a checking account, always use the check register that comes with your checks. This is the small book that has spaces to note the check number, payee, and amount of the check. Every time you write a check, you note this information in the check register, then deduct the amount of the check from the balance in your account. It's important to know how much money you have in your account at all times so you don't spend money you don't have, which can trigger service fees (discussed later in this chapter).

You might find it easier to record checks electronically. Microsoft Office has a check register template you can use, plus you can find check-register freeware on the internet. You even can get an app for iPhone and Android phones to keep track of your checks, which might be the easiest way of all to track your expenditures.

When you get your bank statement, compare your expenditures and balance against the statement provided by the bank. Your figure, and the figure provided by the bank statement, should balance, or be exactly the same. If they aren't, then you need to figure out what went wrong. And here's a tip: if the amounts don't balance, it's probably something you did, since banks use computers to do their work, and computers are rarely wrong. Using an electronic check register is a good way to make sure your calculations are always right.

If you do make a mistake in your addition or subtraction, or you forget to note a transaction, you could find your account overdrawn, which means you've written checks totaling more money that you have in your account. If that happens, the bank will charge you an overdraft fee (known as a nonsufficient funds, or NSF, fee), which can be very expensive.

Overdraft Line of Credit

This feature allows you to borrow money from the bank temporarily in case the balance in your account is not sufficient to cover a check or a debit card transaction. If you have overdraft protection, you'll pay a fee for the privilege, but this fee is usually far lower than NSF fees. You also must repay the money as soon as possible to bring your account back into the black. Talk to your banker or visit your bank's website to learn about the rules and how to sign up.

Debit Card

This type of card, which looks exactly like a credit card, is used to access the funds in your checking account without writing a paper check. (Look for the word "debit" on the front of the card to differentiate it from your credit cards.) A debit card allows you to make an electronic funds transfer from your checking account to the account of the store, restaurant, or other business you wish to pay. This is quick and easy, and works flawlessly unless you forget to note the amount of the sale in your check register. You could end up with overdrafts, and as stated previously, that can be very expensive. Your best bet is to keep all your debit card receipts in one place—maybe a zippered compartment in your purse, or the inside pocket of your suit coat. Then at the end of the day, gather up all the day's receipts and carefully note them in your check register.

When you get your debit card, you will receive a personal identification number (PIN) that you'll use to prove you're the real owner of the account. This PIN will be mailed to you separately from the card to protect your account. Most stores and other businesses will require you to input your PIN into a keypad when you make a debit card purchase.

Never write down your PIN—especially not on the debit card itself. Instead, select a number you can remember easily, memorize that number, and never share it with anyone else. Incidentally, don't choose a PIN that's too obvious, like the last four digits of your telephone number or Social Security/Social Insurance Number, your date of birth, or your address. If your identification is lost or stolen, it wouldn't be hard for someone to guess which number to use to access your accounts. This is also why you shouldn't carry your bank passbook or any other documents (like bank statements) that have your account number on them.

Debit cards are accepted almost anywhere a credit card is, including online. Some debit cards have only your bank's logo on the front, while others have the Visa or MasterCard logo. This allows you to use them as credit cards, in some cases, and offers you special protection if the card is lost or stolen.

You also can use your debit card at an ATM (or an ABM in Canada). You'll need your PIN to access your account. Always be aware of your surroundings when you use an ATM/ABM located outside—even machines that are located on the outside of bank buildings. It's always safer to use ATMs/ABMs that are located in buildings where there are a lot of people around. Likewise, you should avoid using an ATM/ABM at night, even if you can pull right up to the machine and stay in your car while you use it. You never know who's nearby waiting for an opportunity to rob you.

Always remember that a debit card is a direct line to your checking account, and as such, should be treated the same way. Enter purchases in your checking account register, and reconcile (balance) the account when you get your bank statement.

CREDIT CARD

It's just a small piece of plastic, but a credit card is a very powerful thing. The trick is whether you use that power for good—or not.

A credit card is a financial instrument used to buy products and services without cash. In essence, the credit card slip you sign is a promissory note, or a promise that you will repay the credit card issuer for the amount of the sale. Credit cards are usually issued by banks, but there also are companies that do nothing but issue credit cards and rake in fees (examples include American Express and Discover).

Just about everyone needs to have at least one credit card. It allows you to shop or travel without carrying a lot of cash (thieves will notice if you flash a big wad of cash). If you travel, you'll need a credit card when you check into a hotel or when you rent a car. Credit card companies also frequently offer buyer protection, so if something goes wrong with something you've purchased, you may be able to stop payment on the purchase until your concerns are resolved. And believe it or not, if you want to take out a mortgage and you don't have a history of paying credit cards in a timely manner, you may not qualify for that mortgage, because banks want proof that you can handle credit successfully.

There are several types of credit cards. The first is the revolving credit card, which gives back your buying power whenever you pay some or all of the balance owed. For example, if you have a $5,000 limit and you spend $2,000, you have just $3,000 left open to buy. But if you make a $1,000 payment, you immediately have $4,000 open for new purchases.

Other types of credit cards include the following:

- *Store credit card:* These are issued by stores specifically for purchases only in their store. Occasionally, a store will partner with Visa or MasterCard and put one of those logos on the card, which means you can use the card in the store, as well as anywhere else Visa or MasterCard is accepted.
- *Zero-or-low interest card:* This type of card allows you to make a purchase, then pay back the debt over a finite period of time interest-free. Stores

that sell big-ticket items like furniture and electronics are among the stores that offer this type of credit.

- *Rewards card:* This type of card offers cash back or other incentives for using the card regularly. The incentives also may include merchandise and trips. But beware: these types of cards usually have hefty annual fees to pay for the cost of offering such perks.

- *Secured credit card:* This isn't really a credit card at all, but a way to establish credit for the first time, or to repair a poor credit history and re-establish credit. You pay a cash deposit upfront—say, $300 or $500—to have the card, and that becomes your credit line. But steer clear of secured cards that charge an application fee. That fee alone can consume your entire cash deposit. You're usually better off trying for a low-limit store card instead.

- No matter which type of card you get, make sure you sign the back promptly, then look at your monthly statement carefully, both to make sure you know exactly how much you owe and when payments are due, and to make sure there aren't any incorrect or fraudulent charges. If you do find something suspicious, call the customer-service number on the back of your card immediately. If you report fraudulent charges, U.S. federal law limits your liability to no more than $50 on each card, no matter how much is charged. In Canada, it's likely that you won't be liable at all, assuming you've met your cardholder agreement. Check with your bank for details.

CERTIFICATES OF DEPOSIT

Regular passbook savings accounts usually don't pay much interest—in recent years, the rate has been as low as .05 percent. A certificate of deposit (CD) pays a higher interest rate, but there are certain requirements to earn it. To begin with, you'll be required to make a minimum deposit to set up a CD—often $1,000 or more. You also have to tie up your money for a set period of time. Although CDs can have a term as short as thirty days, you'll need a five- to ten-year CD to earn better rates. (Currently, thirty-day CDs are earning just .25 percent on deposits of $95,000 or more.) Just be aware that you won't be able to access your money until the CD matures, or you'll lose all the accrued interest. Still, this is also a simple way to earn a higher interest rate without paying fees.

SAFE DEPOSIT BOX

This is literally a steel box at your bank into which you can place important documents and valuable belongings. It's common for people to use a safe deposit box to store things like marriage licenses, birth and death certificates, insurance policies, mortgage papers, property deeds, stock and bond certificates, jewelry, rare coins, and other valuables. Important immigration papers and documents, including your passport and every document you have ever received establishing your immigrant status, also should go into your safe deposit box. A good rule of thumb for deciding what should be locked away is that if something would be hard or impossible to replace, it should go into your safe deposit box. Make photocopies of these documents, including all pages of your passport, and store them in a safe place in your home, like in a fire-proof box or safe.

However, don't store your will in the safe deposit box. It takes a court-order to open the box after your death if no one other than you has permission to enter the box. Instead, store your will somewhere safe but accessible, and give copies to your executor and/or heirs and let them know where the original can be found. Finally, don't put your green card (U.S.) or permanent resident card (Canada) in the safe deposit box, since you're required by law to have it with you at all times. Make a color copy of your card and store that in your safe deposit box instead.

Safe deposit boxes are rented annually and come in different sizes. When you rent a box, you'll sign a card that will be used to verify your identity the next time you want to access the box, and you'll receive two keys. Only you will have keys to your box—a bank representative literally must drill a hole in the box to enter it if you lose your keys. So safeguard them carefully. Usually, people will give one key to a trusted family member or friend, and keep the other key safely at home.

MORTGAGE AND HOME EQUITY LINE OF CREDIT

Mortgages are a bank's biggest product—and biggest moneymaker. Borrowers who wish to purchase a house, condominium, or other dwelling must qualify on the basis of income and debt in order to acquire a mortgage. See Chapter 13 for an in-depth discussion of mortgages.

A home equity line of credit (HELOC) is a product that allows a person to borrow money against the equity, or ownership interest, in an existing home. The lender agrees to give the borrower a loan against that equity for a certain period of time; usually ten years (120 months). The funds usually must be used for home improvements, debt consolidation, or other major life events (including funding a college education). Since the home is the collateral (security) for the HELOC, it's very important that all payments are made on time. If you miss a few payments, the bank can foreclose, or take your house as payment. You *never* want that to happen.

BANKING FEES

There's an expression in English that "there's no such thing as a free lunch." This is a particularly apt expression when it comes to banks. You might think that because, in essence, you're lending your money to the bank when you make a deposit, the banks would be very happy and grateful. After all, they recognize your contributions to the banking system by giving you interest on your deposits. But it's a fact of life that banks are all about making money, and a significant portion of their profits is derived through fees. Following are the various types of fees you can expect to pay at a bank.

Monthly Account Fees

Smaller accounts in particular may be subject to a monthly account fee, which is a charge for maintaining your account. You might wonder exactly how much maintenance is going on if all you do is leave your money sitting quietly in your account. That's one of the big mysteries of the banking system. The good news is it's often possible to avoid this fee if you have a minimum balance on account. This minimum balance varies by the financial institution and could be as little as $500 or as much as $5,000. Be sure to ask about this when you open your account.

Overdraft Fees

Everyone makes an addition error once in a while, but if you do it when adding and subtracting money in your checkbook register and you end up not having enough money to cover a check (known as being overdrawn), you'll end up paying an overdraft fee. These fees can be quite expensive—as much as $30 or more just for one little mistake. That can really hurt, especially if the check you made the mistake on is really small. Worse yet, let's say you wrote four or five checks to pay your bills, and your account becomes overdrawn. The fee on those five checks could easily add up to $150. What's even worse is that not only will you pay a fee for being overdrawn; unless you have overdraft protection the bank won't pay the check until your account is brought back in line through deposits or fund transfers. That can trigger late fees from the companies you're paying.

Because overdraft fees are usually considerably less than standard NSF fees, it's a good idea to set up overdraft protection at your bank. Alternately, you may be able to ask your bank to set up automatic transfers from your savings to your checking account to avoid triggering overdraft fees.

Banks make a ton of money from fees, so don't make it easier for them to collect. Set up overdraft protection right away.

ATM/ABM Fees

Automated teller machines and automated banking machines are convenient, but beware: if you use a machine not owned by your bank (known as an out-of-network ATM/ABM), you may be charged a usage fee when you make a deposit or withdraw funds, plus your own bank may charge you, too. Typically, these charges are $2 to $5 per transaction. You might even have to pay the fee if you use an ATM/ABM owned by your own bank. Before the fees are charged, you'll be given the option to cancel the transaction. So think carefully about how much you really need the cash before you withdraw it and pay all those fees.

A better time to get cash is when you make a debit card purchase at a store, gas station, or even the post office. These places usually will debit your account for the amount you want (within reasonable limits) without charging a fee. So it might be more cost-effective to drive past the bank and ask for cash back when you buy groceries or do other shopping.

By the way, even though debit cards are accepted virtually everywhere, you still should have a certain amount of cash in your pocket or wallet at all times. There are some things you can't use a debit card for, such as parking meter fees or possibly small purchases (under $5), especially at small businesses. In addition, studies have shown that people generally spend more than they should when they use plastic instead of money. So you might be able to curb your spending by not using your debit card for everyday purchases and instead giving yourself a monthly allowance in cash that you don't exceed.

LATE FEES

Banks charge late (penalty) fees whenever they receive payments after the due date. This applies to everything from payments on credit cards, to loans, lines of credit, and so on. These fees can be pretty hefty. Buy an accordion file with pockets numbered from 1 to 31 so you can sort your bills into the appropriate pocket by due date, then make sure you pay them well in advance of the due date so you'll always avoid late fees. This is especially important if you mail your payments. Always put them in the mail at least seven days before the due date to make sure they are posted and arrive on time. Credit card companies in particular are very unforgiving when it comes to late payments. Alternately, you can set up electronic bill payment at your bank so your payments are posted the same day.

TRANSACTION FEES

Banks are fond of charging fees for basic transactions, too, including transfers, cash advances, and even direct deposits. They also may charge you for transacting business with a teller, as well as for *not* transacting business with a teller (that is, using the ATM/ABM, as discussed earlier). Be sure to read your bank disclosure carefully to ferret out the fee schedule, and consider switching to a bank that doesn't "fee" you to death if your own bank's charges are excessive.

By the way, as mentioned earlier, credit unions don't charge nearly as many fees as banks do, which is another good reason to join one if you can.

INVESTING BASICS

A single chapter in a book isn't enough space to cover all there is to know about investing, especially since the world of investing is quite complicated. So here's just an overview of investing to acquaint you with the concept. Consult with an investment advisor if you need more in-depth information or you're ready to invest.

Stocks

Simply stated, a stock is a share in the ownership of a company. For example, when the online social networking company Facebook went public in 2012, its initial public offering was for 485 million shares at $38 each, which raised $18.4 *billion* for the founder and his associates. If you wanted to become a shareholder that day, you could have purchased one share of stock for $38, ten shares for $380, and so on. In addition to the stock price, you would have paid what's called a brokerage fee to the person (broker) or company who made the purchase for you on the stock exchange.

In fact, stock always must be purchased through established channels; the average person can't just buy a share or two directly from a company. Instead, you'll need a stockbroker, who is a professional advisor licensed to purchase securities on behalf of an investor (that would be you).

There are three types of brokers:

- *Full-service brokers:* These are financial professionals who will meet with you to discuss your needs and help you build a balanced stock portfolio. They can advise you on which stocks look promising and which to avoid.
- *Money managers:* These financial pros generally manage very large or high value portfolios and for this expertise charge high fees usually based on asset value.
- *Online/discount brokers:* These are basically just order takers. You tell them what you want, and they execute the trade with no questions asked or advice offered.

Alternately, you can make your own trades with a few clicks of your mouse. This is the least expensive way to start investing because the fees are so low. For example, you can easily find an online broker that charges just $4.95 per trade (either buying or selling). You usually interact with these brokers online, or you may be able to speak to a live person by phone to make trades. Just remember that they offer absolutely no financial advice.

Once you purchase stock, you can see how it's doing by watching the stock market indexes. In the United States, the two major stock market exchanges are the Dow Jones Industrial Average (which consists of the top thirty ranking "blue chip" companies), and the Nasdaq Composite (a tech-heavy index).

In Canada, stocks are traded on eleven different stock exchanges, including the Toronto Stock Exchange (the largest). You'll need help deciphering what the numbers mean. Ask your broker for help, or search online for information if you're using a discount broker.

Profits paid on stock are known as dividends and are generated by the company from its earnings. These profits are shared among investors and may be distributed to stockholders quarterly, semi-annually, or annually.

Naturally, the IRS and the CRA will be very interested in any profit you earn on your investments. In the United States, you'll receive a 1099-DIV form from the stock brokerage or the company you've invested in that shows how much you earned. This amount must be reported on your income tax return. In Canada, you'll receive a T5 Form for income tax reporting purposes. You also can reinvest your profits into your stock account though a company's dividend-reinvestment program. This defers the tax bite (known as capital gains) until you actually sell the stock.

Sometimes a stock is extremely popular or a company may wish to generate more income by selling more stock. In these cases, the company may decide to split its stock to create more shares. Here's what happens: the total number of shares held in the company is doubled, and the value of each share is cut in half. The newly created shares are then spread out among the existing stockholders. So if you held ten shares of stock at $50, you would hold twenty shares of stock at $25 after a stock split. The lower share price is then more attractive to new buyers, which ultimately (you and the company hope) makes the price go up and the value of your stock portfolio increase.

It's important to note that no matter how well-versed your broker or you are in investing strategies, it's always possible that you could lose part or all of your stock investments. It all depends on the performance of the stocks you own, which can be impacted by many factors, from economic reports to natural disasters. For this reason, it's important to watch your stocks closely and to buy or sell when the timing seems right. Sometimes it's smarter to sell a stock while it's dropping in value than it is to wait for it to recover. Avoid becoming "married" to your stocks because you like the company or because you just don't have time to study the market and move your money around. If you fall into the latter category, it might be better to use a stock broker who can manage your portfolio for you, or at least give you some advice about what to do. It costs more to use a broker than it does to go it alone, but if you're going to lose money on your own anyway, it makes more sense just to pay for a stockbroker's help and advice.

In the meantime, a smart investor learns how to play the stock market by reading and asking questions. Alternately, you can learn a lot without risking any money by using the Investopedia stock simulator at investopedia. com/simulator. When you establish your "account," you're given $100,000 in virtual cash to make virtual trades. It's a fun and educational way to learn the ins and outs of the stock market.

CREDIT PRIMER

We all know that there are things in life worth having that we can't afford right away. They may include an engagement ring for your sweetheart, a college education for your kids, or a home for your family. But even though you can't afford to buy these important things outright doesn't mean you can't have them. The way you get them, of course, is through credit.

Credit may be defined as borrowing power backed by financial trustworthiness. When you borrow money, it's expected that you will repay those funds in full in a certain period of time. Depending on where you borrow the money from, you might not pay any interest (the charge for borrowing money), such as when the money comes from the Bank of Dad; or you may have to pay a certain percentage for the use of the money. That percentage is usually expressed as an annual percentage rate (APR) and can vary from a very a modest amount (6 to 11 percent) to the horrific interest rates charged by credit card companies (29.9 percent or higher). There even are finance companies that advertise on TV that charge the astronomical rate of 355 percent! You read that right—in financial terms, that's known as usury, or charging an exorbitant interest rate. But loopholes in the law allow these predatory lenders to get away with it—at least for a while.

If you stick to reputable institutions like banks and credit unions, you'll get a rate that's much fairer than that. It's then up to you to make payments in full and on time every month, which helps you to build a good credit history. That history, in turn, will make other companies trust that you will pay your debts, and they'll extend credit to you, too.

Of course, that's where people often get into trouble. They open too many credit card accounts with high limits, spend freely, then find they can't pay the money back (possibly because they've lost their job, or because they simply spent too much). If they default on their debts, or fail to pay back what is owed, they do great damage to their credit history and will find it hard, if not impossible, to obtain credit in the future, even for things they may legitimately and desperately need.

YOUR CREDIT SCORE

Your credit score is a reflection of how well you use the credit that's extended to you. (Payments on utility bills like gas, water (*aka* hydro), and power are also considered in your credit score.) In the United States, each month that you have an open credit or utility account, information about how much you pay on that account and when the payment was made (either on time or late—or not at all) is electronically recorded by one of three credit rating agencies or bureaus, either Equifax, Experian, or TransUnion. In Canada, there are two credit bureaus: Equifax Canada and TransUnion Canada. Then when you want to borrow money for a car, a mortgage, your kid's college education, and so on, creditors will look at one or all of these reports and decide whether you look like a good credit risk. They make this decision based on what's known as a FICO score. The better your FICO score, the better the terms will be from the lender. For instance, you may get a more favorable interest rate if your FICO score is good.

FICO scores range from 300 to 850, with the higher scores being the most favorable. You can check your own FICO score right now for free by going to myfico.com/Guest_Home.aspx.

If your FICO score is too low, you won't look like a good credit risk to lenders, and you could be turned down for the loan, credit card, or mortgage you're seeking. Sometimes, though, the bank will relent and give you the mortgage anyway, but at a rate that's a *lot* higher than someone with a great score.

Your FICO score can also be impacted by how many credit accounts you have, how much buying power you have on them (credit open to buy), how close you are to the maximum spending limit with each account, and even how many inquiries are made by lenders.

And here are two more good reasons why you need to take care of your credit: both employers and auto insurance companies base decisions on credit scores. It may not seem fair to lose a job or pay a higher auto insurance rates because you have a lot of outstanding debt, but lenders do that all the time as a way to protect themselves. If it looks like you're too loose with your money, they won't want to take a chance on you.

You can repair your credit history, but it takes seven years for negative information about non-payments or slow payments to drop off your credit history. It can take up to ten years to erase a bankruptcy (bankruptcy is discussed later in this chapter). It's much better to take charge of your credit and spending habits immediately, buy only the things you absolutely need, and limit the number of accounts you have. You could also get a credit card whose balances must be repaid in full every month, like an American Express card. These are all much more responsible ways to use credit, plus it helps you preserve your savings in your own account, not in the account of the bank or other creditor.

The bottom line is you need to use credit responsibly and sparingly. Some credit is an inevitable fact of life—you'll probably need a mortgage at some point, for example—so be sure to make payments diligently and on time, and you'll preserve your good credit and your good name.

BUDGETING

Once you have credit cards and a mortgage and all the other things that come along with home ownership, you need a way to manage your money so you always have enough cash coming in to cover the payments that are going out, as well as some extra to save. The way to do this is to establish a household budget.

Simply stated, a budget is a snapshot of your monthly financial situation. It consists of two things: income and expenses. As long as your income from your job and your investments exceeds your expenses, you're doing fine. But when the gap between the two is too small, or your expenses are higher than what you have coming in, you will find yourself in real trouble, and sooner rather than later.

The main purpose of a budget is to figure out a way to live within your means so you never go into debt. That means you have to be disciplined enough to pay the household expenses and those credit card bills just discussed on time, and preferably, in full.

To make sure you can do this, create a four-column budget either on paper or by using a spreadsheet program like Excel or QuickBooks. From the left, label the columns "Income," "Amount," "Expenses," and "Amount." In the far left column, make a list of your income, which might include wages, overtime, tips, bonuses, child-support payments, pension payments, Social

Security, disability, public assistance, and unemployment payments. Write in how much you received in the next column. Then in the third column over, make a list of your regular monthly expenses. Finally, in the far right column, note how much you spent for each line item that month. Once you fill in all the boxes (use last month's bills and receipts when trying this exercise), tally up each column. Ideally, the "income" column will be greater than the "expenses" column. If it isn't, you need to look for ways to trim your budget so you end up with a surplus of cash each month. Then each month after that, try to increase the amount left over by further eliminating debt or cutting expenses.

On the next page is a simple monthly budget for a family with one wage earner (and therefore, one salary). Notice that "savings account" is listed as a regular expense item so you are always sure to pay yourself first.

Income Sources	Amount	Expenses	Amount
Monthly Salary (after taxes)			
Overtime			
Tips			
Bonuses			
Child support			
Pension			
Social Security payment			
Investment interest/dividends			
		Saving Account	
		Mortgage or rent	
		Utilities	
		Power	
		Natural Gas	
		Water/hydro	
		Phone	
		Insurance	
		Health insurance	
		Transportation: Bus, Train, Light rail	
		Gasoline	
		Tolls	
		Vehicle maintenance	
		Groceries	
		Clothing/uniforms/shoes	
		Entertainment	
		Family activities	
		Child care	
		Child support	
		Credit card 1	
		Credit card 2	
		Credit card 3	
		Loan payment	
Total		**Total**	

You might be shocked when you first see on paper exactly how much you're spending relative to your income. Use that as a wake-up call that you need to do something now to improve your monthly budget. Your financial future depends on it.

BANKRUPTCY

The word "bankruptcy" is enough to strike fear into the heart of any responsible person. Bankruptcy, which is the state of being unable to pay one's debts, represents a personal failure; one that causes guilt and shame in most responsible people. Yet sometimes, it's the only option a person has to avoid crushing debt.

Of course, the preferred course of action is to avoid getting into a situation that would result in bankruptcy. It's important to avoid controllable situations like the reckless use of credit cards. But sometimes, you can be wrecked by situations beyond your control, like towering medical bills or other emergencies. Economic downturns that erode your ability to earn a living, deplete the equity in your home, and erase your buying power are other unavoidable situations. No matter what the cause, bankruptcy changes your life—and quite frankly, sometimes it changes your life for the better. After the initial shame and stigma of the personal failure wears off, you realize you have a chance for a new start, which can lift an enormous weight off your shoulders.

But this is not a testimonial for bankruptcy; it's just a fact of life. So here are the steps involved if you must file for bankruptcy.

In order to start bankruptcy proceedings, you'll start by consulting a lawyer experienced with bankruptcies. He or she can help you decide whether you actually qualify to file for bankruptcy, whether it's the right course of action, and which type of bankruptcy to choose. You can file without an attorney, but it's usually better to have an experienced pro guide you through the process.

In the United States, there are two types of bankruptcy filings. People usually choose Chapter 7 bankruptcy when they're buried in medical debt, they're unemployed and have no resources to pay their bills, or they've run their credit cards up so high that there's no possibility of repayment. Under Chapter 7, assets are liquidated (converted into cash). Assets may include your house, if there's any equity. The money is then divided among your creditors. Usually, they'll get far less than they're owed.

Under Chapter 13, the court oversees the reorganization of your financial life, and you pay your debts back within three to five years. This might be a good choice if you want to keep your home and possessions. But it won't work if you are unemployed or don't have a way to repay debt.

Here's a general overview of the bankruptcy filing steps in both the United States and Canada:

Chapter 7 (United States)	Personal Bankruptcy (Canada)
1. Consult a bankruptcy attorney for advice	1. Contact a federally licensed trustee in bankruptcy to start the process.
2. Complete mandatory credit counseling.	2. File an assignment in bankruptcy document so your creditors can no longer start or continue legal proceedings against you.
3. Fill out the necessary paperwork to initiate the bankruptcy.	3. Attend mandatory credit counseling sessions.
4. File the forms and a petition for bankruptcy in bankruptcy court. At this point, your creditors are required by law to stop any proceedings like lawsuits agains you.	4. Abide by the federal government's surplus income calculation, which is a monthly net amount for a reasonable living standard. You must pay the trustee 50 percent of any surplus income above that monthly net amount, which benefits creditors.
5. Attend a creditors meting to discuss your debt.	5. Stay in touch with the trustee in case you have a means to pay off additional debt.
6. Complete the remaining paperwork and a financial management course.	6. Wait nine months for word that the bankruptcy was granted.
7. Wait sixty days for word that your debts have been eliminated.	7. Restart your financial life by being prudent and careful about future spending and debt.
8. Move on and get your life and financial house in order.	

You can hope that you'll never need to file for bankruptcy. But if you ever do, you can take comfort in knowing that there's a standard process available to help you recover your life and self-esteem so you can move on to better things.

ATTA'S LESSONS

Upon the birth of my first child in 1989, one of my co-workers, who was the bank's financial consultant, handed me a gift for my son: a check for $200. Then he told me to sign it and give it right back to him. I was surprised, but I did it. He informed me that he was going to start an account in my son's name in a child education fund. He also made me sign a form that deducted money every month from my paycheck. That money was deposited into the fund.

Over the years, I increased my monthly contributions, and eventually, I was able to fund my son's entire four-year college education with the proceeds. That money would probably never been there if it hadn't been for the great advice and actions of that professional financial advisor. The point is that while it's important for you to become knowledgeable about finances so you can take control of your money, you also should resist the temptation to do all your financial planning alone. Instead, seek help from a professional advisor. Your bank branch is a great place to start to find help.

Available Cash Assets Worksheet

Accounts	Balance	Interest	Maturity date	Monthly income
Checking				
Savings				
Money Market				
Cash				
Investments				
Cert of deposit				
Treasury bill				
Stock				
Stock				
Stock				
Bond				
Annuity				
Stock options				
Total Assets				

Debt Balance Worksheet
Note the amount you currently owe on the following:

	Balance	Interest Rate
Credit Card 1		
Credit Card 2		
Department Store Card		
Department Store Card		
Car loan		
Car loan		
Car loan		

Financial Planning and Preparation Worksheet

This information will be helpful when seeking
the assistance of a financial planner.

Name_____

Address_____

Phone Number(s)

      Home_____

      Office_____

      Cell_____

Occupation_____

Age_____

Health Status_____

_____

_____

Medications_____

_____

_____

Are your parents alive? ___ Yes ___ No

Mother's health and age _____

Father's health and age _____

If not, cause and age of death _____

_____

Your financial goals:

1. _____
_____

2. _____
_____

3. _____
_____

Have you ever invested in anything other than regular savings or certificates of deposit?

_____ Yes _____ No

If so, did you hold _____ Stocks _____ Bonds _____ Mutual funds (check all that apply)

How did you feel about those investments? _____ Satisfied _____ Dissatisfied

Explain: _____
_____

What year do you expect to retire? _____

Do you expect to receive a pension? _____ Yes _____ No

Do you have 401(K) accounts? List them below:

Company name _____

Balance _____

Company name _____

Balance _____

Are you entitled to receive Social Security payments?
____ Yes ____ No ____ Don't know

How much do you expect to receive each month? _____

How many times have you married? _____

Are you receiving funds from ex-spouse? ____ Yes ____ No

How much? _____

Will payments stop upon her/his death? ____ Yes ____ No

Do you pay alimony? ____ Yes ____ No

Monthly amount _____

Are you paying child support? ____ Yes ____ No

Are you receiving child support? ____ Yes ____ No

How much a month? _____

Do you have money on hand to invest? ____ Yes ____ No

How much? _____

How long are you willing to tie up your money? _____

Do you feel comfortable talking about money matters? ____ Yes ____ No

Do you or other family members expect to receive an inheritance?
____ Yes ____ No

Will any family member(s), physically or financially, help you?
____ Yes ____ No

Are you willing to move someone into your home, if necessary?
_____ Yes _____ No

Do your parents have a long-term health care insurance policy or advanced directive? _____ Yes _____ No

Do you have a will? _____ Yes _____ No

Do you have a trust? _____ Yes _____ No

Do you or your spouse have a long-term care policy? _____ Yes _____ No

Do you or your spouse have disability insurance? _____ Yes _____ No

How much are your deductibles:

     Cars _____

     House Insurance _____

     Health Insurance _____

How long have you/spouse been in your current job?

     Self _____ Years

     Spouse _____ Years

Do you anticipate any career changes? _____ Yes _____ No

When? _____

Children

Number of dependent children _____

Ages _____

How long will they rely on your support? _____ Years

Is anyone currently on disability insurance? _____ Yes _____ No

Have you arranged for your children's college education? _____ Yes _____ No

Are you currently paying for your children's college education?
_____ Yes _____ No

How much? _____

Are you willing to use your retirement funds to pay for your children's education? _____ Yes _____ No

Have you assigned someone capable to take care of your financial business if something happened to you today? _____ Yes _____ No

Chapter 14: Buying a Home

There's no question that home ownership is one of the pillars of the American dream. But in reality, it's the dream of all people everywhere—Canadians included. A home of your own represents comfort, security, and success. For some, it's a place to share happy times with family and friends. For others, it's a hallmark of responsibility and adulthood.

No matter what your home means to you, it's a big step to look for that home, then sign the papers that either makes it your own or gives you the right to live in it for a certain period of time.

While having a house is considered the ultimate in home ownership, not every immigrant is able or wants to own a house—at least, not right away. Maybe you need time to save enough money to make the down payment, which is a partial payment toward the amount you will owe. Maybe a house is just too big for you. Maybe you can't afford the payments and still be able to send money back to the folks in your home country. Or maybe you just don't want the responsibly that comes along with a house, like lawn work, interior maintenance, property taxes, and other time-consuming responsibilities.

If this sounds like you, then buying a condominium or renting an apartment might be better choices for you. In North America, you have plenty of different types of housing to select from, and the right one is out there, waiting for you.

This chapter explores the various types of housing that are available in North America, from modest studio apartments to grand homes situated on large pieces of property. The type of home you ultimately select will depend on your income, tolerance for debt, location, and the number of people in your household.

Because the names of the various home styles are basically the same in both the United States and Canada (with just a few exceptions), they're discussed together in this chapter.

APARTMENT

This type of dwelling is a group of rooms that form a single residence. You'll find a group of apartments located in a single building, from as few as a dozen to as many as a couple of hundred located in an apartment complex. There are three styles of apartments: the low-rise apartment, which is located in a building of fewer than four floors; the mid-rise apartment, which is usually no more than four to six floors high and may have usable outdoor space (like a garden) around it; and the high-rise apartment, which in addition to being in tall building of six stories or more, may have special amenities like a front lobby, excellent views, a fitness room, and even retail space on the ground floor. The number of rooms in an apartment depends on the square footage of the building it's in.

Apartment types include the following:

- *Efficiency/ bachelor/ studio:* This is a small apartment that combines the living room, bedroom, and kitchen into a single room.
- *Convertible apartment:* This is a studio-style apartment that's large enough to be subdivided into different rooms; walls can be permanent or can be temporary structures like screens
- *Loft:* Similar to a convertible apartment, this is an open space in a converted commercial or industrial building. A loft usually features architectural details like high ceilings, concrete floors and posts, and exposed pipes and ductwork. These types of dwellings often are found in urban settings and can be very large.
- *Basement or garage apartment:* Located in—you guessed it—the basement or over the top of a garage, these can be very basic one-room living quarters or beautifully appointed multi-room homes.
- *Duplex:* This is an apartment with two levels connected by an interior stairway.
- *One-, two-, and three-bedroom apartments:* As the names imply, these are apartments with up to three bedrooms, along with a living room, bathroom(s), and kitchen.
- *Classic six and classic seven:* These types of apartments are found in older, renovated buildings, in cosmopolitan cities like New York and Boston. They're high-end and expensive, with multiple bedrooms (two in a

classic six and three in a classic seven), a spacious living area, a formal dining room and kitchen, and a small room off the kitchen known as the "maid's room," which back in the day was intended for the homeowners' live-in staff, but makes a great office or playroom for the kids today. The buildings that house classic sixes and sevens usually have spacious lobbies and a doorman to welcome you home.

- *Penthouse:* This is the expensive luxury apartment on the top floor of a high-rise apartment building. It's considered to be the most desirable space in the building, partly because of the view of the city below it.

CONDOMINIUM (CONDO)

This is a style of home common mostly to North America. Condos are grouped together in a building just like apartments, and may be low-, medium-, or high-rise style. The difference between a condo and an apartment is that everything within the living space—fixtures, flooring, walls, balcony (if you're lucky), and more—is owned by the resident. As a result, you can decorate or alter the space any way you wish. You also may be able have a reasonable number of pets (as long as you clean up after them).

Condos may come with a garage or a protected space known as a carport, which basically is a canopy under which you park your vehicle to protect it from the elements. There's also usually a common area where mail is deposited into individual mailboxes, and there may be other shared amenities like laundry facilities, tennis courts, walking trails, parks, children's play equipment, and an activity center.

Along with your monthly mortgage payment (which is discussed later), you must pay a monthly association fee or strata fee to live in a condo. This fee covers outside services like landscaping, lawn care, snow removal, exterior painting, and roof repairs, and inside services like cleaning and maintenance. This fee easily can amount to hundreds of dollars a month. But if you don't want to take care of that pesky outdoor stuff, then a condo can be a good choice for you and your family. You'll also be responsible for real estate property taxes, as well as interior repairs.

Since you actually own the condo, you may be able to rent it to another person(s) if you wish, for instance if you'll be away for a long period of time. Just make sure you check with the condo association for restrictions. There may be a cap on the number of condos that can be leased in your building.

DETACHED CONDOMINIUM

This is a single-family home that's located within a cluster of other similar homes, whose owners leave the exterior maintenance to a condo association. These types of homes usually have small (or no) yards because they're placed very close together. Style-wise, they can be anything from a modest bungalow (discussed later), to a very large luxury home. Because they tend to be located in or near affluent communities, detached condos allow you to enjoy a better neighborhood and a higher standard of living at a lower price.

TOWNHOUSE

Similar to a condo, a townhouse consists of a row of identical homes with shared walls. The difference between them is that townhouses generally don't have shared common areas. As a result, there's no homeowner association, so the townhouse owner is responsible for all interior and exterior repairs, as well as the annual real estate property taxes.

SINGLE-FAMILY HOMES

As the name implies, these types of homes are meant to house one family, although depending on the home and the number of rooms, they could house a *lot* of family members. There are dozens of types of single-family homes. Some of the most common include:

RANCH/RANCHER

Also known as a rambler or a California ranch or, in Canada, a rancher, the ranch home is a single-story, rectangular-shaped home. It often has a very plain exterior and an uncluttered layout. Sizes run from modest 1,000-square-foot homes to dwellings of 3,000 square feet or more. Ranches commonly have two or three bedrooms, a bath-and-a-half, a living room, and an eat-in kitchen. Depending on which part of the country you live in, a ranch may have an unfinished basement (usually in the Midwest); otherwise, they're built on a foundation known as a slab. Ranches also can have an attached or detached garage, or a carport. They're usually found in subdivisions in urban areas.

Split-Level

Commonly called a tri-level home, a split-level house has staggered floors, meaning the main floor, which has the entryway, is halfway between the upper and lower floors. The main floor usually has the common areas like the living room, kitchen, dining room, and family room. One set of stairs will lead to the upper level, where you'll find two or three bedrooms; a second set of stairs will lead to the basement, which is usually finished (that is, completed like the rest of the house) for use as a den, office, or laundry room. The garage may be attached or detached. Like ranches, split-level homes are generally found in subdivisions in urban communities.

Colonial

Colonial homes are considered the most popular housing style in America, according to *Better Homes and Gardens* magazine. These homes tend to have more square footage than ranches and split-levels (up to 4,000 square feet), and are square with windows on each side of and above the front doorway. Colonials generally have three to five bedrooms, as well as features like a formal dining room, great room, library, den, first floor laundry room, and mudroom. They tend to have attached two- or three-car garages and are located in subdivisions, some of which may be gated communities.

The very largest colonials are called mansions or estates. These homes start at 4,000 square feet and generally sit on a huge parcel of land. They may have luxurious features like a stately exterior with a circular driveway; five or more bedrooms, including a huge master suite; a home theater; and possibly even an indoor pool and an elevator. Some famous actors and recording artists you may have heard of even have a full recording studio and concert stage right in their own home; sports stars have been known to have their own indoor basketball court.

Mansions are usually in guarded, gated communities, and have garages that hold four or more cars—possibly with built-in car-wash bays. It may seem impossible to aspire to own one of these enormous homes, but you never know—you could be destined for great things and may one day have the means to have your own estate.

One type of mansion you may hear about is the "McMansion," which is a negative term for a large luxury home built on a plot of land that's really too small to accommodate it, so it ends up crowding the houses on either side. McMansions often pop up in subdivisions with similar large homes, as well as in older communities that have homes with classic architectural styles; this is one reason why they're so disliked.

OTHER TYPES OF SINGLE-FAMILY HOMES

MULTI-LEVEL HOUSE (CANADA)

This is a term that refers to any home with two or more floors. They're available in many styles, depending on the builder.

MANUFACTURED HOME

This type of home is built very much like a normal single-family home, except that it's assembled in pieces in a factory, then transported to the home site. (You may have heard this type of home referred to as a mobile home, but that term is outdated.) A manufactured home may be placed on a slab, crawl space, or basement on private property that you own or in a manufactured-home community on land that is owned by someone else. If you don't own the land, you'll pay rent to the community. If you do own the land, you'll pay property taxes. In addition, there's always the possibility that your state will charge you a property tax on the home itself. Check with your state's treasury department or bureau of taxation for information.

Manufactured homes can be very basic, with just a few rooms, or can have many rooms with upscale features like vaulted ceilings, fireplaces, crown moldings, and more. What makes them very appealing is that they can cost 25 percent to 30 percent less than a site-built home, according to MSN Money.

CARRIAGE HOUSE

This type of home is actually more like a studio apartment than a house, but since it's a freestanding building, it's discussed here. Originally designed to house a horse-drawn carriage, a carriage (or coach) house is a building that has been converted into residential space. Carriage houses are quite charming and are usually found as outbuildings on the grounds of an estate or a very large home. They can be very small (enough to originally house one or two horses) or very large (enough for a whole stable full of horses). Naturally, the horses don't come with the carriage house anymore.

Bungalow

This is a small, single- or one-and-a-half-story home common in small communities across North America.

Craftsman

Also known as the American Craftsman (and once sold as a kit by Sears, which sells Craftsman tools), this is a small, vintage home with wide porches anchored by columns. Natural materials like wood, stone, and brick were used in the construction of this type of home. They're common in older neighborhoods in North America, especially in the Midwest.

Shotgun

This is a modest home commonly found in the American South. It's a narrow, rectangular structure that features three to five rooms in a row with no hallways. The whole building usually is no more than twelve feet wide and has a doorway at each end of the house.

Saltbox

Very common in the northeast United States, a saltbox is a wood-frame house that has two stories in the front and one in the back. Some companies still build this style of home, but you're more likely to find it in the older parts of town.

Multiple-Family Home

The most common type of multiple-family home is the duplex, which is a single home divided by a common vertical wall into separate side-by-side residences, each with its own entrance. In some areas, the two units are on top of each other (upstairs and down). It's also possible to find triplexes, which have three side-by-side residences. New duplexes and triplexes are more common in Canada; the United States is more a land of single-family homes. But if you want one in the United States, you can still find them in the older parts of many towns.

THINGS TO CONSIDER BEFORE BUYING OR RENTING

Once you've made the decision to find your own home, there are a number of factors to consider before you actually make a commitment. These things include:

- *Buying versus renting:* If you plan to be in your home for more than five years, conventional financial wisdom holds that it's better to buy rather than rent a house, condo, or townhouse. There are a lot of fees associated with mortgages, and it's not worth paying them unless you plan to stay in the house for several years. Of course, if you don't have enough money for a down payment or you just prefer having the freedom to move on to another place when you're ready, then renting might be the better choice for you. You do have to commit to a certain length of time when you sign a lease—usually at least a year; more commonly, three years—but it's easier to break a lease (although not recommended) than it is to sell a house and get out of your mortgage. If you're considering an apartment, then the choice is easier. With very few exceptions (like in New York City, for instance), apartments are rented rather than purchased.
- *Cost:* Even though you will probably take out a mortgage to pay for your new home and the payments will be spread out over fifteen, twenty, or thirty years, the cost of your home is still a huge factor when deciding what to buy. Work with a banker or other financial expert (in Canada, a mortgage broker) to determine how much home you can reasonably afford, then stick to that price range when shopping. You'll find more information about how banks determine how much they'll lend you in the discussion of mortgages later in this chapter. Remember, too, that there are many other costs associated with home ownership, from utility bills to taxes, home improvements, and more. You also have to feed your family and pay for clothing, school expenses, and other bills. You must

factor in all these expenses to make sure you're really financially able to handle them and a mortgage, too.

- *Financial stability:* It's crucial that you have a stable job and savings before you buy a house, because if you miss payments due to a job loss, for example, you'll lose your house, too, and all the equity you may have built in it. For this reason, it's a good idea to consult with a financial expert before you buy. In addition to looking at your financial situation and counseling you about whether you can manage all the costs associated with home ownership, he or she can help you draw up a budget. In addition, you need a plan that will allow you to support your family for a minimum of six months if you lose your job and income. A financial expert can help you figure that out, too.

- *Size:* Depending on the living arrangements, you may need a larger home, especially if you will be living with many people. While homes in North America are meant to be single-family dwellings, it's not uncommon for more than one immigrant family to live together temporarily.

- *Living with family or friends comes with many benefits.* You not only save on rent and other expenses, but there's the sheer joy of having their company and ongoing support. For many immigrants, living temporarily with family is a proven good practice and an excellent way to get settled in your new land.

- *Location:* If at all possible, you should select a home that's close to your job. That will make getting to work easier and will give you more time to relax at the end of the day instead of sitting in traffic. However, if you live in a large, sprawling urban area like Los Angeles, you may have no choice other than to commute. So other things to consider when choosing the location of your new home are the quality of the local schools, the proximity of shopping (grocery stores, convenience stores, malls/clothing stores), and the distance to medical facilities and physicians' offices. Also consider the community where your prospective home is located. Does it offer activities for families? Are there convenient travel routes in and out of town? Is there adequate public transportation? Are the streets safe? These are all important considerations.

BUYING OR LEASING A HOUSE

Unless you are fortunate enough to have funds to purchase a house out-right, for most buying a home is a matter of qualifying for and obtaining a mortgage from a bank or other financial institution (discussed later in this chapter), signing papers, and making monthly mortgage payments. You'll also have to pay property taxes, and utility, and other household expenses. In addition, you'll be in charge of all the outside work, including cutting the lawn, weeding, trimming bushes, weed-whacking, and so on. If you live in a subdivision that has a homeowners' association, you'll be required to pay a monthly or annual homeowners' fee, which usually covers landscaping around the entrance to the subdivision, snow removal, watering, and other beautification/maintenance projects.

If you don't have sparkling credit or you just aren't ready to buy, you still can get into a home of your own by leasing it. With a lease, you're committing to a long-term contract to stay in the house and make the payments. When you rent, you're planning to stay for a shorter period of time, say, thirty days. A rental agreement does renew automatically at the end of the rental period if you give written notice that you wish to stay. Renting can be the way to go if you're not ready to buy but need a place to live right away.

If you own your home, you're free to do any redecorating, remodeling (once you get the approval and permit from your local city planning department), landscaping, or other beautification work you wish. If you're leasing or rent-ing, you probably won't have that freedom. Check the terms of your lease or rental agreement to be sure.

BUYING OR LEASING A CONDO OR TOWNHOUSE

Although it's possible to rent a condo or townhouse, it's much more common for people to buy these types of homes. You can buy a condo or townhouse with cash, of course, but you're much more likely to need a mortgage, which allows you to pay for the house using money from a lending institution like a bank and pay the money back over time. Mortgages are discussed later in this chapter.

As with a house, you can only make improvements or redecorate a condo or townhouse if you own it. It's hands off for people who lease or rent.

The Pros and Cons of Buying a Home

Pros:

- Buying is an investment in your future. If you make significant payments—that is, payments above the cost of mortgage interest alone—you'll build equity in the house faster as long as the housing market remains strong.
- You'll own the house and property outright once the mortgage is paid off. If you sell the house before it's paid off, you may get the equity back, based on local market conditions. When you rent, your money goes to the landlord—you'll never see it again.
- Your home's value will rise in a strong housing market.
- You have the freedom to do what you want with your home—remodeling, redecorating, and otherwise improving your home and property.
- You don't have to deal with landlords or leasing agents.
- Home ownership gives you the opportunity to become part of a community made up of local schools and shops while creating a support system of friends.

Cons:

- You have to qualify for a mortgage, based on your income, debt level, and credit score. You may have to settle for less house than you really want if any of the three factors are out of line.
- You'll be locked into a fixed payment every month for years until you sell the house. Renters have the flexibility to contract for either months or years, allowing them to test out an area before committing to a long-term contract or buying a permanent home.
- The value of your home may go down in a weak housing market.
- Mortgage interest, property tax, insurance, and maintenance costs tend to be high. Although you can get a federal income tax deduction for mortgage interest and property tax, the cost of insurance and maintenance can never be recovered.

RENTING AN APARTMENT

Apartments are rented for a certain length of time—usually three years, but as few as one year, in some situations. Rent payments are usually due on the first of the month, and you're likely to have to pay the first and last rent payment when you agree to take the apartment and sign on the dotted line. You will also have to provide a security deposit, to pay for any damage to the apartment above normal wear and tear (such as gouges in the walls or flooring). The deposit also covers key replacement, painting, carpet cleaning, and other services necessary to prepare the apartment for the next tenant.

The landlord will have the apartment freshly painted and cleaned before you move in. As a resident, you're usually not allowed to paint, wallpaper, hang pictures, or otherwise alter the living space in any way. Because you don't own the apartment, you will call the building superintendent (or perhaps the landlord) when repairs are needed to the plumbing, appliances, and so on.

Apartments come either unfurnished or furnished. If the latter, then you're stuck with whatever furnishings are in the place, no matter how much you hate them. The only thing you can do with furniture you don't like would be to store it in an offsite storage unit, then bring it back before you move. (But hands off the draperies—you're stuck with them.) Do let your landlord know what you're up to. The landlord is prohibited by law from entering your apartment once you've moved in, but he or she could get very upset seeing the furnishings on the way out the door. Make sure you discuss what you're doing with the landlord first.

Some apartments come with all utilities included in the monthly rent payment. Others may require you to pay for electricity, water (hydro), and gas or heating oil. You are responsible for your own landline phone, cable TV, and internet service bills.

Pets are often not allowed in apartments, but there are exceptions. So if you're bringing Fido or Fluffy, be sure to ask if she's welcome. Most landlords also won't allow you to have long-term guests. If you are expecting someone from your home country to come for a long visit, be sure to check your lease first, because if there's a clause prohibiting guests, you could lose your lease due to noncompliance.

Some apartments also may have a nonsmoking policy. If you or a family member smokes, be sure to ask before you make any commitments. Finally, when it's time to move, it's customary to give at least a month's notice before you actually move out.

THE MORTGAGE PROCESS

A mortgage is a loan secured by property or real estate like a home. With a mortgage, the lender (a bank or other financial institution) gets a promise in writing from the borrower to make monthly payments until the mortgage amount is repaid, usually within fifteen, twenty-five, or thirty years. It's important to note that although people are said to be "homeowners" while they're making payments, technically, the bank is the actual owner of the home. If you, as the borrower, default (stop making payments) on the mortgage, the bank can swoop in, claim the home, and evict you and your family.

This is the last thing you want to happen as a homeowner. That's why it's important to have a stable income and a consultation with financial advisor to make sure you're in a position to make payments regularly and faithfully. In the discussion of mortgages that follows, it's assumed that you have the means to make mortgage payments and cover all the other expenses associated with home ownership.

Types of Mortgages

Looking for the right mortgage is the important first step in the home-buying process. Banks and mortgage brokers provide various options that will have huge impacts on your overall costs and the interest rate you'll pay for the life of your loan. The various types of mortgages include:

- *Government loans:* Both the United States and Canada have government loan programs for their citizens, which are insured by their respective Federal Housing Administrations (FHA). In addition, the Veterans Benefits Administration in both countries offers loans for military veterans. Such programs usually require minimal down payments (3.5 percent in the United States, 5 percent in Canada for FHA; zero and up for veterans' loans). These are great options for people with low incomes or less than perfect credit, as well as those who can't qualify for private mortgage insurance (discussed in Chapter 20). Talk to your mortgage banker about your options.
- *Fixed rate mortgages:* This type of mortgage has a guaranteed interest rate during the entire life of the home, which means your payment (including principal and interest) will not change during the loan term.

This can help you manage your payments better, because you always know exactly how much you must pay. Typically, banks offer terms of thirty, twenty-five, fifteen, ten, and five years.

Here's a table that shows how much the term of a loan impacts the amount of money you must pay over the life of a fixed-rate $200,000 loan at an interest rate of 5 percent:

Term	Monthly payment (principle and interest)	Total loan amount at end of loan term	Total interest amount
30 years	$1,073.64	$386,510.00	$185,511.00
25 years	$1,169.19	$350,754.00	$150,754.00
20 years	$1,319.91	$316,778.00	$116,778.00
15 years	$1,581.59	$284,685.00	$84,685.00
10 years	$2,121.31	$254,964.00	$54,964.00
5 years	$3,794.23	$226,455.00	$26,455.00

- *Adjustable Mortgage (ARM), U.S.; Variable Interest Rate Mortgage, Canada:* With this type of loan, your interest rate may fluctuate based on the movement of financial indices. The benefit of such loans is the lower initial interest rate, which in turn will help you buy a bigger or more expensive home. In addition, if interest rates decrease, the adjustable mortgage rate will decrease as well. However, the rate is just as likely to increase, which can make your monthly payment much higher. If you're not much for risk, you should avoid an ARM.
- *Combination rate mortgage (Canada):* This type of mortgage helps you manage your interest, yet it allows you to take advantage of short- and long-term rates while having a stable principal and interest rate.

Keeping a Lid on Mortgage Costs

While it's exciting to think about having your own home and the freedom that comes with it, don't ever take on a larger mortgage payment that you reasonably can afford. Your banker actually will have a lot to say about how much buying power you have. He or she will consider your debt-to-income ratio, which is a comparison between the amounts of money you earn versus your debts, including your prospective mortgage payment, as well as your car payment(s), credit card debt, and household expenses. Typically, the guideline is 33/38, where your housing costs total no more than 33 percent of your monthly gross (before tax) income, and your monthly consumer debt is no more than 38 percent. You may be turned down for the mortgage if this ratio is too high. There are exceptions. In the United States, for example, the qualifying ratio is 29/41 for an FHA loan; for a U.S. VA loan, the only ratio that counts is a 41 percent consumer debt load.

Even if you don't meet these requirements, there's still hope. If you can come up with a large down payment or your credit is A-1, these ratios may be flexible. Your banker will determine whether you qualify.

It's always a good idea to get prequalified for a mortgage before you start shopping. This indicates to the sellers that you're a serious buyer and prevents you from looking at homes that are out of your price range.

FINDING A NEW HOME

The easiest way to find a new place to live is to use a realtor, also known as a real estate agent. In the United States, a realtor will help you prequalify for a mortgage so you know exactly how much house you can afford. In Canada, a realtor can connect you a mortgage broker who will make this determination. He or she also will locate homes in your price range and target area that have the features you want. You then will visit each property personally to inspect it and determine which one meets your needs.

Realtors charge a commission for their expertise. Although it can vary, the average commission rate in the United States is 6 percent, although it can be higher or lower depending on where you live (the rate is based on the selling price in Canada). Although you don't have to worry about where the fee goes, the fact is that it's split between your realtor and the realtor who represents the seller. Because realtors are independent contractors, you may be able to negotiate the fee. It never hurts to ask.

Alternately, you can look for and negotiate a home sale on your own. However, even a native English speaker will find it difficult to decipher the terms and other legalese in a real estate sales contract. It's usually a better idea not to do this on your own and pay the commission instead.

To indicate your interest in a home, you'll submit an offer through your realtor. If you really want the home, you should offer at least 90 percent of the asking price, if not the full price. If you're a gambler and want to get a really good deal, you can offer less, but don't be surprised if your first, second—or fifth—offer is rejected. If you offer too little, you run the risk of offending the seller, which could scuttle the deal. Your realtor will be the go-between for all the negotiations and counteroffers.

If you've been prequalified for a mortgage, you can now approach the bank to get the paperwork started. Within three days of applying for the loan, your lender is required by law to provide you with a Good Faith Estimate (Good Faith Estimation in Canada), which gives the purchase price of the home, the interest rate, and an accounting of all the fees you'll be required to pay at closing. These fees, which are required by your bank and local government, can be truly mind-boggling and may include a loan origination fee (for processing your paperwork), an appraisal fee, a survey fee, title insurance, escrow deposit (for property taxes and private mortgage insurance), and plenty of others. These fees are not negotiable, although you may be able to get the seller to pay them for you if he or she is especially motivated to sell. As mentioned earlier, it never hurts to ask. Keep in mind, too, that these fees are just an estimate—they may be higher or lower at closing time, so don't write a check until you get to the closing.

THE MORTGAGE CLOSING PROCESS

Once the home sale has been negotiated, your banker will get to work finalizing the details of your mortgage. The process culminates in a loan closing at your bank. You can expect to sign a lot of documents, then turn over a check to cover the closing costs, which typically amount from 2 percent to 5 percent of the purchase price. Once the mortgage papers are signed, the fees are paid, the hands are shaken, and the keys are passed over, you're a home owner. Congratulations!

ATTA'S LESSONS

Even as a single young man, I knew how important it was to own a home. In fact, not having a home to call my own was one of my biggest concerns and nightmares when I immigrated to the United States. But even though I worked in a bank and dealt with financial matters related to home ownership all the time, I made the huge mistake of not investing soon enough in a home. Instead, I spent way too much money on rent and possessions for a good ten years instead of investing in real estate.

Eventually, I was able to buy my first home, but it happened at the time when home prices had risen significantly. With a little planning, I could have owned a comfortable home and had enough left over for other real estate investment opportunities a lot earlier.

Many immigrants fall victim to the same kind of situation. Home ownership and real estate investment should be prime priorities for everyone. Invest wisely, and then put yourself on an accelerated payoff plan so you can own your home in a maximum of ten or fifteen years. Being a homeowner with a mortgage for up to thirty years, during which time you pay tons of money to banks and lenders, is not really home ownership, but home "rentership." You want the property to be yours free and clear of any debt as soon as possible. Learn about what it takes to own your home and put a plan in place to make it happen.

Real Estate Inventory

Whether you're considering buying a new home or you wish to remain in the same place, it's a good idea to take stock of your real estate holdings so you can see at a glance exactly what you have. Answer the following questions as a starting point:

Question	Response
Do you rent or own your home?	
What is the current value of the home you own?	
When did you purchase your home?	
What was the purchase price?	
Did you invest the net gain from a previous home in your current residence?	
If so, how much did you invest?	
Do you have records of all improvements made to your home(s)?	
If so, where are those records kept? (Use the worksheet on page 215 to note major home improvements).	
What is your current mortgage balance?	
What is the interest rate?	
Do you have a home equity (second mortgage) on your home?	
What is the interest rate?	
How long do you plan to stay in your current home?	
When do you plan to pay off your mortgage?	
What are your plans for selling this home?	
Are you interested in buying a second home, or do you own one already?	
If yes, what is the value of your second home?	
Do you have or plan to invest in commercial?	
What price range are you considering?	
What type of property are you considering?	

Home Improvement Worksheet

Note all major home improvements you've made to your home on this worksheet. Use any remaining lines for planned home improvements.

Date	Home Improvement Description	Cost

Chapter 15: Time Management and Organization

Have you ever felt that, if you just had a few more hours in the day, you could get everything done that you set out to do? That's a pipedream, of course—everyone has the same twenty-four hours a day to get the things done that are necessary to keep one's home life, work life, and personal time on track and organized.

Everyone knows that time is a precious resource, which is why we have multiple clocks in our homes, watches on our wrists, and timers on our phones. We watch the clock to manage our time, keep us on schedule, and determine when enough is enough. But even when we manage our time carefully, it's not uncommon to feel overwhelmed or stressed out. That's because what we're really doing is dealing with time *mis*management issues that come from trying to stuff too many activities into a day that's already stretched to the limit.

But there are simple ways to manage your daily life successfully without feeling exhausted, tired, and frustrated, and it starts with good organization. American statesman Benjamin Franklin said, "Do you love life? Then do not squander time, for that's the stuff that life is made of." On that note, here are a few proven ideas and tips to help you improve your time-management skills and your ability to increase personal productivity.

EFFECTIVE TIME MANAGEMENT

You may have a great memory, but unless it's photographic (and few are), then you need to get into the habit of writing down and tracking your activities rather than relying solely on memory. If you're like most people, you have a lot to think about in a typical day, and keeping mental track of your schedule isn't the best use of your brain power. Get yourself an organizer or an app for your smartphone to help you stay organized and punctual.

Once you have that organizer in hand (or in the cloud), fill it with activities. Be sure to note every activity in your life, from appointments to deadlines. Then set priorities for yourself for the day, week, and month. Note memorable occasions (birthdays, anniversaries, and so on), business meetings, and recurring activities like your children's extracurricular events. That way, you won't miss an important deadline, family function, or any of the important things on your schedule.

Next, take a moment every morning to plan out the day's activities. It's easier to stick to a schedule when you have a general idea of what needs to be accomplished that day. To keep yourself on track, try allotting a specific amount of time to each major task, like one hour to return phone calls in the office or two hours to whip the house into shape before company comes. By segmenting your time this way, you can keep your activities under control and prevent them from taking longer than they should. Of course, you don't have to be totally regimented about this, but having a general idea will help you accomplish what you set out to do.

It's also a good idea to learn how to use the calendar tool on your smartphone, home computer, and other electronic devices to take and make notes on things you need to get done, then pay attention when you receive an alert.

Be a clock watcher, but in a good way. Be aware of the time as you work so you know whether you have to speed things up or if you can do them in a more leisurely fashion yet still meet your personal deadlines.

Get into the habit of carrying a small notebook or scratch pad with you, or use your smartphone's note-taking function to jot down important ideas, action items, and appointments that you don't want to forget. Be sure to transfer those notes to your master schedule so you don't miss a deadline or event.

Create a "to do" list on paper or electronically, then check off the completed items as you finish them. This will give you a sense of accomplishment and energize you for the next task.

Use a digital recording device to record your ideas on the go. (This is a better idea than trying to recall a great idea later from memory.) Such recorders are inexpensive and can hold a lot of data. Just remember, though, that you will have to listen to the recording later and either transcribe the information verbatim or jot down the most pertinent points. This takes time out of a busy day that you may not have. And by the way, you can use your smartphone as a digital recorder, but doing so will decrease battery life faster than normal.

Plus cell phones emit pulsing signals when they communicate with local cell towers, which can be picked up by the digital recorders others are using around you. In effect, your smartphone will ruin those recordings. So if you do use your cell phone as a recorder, place it as far away from any digital recorders in the room to keep the peace with your coworkers.

Having all these strategies in place and working for you is one thing; not overextending or over-committing yourself is another. Determine that's important and what's urgent. There's a difference between the two, and prioritizing tasks this way will help you stay in control and not feel as though you're overtaxed. In addition, avoid activities that don't match or help you achieve your goals. Everyone gets tasked with busy work (or nonessential activities) from time to time, but if you schedule too many of them, the important things on your list will go begging.

Learn to say no. Sometimes, you just can't take on one more thing, or you've been asked to do something that is so outside your realm of expertise that it would be difficult or impossible to do it well. You know your capabilities, so don't accept a job or task just so you don't disappoint someone. That person will be far more disappointed when you can't deliver what you've promised.

Finally, work some time for yourself into your schedule. You probably won't have to go so far as to actually schedule the time, but do leave some time here and there to take a break, read a book or newspaper, and otherwise take care of yourself. There's an expression in English: "All work and no play makes Jack a dull boy." Don't be a Jack—give yourself a break.

EFFECTIVE ORGANIZATION

It may sound strange, but being organized on both a personal and professional level can really help you have a successful life. Just think about it: how much time do you waste looking for the things you need? This is just one sign of unstructured living that can torpedo your efforts to be productive and successful.

But being organized is not just about labeling, color-coding, or filling file cabinets. It means creating a system that works well for you and allows you to access the items you need when you need them, both efficiently and without wasting time.

FILING SYSTEM

Every good organizational system starts with an efficient filing system. Start with a simple accordion file, which is available from any office supply store, or a file cabinet, and create a separate file for each of your household expenses. For instance, you'll need a file folder or slot for each utility bill, including the gas, electricity, water, phone, and cell phone bills. Next, create additional file folders for:

- Health care-related information, such as physician, dentist, prescription, and hospital bills and receipts;
- Credit card statements; make a separate file for each credit card company;
- Car-related information, such as repair bills and car titles;
- Insurance-related information, including home, life, and auto-insurance policies, bills, and receipts;
- Mortgage paperwork, including deeds, payoff documents, and property tax bills;
- Income tax paperwork, including W-2s, 1099 forms, T5s, receipts, past tax returns, and estimated tax payment proof (if you're self-employed).

Next, set up separate files for personal documents, including family birth certificates, naturalization papers or permanent residence cards (*aka* green cards), Social Security cards, passports, baptism records, marriage certificate, adoption papers, powers of attorney, and death certificates. Be sure to safeguard these items—if they fall into the wrong hands, you could have a serious problem with identify theft.

As part of the organization process, scan your personal information and print a couple of sets of backup copies, including one for your safe deposit box at the bank, and one for a locking, fireproof box that you keep in an inconspicuous place at home. This way, you're covered if anything happens to your master file.

Organizational experts say that 90 percent of everything we file away is never accessed again. For that reason, invest in a document shredder and purge and shred your files with personal information on a regular basis; say, every three years. That's the length of time the IRS generally requires taxpayers to keep tax return materials like 1040 forms and receipts, so the same guideline works for most other paperwork. (See "How long should

I keep records?" on irs.gov and cra-arc.gc.ca/menu-eng.html for exceptions to this rule.) Documents you should keep indefinitely include mortgage papers, naturalization paperwork, personal residence cards, estate-planning documents, life insurance policies, and pension documents. Some advisors also suggest keeping copies of tax returns indefinitely, even though the IRS advises differently. Scan them and file them electronically, then shred the originals to cut down on clutter.

Be sure to inventory the items in your safe deposit box and keep a copy of the list and a spare in a secure location (not just in the box itself). Also be sure to note the location of your safe deposit box key, or you'll be at the bank paying a fee to have the box drilled when you can't find it.

Finally, take advantage of online bill-paying tools from your bank or credit union, which make bill paying go faster because you won't have to spend time writing checks. You'll also save the cost of stamps and the time it takes to mail the bills. Also, sign up for free payment alerts that are emailed or texted to you by your bank and credit card companies. They remind you when payments are due, which in turn helps you avoid paying late fees. To protect the integrity of your personal data, password-protect your computer and smartphone to prevent unauthorized users from accessing the information.

ELECTRONIC ORGANIZATION

Home Computer System

If you don't already have a computer or you don't know much about computer equipment, it can be overwhelming trying to choose from among the many products on the market. For this reason, it's best to consult a computer-savvy family member or friend to help you buy and install the right system. Barring that, you should ask a lot of questions at the computer or office supply store to make sure you're getting the right equipment, then pay extra to have someone install the software you need. For a fee, some electronics stores like Best Buy will even send someone out to your home or office to set everything up. Alternately, a computer consultant (whom you can find on yellowpages. com or in the phone book) can get your system up and running. Don't try to cut corners on this—it's worth the cost to have everything set up right—and you'll save yourself a *lot* of aggravation.

Likewise, don't skimp on your computer system to save money. Computers are pretty inexpensive these days, and it's tempting to buy the cheapest one on the market. But there's a lot of difference between that bargain-basement computer and one that's even just slightly more. Case in point: you can buy a low-end Gateway computer for a under $300. It comes with a 500GB (GB stands for gigabyte) hard drive, which sounds pretty impressive until you discover that most computers now come with 1TB (TB stands for terabyte, which is 1,000GB) of memory, or a little over twice as much memory, for only about $100 more. You might be able to live with the 500GB just fine, but the lower priced computer also doesn't come with a wireless internet card, which will cost you—you guessed it—about $100. So if you just bought the next model up, you'd have the card installed already and you could get on the internet right away, instead of spending time trying to figure out how to make the computer work with the parts you bought separately.

If you're buying your first computer, you need to figure out whether a desktop model or a laptop will suit you better. If you will be doing most of your computing in your home office or in the spare bedroom, for instance, then a desktop (*aka* "tower") model is probably your best bet. And by the way, a desktop computer doesn't have to be right on the desk. It can go wherever the wires reach to connect it.

A laptop is a great choice if you think you'll be using the computer on the go, or if it will be moving from room to room in your home. This is an important consideration if you have several people who will be using the computer throughout the day. Laptops cost more than desktops—a lot more, if you decide to purchase a MacBook, for example—but the mobility is a definite advantage.

There's one more type of computer that bears mentioning: the iPad. You've probably seen the commercials about how great an iPad is and how much it can do. And they're right. But iPads and other tablet computers are used mainly for entertainment and accessing the internet. They do come with a virtual keyboard, meaning you tap on an onscreen keyboard, but they're difficult to use if you have a lot of typing to do. You can buy an external keyboard, but that gets hard to carry around. If you really want a tablet because they're cool, a Microsoft Surface might be a better choice because it has a snap-on keyboard that is actually made for word processing.

But let's say you want to use your computer to keep yourself organized rather than for entertainment (and yes, for the occasional computer game).

Some basic features you should look for include at least a 500GB hard drive (although that 1TB mentioned earlier might be a better choice), built-in wireless networking, and a multi-format DVD/CD-RW drive. Add in a wide-screen monitor, or purchase a tower/monitor package, and you're good to go.

Also make sure the computer has enough USB ports, which are the slots into which you will plug peripherals like printers and a mouse, as well as flash drives. It's helpful to have the ports right on the front of the computer for easy access. You also can buy a USB hub, which plugs into one of the USB ports and gives you up to ten additional ports.

You'll also need a printer, and it's generally best to go with a wireless printer so you don't have a lot of dangling wires connecting your printer to your tower. A wireless printer gives you the ability to send documents from your laptop to your printer, no matter where it is in the house. Wireless printers generally are more expensive than wired models, but the convenience makes it worth it. Other than that, there is very little difference in quality between average home printers these days; the price is more about the number of features it has, the number of pages you print every day (usually not a consideration for a home user), and how fast the pages print. Other features like duplex printing (which allows printing on both sides of the sheet) can also send the cost up.

One type of printer worth considering, especially if space is tight, is a multifunction printer/copier/scanner/fax machine. These are quite inexpensive, starting at less than $100, and are great, because they do a lot yet have a small footprint (that is, they take up less space on your desk). But there's one drawback: if one of the functions goes bad—say, the printer doesn't work well over time—you won't be able to receive printed faxes. But for the occasional user, a multifunction machine is a great and inexpensive choice.

A standalone scanner is another great tool for home organization. With a scanner, you can take pictures of (or scan) different-sized documents up to 8.5-by-11-inches, then save them for long-term storage by date or name. This significantly cuts down on paper documents in your home, which translates into less clutter.

One really useful type of scanner is the sheet-fed document scanner. This type of equipment has a hopper, or sheet feeder, on the top, so all you have to do is load the documents, and click or press a button, and they feed through automatically. A sheet-fed scanner allows you to scan documents of all sizes, including business cards, receipts, and letters, all at the same time (although it's usually best to scan them in same-size batches to avoid jamming). The documents are saved to a file on your computer, where they can be retrieved easily. Two such scanners to check out are the Fujitsu ScanSnap and the NeatDesk. They're a little on the pricey side—starting at around $260 for the lowest price ScanSnap—but they scan documents fast and really help to reduce paperwork and clutter, so the cost is worth it.

If you're on a budget, a flatbed scanner works just as well. It does take longer to scan documents and they have to be loaded manually, one at a time. But the result is the same: less paper to manage, less clutter in your office, and more satisfaction with your workspace.

Anti-virus software is right at the top of the list of must-haves for your computer. Most new computers come with a trial version that is good for about ninety days. But you absolutely must buy the full program once the trial expires so your computer is protected when you're online or if you transfer files from other computers via a flash drive or CD-ROM. A computer virus can decimate your system, and anti-virus software is the only way to protect it. Some cable systems like Comcast provide anti-virus protection free with their monthly service, so check into that before you purchase an anti-virus program.

Once you get your computer up and running, you'll be in business, so to speak. Just remember to save your work frequently as you're word processing or scanning so you don't lose anything important if the power suddenly goes out (it happens). Also, back up your computer files regularly—say, once a month or so—on external media like a flash drive or CD, or pay a company to do the job for you. (You simply email your files and they'll provide you with a backup.) This is important because if your computer crashes (stops working) or it's damaged in any way, you'll have separate copies of your files and you won't lose any valuable information.

Online/Internet Safeguards

No doubt one of the reasons you plan to buy a new computer or you use the one you have is so you can "surf," or explore, the internet. But there are important safeguards you should take to keep your personal and private information safe from prying eyes. They include these steps:

- *Avoid using obvious passwords, such as your birth date or your children's names, for any password-protected account.* Naturally, this includes your credit card and bank accounts, but also should include simple things like your library pass. The best passwords are words that don't exist in the dictionary (including words in your native language) or are a combination of letters (both upper and lower case), numbers, and symbols. For example, a password like happy_camper can be made stronger by typing it this way: haPpYCamPEr. Add in a number or two (haPpY67CamPEr), and you'll make it virtually hacker-proof.

- *Never click links you receive in unsolicited emails, even from people you know.* A person's email account could have been hacked, and those links could lead to a computer virus that can damage or destroy your computer and the data you've saved. This is especially important when it comes to emails from banks and other financial institutions. If you wish to visit a site for which you've received a link, go directly to the website instead.

- *Watch out for phishing attempts, which is when someone fraudulently poses as a real financial institution (typically) for the purpose of stealing money or identities from unsuspecting people.* Phishing is a big problem, so you'll probably get plenty of these emails. (One "famous" one is the Nigerian-prince-phishing email, in which a person claiming to be a prince wants to give you a huge amount of money if you send him a few thousand dollars in advance. Don't do it.)

- *Never, ever provide your password, personal information like your birth date, Social Security Number, or account numbers to someone who requests them by email.* Your bank or credit union will never ask for information this way. Criminals are so clever that when you click the link in such an email, you'll be taken to a website that looks just like your bank or credit union's website, and if you log in, you open the door for crooks to steal your information, then drain the cash from your accounts or open new credit cards or other accounts. If you're in doubt about whether an email is real, call the financial institution directly. Another way to check whether an email is a phishing attempt is to go to Snopes.com or rcmp-grc.gc.ca/scams-fraudes/phishing-eng.htm; they usually can give you the background on any suspicious email you receive.

PROFESSIONAL ORGANIZATION

No matter what type of work you do, staying organized is key to getting things done right and on time. So no matter whether you work in an office building or at a discount department store, below are some suggestions for keeping your work life on track.

Designate a place where you can routinely put the things you need for your job so you can grab them quickly on the way out the door. Maybe it's a portfolio for a client meeting, the apron you wear while serving at a restaurant, or your reading glasses. If you put these things in the same place every time you come home from work, you'll find them again easily the next time you leave. Important note: if leaving things around in the open is too unsightly, drop everything into a basket, then tuck the basket away in a closet or the mudroom where it will be easily accessible.

Plan your wardrobe in advance. This may sound crazy, especially to men, but if you know what you're going to wear the next day, you can be assured that you'll look your best. That's because you'll know before you put a shirt on that a button is missing, or that a stain didn't come out of the fabric when you washed it. You don't want any surprises when you get to work or school. Planning in advance also keeps you from wasting time in the morning searching for a particular garment, socks, shoes, or other apparel.

Leave early enough to get to work on time—or better still, leave a little earlier. That way, if traffic is slow, you'll still be on time, you'll have time to pick up your favorite cup of coffee at the drive-through window, or you'll have a few free moments to look at the newspaper before work.

Make a list of everything you have to accomplish that day, then prioritize the list according to the importance and deadline of each project. It's easiest to do this on a computer because you can move things around, but a simple list numbered by hand also works. As stated earlier, it also helps to look at the big picture and make a weekly and monthly list. In general, you should strive to do the most important task of the day first, when you're sharpest and most alert. Of course, if you're more of an afternoon person rather than a morning person, switch the times so you're at your best when you tackle the big stuff.

Set up a filing system in the office similar to the one you have at home. Being organized on the job will make it easier to accomplish tasks, because whatever information you need is right at hand.

Use the calendar function on your smartphone or a planner to note business appointments, and set a timer to remind you when it's time to go. Make sure you build in some free time in your schedule as well, because unexpected things can crop up, plus you need a break from time to time.

Try to complete one task before going on to the next. It's true that sometimes you have to multitask to take care of things that crop up, but whenever possible, finish what you start. You'll have a feeling of accomplishment as you check another project off your list.

Stay off social media sites like Facebook and Twitter during business hours, and don't send personal texts. Work is just that—work. Social media and texting distract you from that work and turn you into an underachiever—something the boss will notice.

Finally, take a break between projects. You deserve it.

ATTA'S LESSONS

Almost everyone procrastinates once in a while, but rarely does procrastination become a life-threatening situation, as it was for me. In the mid-1970s, I had an amazing opportunity to travel to Bangkok for an excellent hotel-management training program. But as I was happy with my job managing a soccer club in Afghanistan at the time, I procrastinated about making a decision and eventually wasted a great opportunity.

Big political changes took place in Afghanistan shortly after that, which altered the course of life for millions of people, including me. I faced numerous life-threatening challenges before I left the country and became a refugee, first in Germany, and ultimately, in the United States.

The experience taught me a huge lesson: don't think of time as money only. You can earn money and buy all the amenities in life, then replace them if they are taken from you. But when time is wasted, it is gone forever. I have since become a firm believer that human beings need no more than seven to eight hours of sleep a day, and that the rest of the time should be dedicated to constant, productive work, and service in which you reach out to others and make a difference in their lives. Too many people waste precious time every day, either by procrastinating or sitting idle. Our world would be a much healthier place if we all got off our couches and got engaged.

There are so many opportunities lying ahead of us. But procrastination steals those opportunities from us and must be avoided.

Chapter 16: Managing a Household

Once you're in your new home, you'll have many responsibilities—and expenses. This chapter covers general household activities, as well as what you'll need to do when the time comes to sell your home, sweet home.

WELCOME TO THE NEIGHBORHOOD

Although it won't be one of the first things you do when you enter your home for the first time as new homeowners, part of the fun and excitement of moving into a new neighborhood is getting to know the people and places around you. In particular, kids like to know who lives nearby because they'll be looking for instant friends in their new neighborhood. But unfortunately, many societies today are very insular; people tend to mingle only with those they know very well, like family members and friends. But you can break through the barrier if you make the effort to get to know your neighbors and become part of "the 'hood,'" as some say.

There are many ways to get to know your neighbors. For example, The Welcome Wagon, a group of volunteers who drop in on new neighbors to welcome them, will probably arrive at your door after you've moved in, but don't wait for them. Instead, go out and meet people yourself and make sure your family comes with you. Shake a few hands, make small talk, and exchange phone numbers or email addresses. Offer to look after their homes when they're away—maybe pick up the mail, look in on pets, or keep an eye on a vacant house to head off mischief—and they'll probably feel compelled to do the same for you.

Other ways to meet your neighbors include:

- Take a gift to your next-door neighbors. It can be something small—maybe a favorite homemade pastry or a small token from your homeland, like a scarf or an inexpensive piece of jewelry. The idea is to reach out to the people around you.

- Walk around the neighborhood. That way, you can introduce yourself to anyone who happens to be outside. When you meet someone you like, invite him/her/them over for a drink. They'll be as interested to know about you and your lifestyle as you'll be about theirs. Drinks can include coffee and soft drinks—you don't have to serve alcoholic beverages.
- Arrange a play date. Mothers *love* having a place to take their kids for a while, and offering your backyard for a play date with their kids could make you instant and fast friends forever.
- Organize a block party. This kind of party is open to anyone who wants to come. It's held outside, sometimes right in the street if there's not too much traffic (like on a cul-de-sac). Just crank up some music, set out some soft drinks and coffee, and invite people to bring their favorite dishes (a process known as a potluck). This is a good time to showcase a favorite dish or two from your own culture. Be sure to enlist the aid of a couple of neighbors to help, since you'll be the new person on the block and you'll want to meet as many people as possible.

GETTING ORGANIZED

When you first move into your new home, a little household chaos is to be expected. But once you've had time to get settled, you'll probably find that you won't have any patience for clutter. To keep your home and life organized and tidy, try these tips.

Set up a schedule to deal with routine household chores. For instance, always run the dishwasher at night, then empty it the next morning (this is a great chore to assign to your kids). Do the laundry on Saturday mornings, followed by the vacuuming. Get the kids' lunches, gear, and schedules sorted out on Sunday night so everyone can grab and go on Monday morning. Sit down with your kids at the same time each day to help with homework.

Activities like these add up to an efficient, well-run home. You don't have to be fanatical about keeping to a schedule, but adopting one will help your household stay on track and your environment stay clutter-free and clean, even if you have little ones. Even the youngest (say, two years old and up) can take some responsibility for keeping the house tidy. Your toddler may only be capable of dropping his toys into the toy box before bedtime, so assign that task to him and work with him to make it happen, even if he fusses.

Gently emphasizing the need for tidiness will set up good habits that will last a lifetime.

Establish a central place for posting family messages. This can be a simple write-on/wipe-off board or calendar on which everyone can mark his or her activities. This will keep the counters free of notes and loose papers and will keep everyone on time. Assign a different colored marker to each family member so you can see at a glance who needs to be where and who needs what done when it comes to school project due dates, appointments, and deadlines.

Place a box or other receptacle somewhere handy where all the incoming mail can be deposited. Then once a day, go through the box and weed out the bills from the junk mail. Immediately toss or shred the mail you don't want, and put the bills and other mail you need to keep in a folder so it can be handled properly.

File important papers right away. You'll recall from Chapter 3 that there are a number of different immigration and citizenship documents that should be filed away indefinitely. This goes for other important paperwork, too, like tax-deductible receipts, doctors' bills, your children's artwork—in short, anything you may want or need again later.

Don't let the paperwork get out of control, because there never will be enough time to deal with it if the pile gets too large. A good way to file bills is to use an accordion-style folder with twelve slots so you can file paperwork by the month.

Designate a central place where keys can be dropped when someone enters the house. A simple basket will do the trick and will eliminate those frustrating searches for keys when you're on the way to work.

Hang up coats, hoodies, and other outdoor gear the moment you come in the door. Install a coat rail (a board with a series of hooks screwed into it), or make some space in the closet nearest the main entry so everyone is encouraged to hang, store, and put their things away before they go any further.

Recordkeeping Guidelines
(chart on next page)

Use these lists to determine how long you should keep important papers. Rely on online recordkeeping whenever possible to limit the possibility of identity theft, as well as to cut down on the amount of paper in your home and home office.

Retention Time	Type of Record	Availability of Online Access (Y/N)
1-3 Months	Grocery Receipts	N
	Receipts for Cash Purchases	N
One Year	Gas Bill	Y
	Electric Bill	Y
	Water/Hydro Bill	Y
	Phone Bill (landline)	Y
	Cellular Phone Bill	Y
	Trash collection Bill	Y
	Cable TV Bill	Y
	Major Purchases	Y
	ATM Receipts	Y
	Bank Statements	Y
	Cancelled Checks	Y
	Social Security Statement	Y
	Brokerage Statement	Y
	Credit Card Bill	Y
7 Years	Tax Returns	N
	401(K) and Retirement Portfolio Statements	N
Forever (preferably stored in a safe deposit box)	Life Insurance Policies	None of these are likely to be available online
	Adoption Papers	
	Home Appraisal (for as long as property is owned)	
	Deeds	
	Citizenship Papers	
	Birth Certificate	
	Marriage Certificate	
	Divorce Papers	
	Military Records	
	Power of Attorney	
	Will(s)	
	Living Trusts	
	Custody Agreements	
	Jewelry Certificates (while owned)	
	Antique Item Records (while owned)	
	Warranty Papers (while owned)	

Health Care Records

Retention Time	Type of Record	Availability of Online Access (Y/N)
Until reaching age 25	Vaccinations (children)	N
8 years	Hospital records (tests, treatments, surgeries)	N
10 years	Vaccinations (adults)	N
25 years	Maternity records	N
	Mental disability	N

CARING FOR YOUR HOME

There's nothing like a neat, clean, sweet-smelling living environment to keep your spirits high and give you a sense of accomplishment. Here are some tips for making that happen.

Clean as you go. Don't let dishes pile up in the sink; wash them immediately or stack them in the dishwasher. Wipe the mirror and shower door in the bathroom after every shower you take so they look clean at all times. Put away laundry as soon as it comes out of the dryer or in from the laundromat. You'll be surprised how much you can get done in small increments each day.

Do a more intensive spring cleaning once a year. If you use the incremental approach just mentioned all year long, you'll find that this deep cleaning will go much faster.

See if your community has a recycling program, then use it faithfully. Recycling aluminum cans, bottles, and paper (newspapers, junk mail, and loose paper) is good for the environment and will give you a sense of pride that you're protecting Mother Earth. You can buy recycling bins from Target or from home improvement stores like Home Depot for your basement, mudroom, or garage, or you can simply place some appropriately labeled large cardboard boxes where everyone can find them.

In Canada, residents are required to use "green bins," which are special composting containers used to collect organic waste like food scraps, grass clippings and other yard waste, floor sweepings, fireplace ashes, and even pet waste like used kitty litter, to name just a few of the biodegradable items. The bins are emptied separately from the regular trash each week. For more information on what goes into a green bin, check with your city government.

CARING FOR THE OUTSIDE OF YOUR HOME

A well-cared for yard is a source of pride and reflects well on your family, too. Plants and trees, bushes and fences add a lot to the curb appeal and contribute to the value of your home, but only if they're well-tended. Establish a regular schedule for mowing, trimming, edging, and weeding every week, or pay someone to do it for you. Also, water your lawn, plants, and garden regularly to help them flourish. Just be aware that some communities have water restrictions that prevent you from watering except on certain days or at certain times. Check with your municipality to learn the rules.

If you need to add some curb appeal to a too-drab yard, head for the local nursery and check out the offerings. Try to add flowers and bushes that bloom at different times of the spring and summer so you always have a pop of color accenting your yard and home. A good time to buy plant material is in the fall, when nurseries clear out their inventories. If you live in the northern states or provinces, be sure to purchase only plant materials that are hardy enough to survive the winter. A nursery employee can give you some advice on what to buy.

Don't forget to tend to the hardscaping in your yard as well. Hardscaping refers to the inanimate materials in your yard: the brick pavers, flagstones, brick borders, retaining walls, and so on. One way to install new hardscaping on a budget is to prowl through home and demolition sites for discarded bricks, stones, and other materials you can have for free (but always ask first, of course.) Reclaimed brick and other recycled materials used for landscaping borders and pathways can give your yard a unique and distinctive look. Look for free landscaping plans on the internet or check with your local nursery.

CUTTING HOME UTILITY BILLS

Utility bills can creep up on you and become sky-high before you know it. It's important to keep an eye on your spending and use the following tips to lower your bills:

- Turn the lights off (and instruct your kids to do the same) whenever you leave a room.
- Maintain your air-conditioning system to keep it operating at peak

efficiency. Schedule air-conditioning-system maintenance, and keep filters clean to increase efficiency.

- Replace furnace filters at least once a year. Have an annual inspection to make sure the furnace is working properly and isn't emitting any noxious (dangerous) fumes.
- Close vents in rooms that aren't in regular use. There's no need to heat or cool them if no one uses them.
- Use ceiling fans to circulate warm interior air in the winter and cool air in the summer, rather than running your heating and cooling equipment 24/7. This is an especially effective technique at night.
- Caulk and seal around windows and sliding doors to keep drafts out and seal cool or warm air in.
- Replace your windows, when the time comes, with energy-efficient models.
- Insulate your attic and around doors and windows.
- Keep your shades drawn in the warmer months to keep out sizzling summer heat; and open them wide in the winter to allow sunlight in.
- Replace old appliances with newer, energy-efficient models when your budget allows.
- Install a programmable thermostat, and set it to dial down the temperature for those times when you and the family are away during the day and while you're sleeping at night. If you don't have a programmable thermostat, get into the habit of dialing up and down manually every day to save on energy costs.
- Unplug any electric device or appliance that you don't use regularly (such as recharging stations, curling irons, and other small appliances), since they continue to draw a little power even when they're turned off. Alternately, plug small appliances into power strips that can be turned off when the appliance is not in use. (Warning: don't try this with major appliances that draw a lot of power, like a vacuum cleaner or space heater. They can overheat and possibly start a fire. For the same reason, never leave a space heater running when you leave a room. A child or pet could tip it over and start a fire.)
- Avoid cellphone plans with unlimited talk and text, especially if you don't use your phone much, because these plans cost the most (often more than $100 a month). Instead, sign up for a plan that gives you a set number of minutes a month, as well as free evening and weekend

minutes. Cell phone companies don't advertise these plans much any-more, because they want you to sign up for the pricier unlimited plans, so always ask about them. You can also switch to a no-contract company like Consumer Cellular, which charges as little as $10 per line (plus taxes) each month, offers a free phone, and will port over (transfer) your old cellphone number at no cost. If you absolutely must have texting as part of your cellular package, go for a shared family plan, then establish limits for each person so usage is divided fairly.

Finally, always check the charges on each of your monthly bills carefully. While computers do the work when it comes to logging charges and sending statements, a human being still has to make the computer run, so there's always the possibility that a mistake has been made. Watch for cellular data charges, in particular. Hackers have figured out how to highjack phones and use hundreds—or thousands of data minutes, which can cost a small fortune.

REFINANCING YOUR MORTGAGE

Refinancing is the process of replacing an existing debt with a new debt that has more favorable terms. While you can refinance many things—your car loan or installment loans, for example—it happens most commonly with residential mortgages.

Refinancing your mortgage often makes very good financial sense. You can refinance to lower your interest rate, which, in turn, can mean a reduced monthly payment. You can also refinance to reduce the length of the mortgage term. For instance, you could refinance the twenty-three years remaining on your loan to fifteen years. This would increase your monthly payment, but would dramatically decrease the amount you will pay in interest over the life of the loan. You also can refinance to switch from a variable rate mortgage to a more stable fixed-rate mortgage. Finally, you can refinance and consolidate debt, which helps to reduce the monthly interest you pay on credit cards and other debt.

The prospect of saving all that money probably sounds great, but the reality is refinancing isn't for everyone. To begin with, there are fees associated with refinancing that you'll have to pay out-of-pocket or add to your new mort-gage amount, which sends your balance in the wrong direction. In addition, if the difference in the percentage rate you're currently paying and the proposed new rate is very small, there's definitely no point in refinancing.

Speaking of the interest rate, conventional wisdom used to hold that a refi (short for "refinance") made sense only if it would lower your interest rate by at least two percentage points. While that's a reasonable guideline, the real issue is how long you plan to stay in your home. If you're planning to move in a year or two, for example, you won't have enough time to break even on the costs of the refi, and in essence, you'd be throwing away your money. Here's why: let's say you have a thirty-year $200,000 mortgage with an 8 percent interest rate. Your monthly payment would be $1,468. If you refinanced at 6 percent, your new monthly payment would be $1,199, for a savings of $269 per month. That looks pretty good on paper. But assuming that your new closing costs amounted to $2,000, it will take just over eight months to break even ($269 x 8 months = $2,152). If your intention is to stay in your home a minimum of eight more months, then a refinance might be appropriate. If you planned to sell the house before then, you might not want to bother refinancing.

SELLING YOUR HOME

This chapter has centered on strategies you can use to keep your household well-organized. But there will come a time when you'll want to sell your home. Maybe you'll find that you've outgrown the space and need more room—or conversely, maybe your family has shrunk and the space is now too large. Maybe you've been transferred to another city. Or maybe you just want to be closer to relatives who have moved away.

Whatever the reason, you may find that the process is easier said than done. Since the 1990s, the economic mood in North America has swung from high flying and prosperous to depressed and conservative. That has affected home sales to the point that millions of homes in the United States, in particular, have lost a significant amount of value. According to CoreLogic, a leading provider of consumer, financial, and property information, about ten million mortgages, or nearly 20 percent of the U.S. total, are "underwater," meaning that homeowners owe their banks more than the home and property are worth. These figures have declined in the past few years, but continuing rounds of foreclosures have depressed housing prices further.

This is just a fiscal cycle, of course, and the economy, as well as the housing market, eventually will recover. But until they do, the key to selling a home is to make it look as appealing as possible to buyers so you'll get the sale—and get the selling price you want. So here's what to expect when you sell your home.

The Real Estate Sales Process

Once the decision has been made to sell your home, the first thing you should do is hire an experienced realtor. As you may remember from Chapter 14, a realtor is a sales professional who specializes in home sales. He or she will know the local market and will be able to analyze recent sales data to help you set a price that's neither too high nor too low. The realtor is also the person who will screen buyers, escort qualified buyers through your home and point out all its best features, and steer those prospects toward the right financing. For all this expertise, you will pay a percentage of the final sales price to the realtor—usually around 6 percent, although the figure can be higher or lower depending upon where you live. (In Canada, it can be as little as 1 percent.) That 6 percent probably sounds like a lot of money, and if you do the math, you'll see that it is. For example, a 6 percent commission on a house that sells for $250,000 is $15,000. But if you want to sell your house as fast as possible and for the most money possible, you should hire a realtor. And by the way, a realtor only gets paid if your house is sold, so in essence, you're getting the services of this experienced professional free until the purchase contract is signed by the buyer.

To find a realtor you can trust, start by asking your friends and neighbors for referrals. Once you have a few names, call each realtor or stop by in person and tell him or her a little about your house. Don't ask about setting a price yet; the realtor needs to inspect your home before that happens. Instead, use the time to size up the realtor. Consider whether he or she seems interested in helping you, not just in making a quick sale. Your realtor also should be friendly and respectful.

Once you find a realtor you're comfortable with, you can engage his or her services. This is done by signing a seller listing agreement, which typically covers a period of sixty days or so. If your house doesn't sell in that time, you can sign a new contract for another sixty days, or switch to another realtor. But be patient. A realtor will work hard for you, but it takes time to find the right buyer. Don't get upset with the realtor if he or she doesn't sell your house as quickly as you had hoped.

After you've agreed to work with a realtor, he or she will look at comparable properties in the area and the price they sold for to determine the price at which your home should be listed. It's quite likely you will disagree with your real estate agent. You'll probably think that the suggested listing price is far below what the home is worth. But don't forget that you've probably attached an emotional price to the house, which doesn't mean anything to anyone except you. It's always better to trust your realtor's judgment. Not to mention: a too-high selling price is one of the biggest obstacles to a sale. So really listen to your realtor and set your listing price as he or she recommends.

In addition to listing your house with the Multiple Listing Service (MLS), he or she probably will advertise your home online or may put a box in front of your home full of fliers describing the home's features and possibly giving its price. You can control how much or how little you want to say on the flier. Just talk to your realtor.

You'll usually have a window of opportunity to spruce up and fix up your house to make it look as appealing as possible. Your realtor will likely make some suggestions about what you should do. The first thing on the to-do list is usually to reduce clutter. Reducing clutter automatically makes your house look larger, which is something virtually all buyers will like.

Both your realtor and other realtors who represent buyers will bring them in to show your home. As a matter of courtesy, the realtor will call you to tell you there is a showing lined up. But you don't have to be home during a showing. Rather, with your permission, the realtor will install a small key safe known as a lockbox on your front door (usually the knob) so he or she, as well as other realtors, can enter the house even if you're not at home. (You can choose not to have the lockbox, but that means you or someone you know will have to be at the house to let the realtor inside.)

If you're at home during a showing, it's usually best to leave the premises while the prospective buyers are in the house. Otherwise, they may feel intimidated with you lurking in the hallway and may cut the showing short, which potentially could result in a lost sale. In addition, it can be hard to hear a prospective buyer's negative comments about the house you love ("The kitchen is too small…" "I hate that color…" "What were they thinking?") Instead, go out to the backyard, walk around the block, take your kids out for ice cream—anything that will keep you (and your pets) away from home until the realtor has left with the client(s). If you must stay in the home during the showing, don't answer questions from the buyer about why you're selling. The buyer may be trying to figure out ways to get you to bring the price down by exploiting your reasons. Instead, say something noncommittal like, "It's time to move," and let it be.

After one showing or many (more likely the latter), someone will be interested in your home and will make an offer through the realtor (either yours or his/hers). That offer will be put in writing, and your realtor will examine it and then present it to you. The initial offer is likely to be for less than the full asking price. But you are not required to accept it; rather, you can make a counteroffer somewhere between your original price and the price the buyer is offering. Your realtor will help you decide on the amount. Sometimes these offer/counteroffer negotiations can go back and forth several times until you both arrive at a price on which you can agree. Or sometimes, you won't come to an agreement, and the buyer will walk away. If that's the case, the realtor will go back to work to find you another buyer.

In some real estate markets, bidding wars break out over really desirable properties, causing them to sell for more than the asking price. (Just watch the HGTV show "Property Virgins" for a look at what can happen.)

Once you have agreed on a price, the deal is almost done. Almost. There's still the matter of a pest (termite) inspection, an appraisal by the buyer's financial institution, and other financial tasks. But once all the details are taken care of, you'll head for the closing—only this time, you'll be sitting on the other side of the table and handing the keys over to a happy buyer.

You'll receive a check from the buyer's mortgage company, minus the remaining balance on your own mortgage, the realtor's commission, and other fees. But the remaining funds are yours to use toward a new home (possibly as the down payment). And in fact, that's what you should do with the money in most cases. Gains on the proceeds of your home are considered capital gains (profits on the sale of an asset), which means you have to pay taxes on them. However, if you reinvest into another home, you may be able to exclude up to $250,000 of that gain from your income, according to the IRS. See IRS Publication 523, *Selling Your Home*, for more information, or talk to your accountant or tax consultant.

In Canada, if you are selling your principal residence, you may be eligible for the principal residence exemption, which eliminates all or part of the capital gains. See the Canada Revenue Agency website at cra-arc.gc.ca for more information or speak to your tax advisor.

So that's it. Your house is sold and you can start the process of being a buyer again. You also can start looking for a home before yours is sold. But because many home purchases are contingent (dependent) on the sale of one's house, it's sometimes not a good idea to look, because you may fall in love with a new house and not be in a position to make an offer on it. Worse yet, you could end up paying two mortgage payments at the same time: one for the home you already have that hasn't sold yet and a second for your new place. If negotiations drag on or you have trouble selling your home, you could end up spending a lot of money juggling the mortgages. So exercise caution when you're shopping for your new home, and avoid making an offer until it's fairly certain (like when there's a closing date) that your house really has been sold. Buyers have been known to pull out at the last minute or have their financing fall through, and you wouldn't want to be disappointed. This is another good reason to use a realtor. He or she can vet prospective buyers to make sure they have the means and a prequalification in hand when they're shopping.

Selling Tips

There are many things you can do to make your house look great before buyers ever walk through the front door. Most are easy and low-cost, and can make the difference between a house that sits on the market and one that's snapped up right away.

Make It Sparkle

You'd be surprised how many people put their homes up for sale without ever picking up a dust rag or washing a window. Take the time to clean your home thoroughly. Polish every surface and fixture, knock down the cobwebs in the highest corners, and get the carpeting cleaned—in short, do a top-to-bottom cleaning. If your schedule will keep you from doing a thorough job yourself, hire a cleaning service to come in and do the work for you. Then when everything is clean and polished, make sure everyone in the family helps keep it that way.

Get Rid of Clutter

Clutter is one of the banes of home sales. When you live with clutter, eventually you don't even see it any more—but a prospective buyer definitely will. So start throwing away things as soon as you know you want to move. Consign things with value to a donation pile, list them on Craigslist or eBay, or have a garage sale. You can even rent a storage unit and stash things there temporarily. Just do whatever it takes to spruce up, clean up, and declutter. With less clutter around, your home will also look larger, which is always a selling point for a buyer.

If you've been using a bedroom as a home office, *repurpose* the room and remake it as a bedroom while your house is on the market and buyers are coming through. People prize bedrooms more than they aspire to having a home office. By the same token, if clutter has overtaken your garage and you can't park a car (or two) inside anymore, move out the excess stuff so you can show off just how large and spacious it is. The same thing applies to a basement and finished attic space.

It's also a good idea to remove exceptionally large pieces of furniture, which may make rooms look smaller than they really are. You might not object to squeezing past the end of an heirloom armoire in your bedroom, but a buyer is going to see a room that's too small for his or her furniture.

You might also consider using the services of an interior redesign professional or a home stager to show your house to its best advantage. An interior designer will rearrange your furniture and accessories to show off the space to its best advantage. You'll be amazed at how warm stylish, chic, and comfortable rooms will look once an interior redesigner works his or her magic. For a lead to an interior redesigner, talk to your realtor.

Remove Personal Photos and Mementos

You might really enjoy seeing a wall full of smiling photos of your kids every time you come through the front door. But buyers aren't interested in your family—they want to visualize what your home would look like with their photos on the walls and their possessions in the rooms. So as hard as it may be, take down those photos and pack them away. Remove other personal possessions like trophies or the crayon drawings on the refrigerator door and store them away, too. You may not like removing your personal stamp from your home, but, let's face it: you've already decided to distance yourself from your current home by moving, so remake it now so it will be easier for a buyer to imagine living there, since that's the whole point of them coming through your home.

More Easy Home Selling Tips

- *Paint rooms in neutral colors:* You may prefer green walls or black moldings, but most people can't see past details they don't like, even if they intend to repaint after they move in. Neutralize your home for them so they'll focus on the living space, not the décor.
- *Play some music:* Just before a showing, turn on some soft music to make the environment seem cozier. Avoid ethnic music (not everyone will like it), and turn the TV off.
- *Offer a home buyer's warranty:* Even though real estate is sold as is, buyers will sometimes complain after the sale about things like a water heater that has failed or air conditioning that doesn't kick on. So offer a home warranty (available through your realtor, usually for a few hundred dollars) to head off those complaints. In addition, the warranty is a positive selling point, since it demonstrates that you are confident in the house's ability to meet the buyer's expectations.
- *Inform buyers about the monthly bills:* Buyers will want to know how much it costs to heat the home, what the water rates are, how much the summer and winter taxes are, and so on. Help them out by creating a spreadsheet showing the various costs for the past few months or leave copies of recent bills for them to look at. Just be sure to black out your account number and name on any bills you leave out for inspection.
- *Improve curb appeal:* Cut down or shape overgrown bushes, install a new mailbox or door hardware, repair screens, and carry out other changes that will make your house look fresh and new.
- *Don't be offended by the realtor's suggestions*—he or she is on your team and wants to sell your house as much as you do. So if the realtor makes suggestions you don't agree with, it's usually best to take a deep breath and go with them.

Chapter 17: Home Life

A loving and close-knit family can be one of the most precious things you'll ever call your own in this lifetime. Sure, from time to time, we all get angry, exasperated, and upset with our spouse, significant other, children, or other members of our extended family. But our family members are dear to us because they are our support system. They stand by us when we're having everything from a bad day to a bad life. They show us in a hundred ways how much they care about us and want what's best for us. And, of course, we do the same thing for them.

Family members who share the same social beliefs, and nurture and care for one another are said to have family values. These values are an unwritten set of rules and ideals that the family lives by, which provide the emotional and physical basis for being together. We develop family values based on our personal history, our precious traditions, our religious beliefs, and our cultural heritage, and we pass them down from generation to generation. A person who lives by a set of family values, which protect and cherish the family, tends to be an honorable and respectable person—both someone you aspire to be and someone you would like to know.

In North America, family values refer to the nuclear family; that is, a family consisting of two parents (usually married) and their children. But increasingly in North American society, nuclear families consist of adults in nontraditional relationships, including parents with blended families (which result when adults with children from previous relationships marry and combine their families), unmarried parents, and even same-sex couples who may or may not have entered into a civil union or marriage. This is not to say that people in North America don't cherish their extended family; but native U.S. and Canadian people tend to live in single-family homes, then come together for holiday celebrations and big, noisy family gatherings when time allows rather than living together.

But even if you live by a set of cherished family values, it's human nature to get so caught up in work life and other activities that you end up neglecting your family. However, focusing too much on the pursuit of more money, more material things, a better job, and a more rewarding career to the exclusion of all else is never a good thing because this can cause you to forget that your family should come first. Worse yet, when you get stuck on this treadmill of pursuing material things, you quickly find out that your life is without real balance, and your family support erodes. Ultimately, living this way can cause stress, discontent, and even declines in physical health.

This chapter covers ways to maintain a strong family network, even in the face of challenges. And because the world is not perfect, the chapter also touches on the darker side of family life, including shameful behavior (such as child abuse) that no one likes to talk about, even though it does exist, even in the best families.

PERSONAL RULES TO LIVE BY

Here's a list of common sense "rules" that can help you to maintain and build harmonious relationships:

- Love your family unconditionally, even when someone makes a mistake or does something you don't like or you disagree with. Acknowledge the mistake, forgive the transgressor, and let it go. You can offer suggestions for improvement, so the same mistake doesn't happen again, but don't feel badly if your advice isn't taken immediately. The person who made the mistake may be feeling embarrassed or resentful about the mistake or may try to ignore it all together.
- Show consistent respect toward all family members. This means valuing the thoughts, ideas, and goals of every person. You can provide helpful input when you disagree with something a family member does, but you must accept each person as an individual with individual thoughts and beliefs. This will strengthen familial bonds.
- Make the most of every special occasion and holiday. Have family gatherings and celebrations regularly, and strive to make them happy events. Put aside disagreements, at least for the day.
- Keep those family events simple. Get-togethers are not about impressing each other with lavish menus and gifts; rather, they're about spending quality time with each other.
- Make honesty the foundation of your family. This means not telling anything less than the truth (even to yourself), not having a hidden agenda, and not glossing over or distorting reality to make it more palatable or

appealing. Being truthful leads to trust and integrity, and builds character, which are traits every family member should aspire to. Toward that
end, teach your kids and show by example that they never have to lie or
say something to impress another member of the family or anyone else.

- Value the opinions of others, even if you don't agree with them. This is
crucial. When you respect others, you will be respected in turn.

- Be ready to give, give, and give again. The world does not revolve around
you. Promote the idea of "we" versus "I," because as the saying goes, there
is no "I" in "team." This promotes generosity and allows family members
to help each other without expecting something in return.

- Maintain strong lines of communication. Consistent communication
among family members results in commitment to each other. It's what
not only keeps the familial bond strong but promotes a sense of belong-
ing and commitment among family members.

- Be responsible. A responsible person is a trustworthy person; someone
the family can count on, no matter what happens. Taking responsibility for one's own actions, no matter how difficult that may be, shows
integrity and strength of character, and provides a good example for your
children.

- Build on old traditions and celebrate new ones. Don't forget: you're in a
new land, and the traditions and cultures here are different. Retain your
family traditions by all means, and celebrate them joyously. But be open
to new ones as well. You don't have to give up your cultural identity to
celebrate Christmas or Easter if you're not a Christian, or the Fourth of
July or Canada Day if you're not yet an American or Canadian citizen.
It's the spirit of the holiday that's important, not its name.

PROTECTING YOUR CHILDREN

Despite the fact that family members should be cherished, the sad fact is that
not everyone honors their children as they should. You need only read the
newspaper or watch the news to know that crimes against children—truly
unspeakable crimes—are on the rise. Call it desperation in a bad economy,
bad luck, plain ignorance, or true evil, the reality is that people hurt and
exploit children—both their own and others unrelated to them—every day,
which, of course, leaves an indelible mark on the children's psyches. And it's
not just about physical injury; rather, psychological harm can scar a child
forever, whether it's inflicted by a family member or a complete stranger.

Unfortunately, children around the world today are in more danger and are more vulnerable than ever. A lack of enforceable international laws and an increase in crimes such as kidnapping, rape, gang violence, and enslavement, as well as natural disaster, wars, and even parental abduction make children easy targets. Forcible recruitment of child soldiers by national armed forces and child labor are also rampant in various parts of the world.

Therefore, it must be our highest priority and responsibility as adults and parents to do our part to prevent harm to our children. We cannot be complacent about child abuse and other dangers, because to do so increases the risks our children face and escalates their vulnerability.

Here are some steps you can take to protect children of all ages.

HOME SAFETY

Teach your children how and when to dial 911. Stress that they are to call only in an emergency. Explain what an emergency is and give examples they can understand.

Teach your children that they should call you if they're in personal danger, but give them strict rules on what constitutes an appropriate situation to call about. For example, if someone seems to be following them at the mall, they should definitely call immediately. But if they're fighting over a toy, they don't need to call you—they need to work it out themselves without coming to blows.

Have your children call or text you to let you know they've arrived home safely. Alternately, you can install a home-security camera system so you can see exactly what they're up to, right from your smartphone and computer. Cable TV systems like Comcast offer such systems as part of their monthly services.

Tell your children to be observant when entering the house alone. Inform them that if they see any signs of forced entry (such as a broken window) or if they encounter an unlocked door, they should go immediately to the nearest neighbor's house to call 911.

Tell your children that they should never open the door to a stranger, including a delivery person. Install a peep hole or a closed circuit TV system so they can see who's at the door without opening it.

Instruct your children that if they are in the house during a break-in, they should hide anywhere other than in the master bedroom, since that's where thieves are mostly likely to go first in search of valuables. They should remain hidden until the intruder leaves.

Establish a network of trusted adults your children can call, besides you, in an emergency. Compile and post a list of their contact numbers, and place copies in various locations around the house. Also download the list to their cell phone.

Become acquainted with your neighbors and ask them to keep an eye out for your children. If something doesn't look right—maybe they witness your child getting into a strange car or a loud party starts while you're at work—ask them to call you or call the police, depending on the situation.

Choose caretakers such as babysitters carefully. Be sure to obtain proper references from family, friends, and neighbors, and call the references personally to verify that the babysitter is reliable and trustworthy. Insist that babysitters come to care for your kids, not to talk on the phone, fool around with a girlfriend or boyfriend, or otherwise act out.

Keep hazardous materials secured and out of reach. This includes caustic substances like household cleaners and bleach, and poisons like insect and rodent killers. Put safety latches on cabinets so little kids can't get in.

Keep an EpiPen Jr. on hand in case of a life-threatening allergic reaction (known as anaphylaxis) from bee stings or other causes. Seek immediate emergency treatment after you've administered the EpiPen.

Know your child's food allergies and keep those foods out of sight or out of the house completely. Avoid giving nuts, small candies, raw carrots, and other small, hard foods to kids under the age of four, as they can easily choke on them.

Media Safety

'Television (TV)'

There are many TV and cable programs with content that is unsuitable for children. Use your TV or cable system's V-chip to set parental controls on programs you deem are not wholesome or age-appropriate. Also, if you have a device in the house like an iPad or Kindle Fire, you can limit your children's time and access there, too. Use either the internal parental-control settings or download an app.

Secure your TV set so it can't tip over. The average flat-panel TV weighs fifty pounds, and the website TVSafety.org says that every three weeks a child is killed in the United States by an unsecured TV set. To prevent a tragedy, have your flat-panel TV professionally installed using the right wall mount for its size. Alternately, you can use a furniture mount system, or FMS, which attaches the TV to the back of a piece of sturdy furniture like an entertainment stand. It's not beautiful, but it works.

'PHONE'

Instruct your children never to tell a caller that you or another responsible adult is not at home. Instead, tell them to say that you can't come to the phone at that moment and offer to take a message.

Make sure your children understand that it's never acceptable to use a cell phone to bully others. Also, impress on them that they must not use their phone to take pictures, post anything, or send texts that are suggestive or otherwise unacceptable.

'INTERNET'

Limit the amount of time your children spend on the internet, and monitor their usage. Also, stress that they should never agree to meet anyone they "friend" on Facebook and elsewhere on the internet without adult supervision.

Make sure your kids understand that they must never share personal information, such as last names or phone numbers, or similar information about their parents or other family members, on Facebook and other websites.

Tell your kids never to click links or ads that promise free prizes, apps, or other things, even if the links or ads come from someone they know. Share with your kids details about the danger of clicking links in emails, which can contain viruses or other malware.

Observe minimum age requirements on sites like Facebook and Twitter. The restrictions exist for a reason.

STRANGER DANGER

It's a sad truth that children today are in danger more than ever from adults who want to do them harm. In fact, child kidnapping has become such a problem that the U.S. Department of Justice instituted the "Amber Alert System," a nationwide missing person's network, and as a result, kids are being rescued safely more often. If you'd like to be part of the Amber Alert network and receive alerts on your phone, sign up at amberalert.gov in the United States and wirelessamber.ca in Canada.

Protect your children from "stranger danger" by sharing the following information:

- Tell your children whose homes they are allowed to visit, and make sure you know who is at home when they're there. Insist that a responsible adult be present when your child is visiting.
- Never drop children alone at malls, movie theaters, video arcades, or parks. Accompany them yourself, or make sure they're in the company of another trusted adult.
- Have your children walk, bike, or take a bus with a friend or a group of friends rather than going alone.
- Never allow kids to go anywhere without parental permission or to go with unknown friends.
- Don't allow children to hitchhike under any circumstance. If they are suddenly without a ride home, tell them to call you or another trusted person. Even calling a taxi is preferable to allowing your child to take chances hitchhiking.
- Make sure your kids know they should never approach a car when the driver is unknown to them. Warn them that strangers may try to lure them into a car by asking for directions, offering candy, pretending to be looking for a lost dog, and so on.
- Tell your children to say "no" to strangers who offer them a ride; tell them to then run to a safe place.
- Walk the route to and from school with your children so you can make note of landmarks and point out safe places where they can run if they are being followed and need help.

OTHER PRECAUTIONS

- Teach children at any early age how to recite their full name and home phone, and tell them when it's okay to give that information out.

- Teach your children never to allow anyone to touch them inappropriately or make them uncomfortable. Give them specific examples.
- Check the FBI's sex offender registry (fbi.gov/scams-safety/registry), which has links to the sex offender lists in all fifty states. You can check to see whether there is a registered sex offender living in your neighborhood. Unfortunately, the Canadian National Sex Offender Registry, under the aegis of the Royal Canadian Mounted Police, is not accessible by the public. So if you have a concern about a neighbor in Canada, you'll have to call the local police for information.
- Never leave children unattended inside locked automobiles. The temperature in a closed car can quickly rise to 120 degrees on a summer day, causing heat stroke, seizures, and death. This goes for pets, too.

RULES AND DISCIPLINE

When we're busy, it's tempting to allow rules to be broken or discipline to slide. But your kids will come to no good if you don't give them rules and set restrictions. Begin by setting clear expectations and boundaries for your children. They won't know what's appropriate if you don't tell them.

It's also important to be consistent when you establish those rules. In particular, don't allow too many exceptions from the rules, because it's confusing to children and could encourage them to act out inappropriately. Kids need the structure afforded by a list of rules to live by.

It's also important to discipline your kids. Parents with a strong sense of discipline and habits raise disciplined kids. Discipline also teaches kids that they must take responsibility for their own actions, and there are consequences—usually unpleasant—if they don't.

Finally, be an involved parent. This means knowing your children's daily routines and what they're doing at any given time. The idea isn't to be a watchdog, but to be a loving caretaker.

PERSONAL SAFETY FOR EVERYONE

Kids aren't the only ones who need to be careful in today's world. Every member of your family—that means you, too—needs to take precautions against danger situations every day. This is not to say that danger is lurking around every corner—far from it. But many crimes are crimes of opportunity. For instance, a woman talking on an iPhone might have it snatched right out of her hand by someone riding by on a motorcycle (a crime known as "Apple picking"), or a man sitting in his car making notes before a business meeting might be held up at gunpoint or carjacked.

You can avoid scenarios like these by paying attention to your surroundings at all times. That means not focusing on texting or talking on the phone to the exclusion of everything else around you. Also, if someone or something looks suspicious, remove yourself from the situation immediately. If possible, head to the nearest police station. Someone bent on harming or robbing you isn't likely to follow you there.

Don't go alone into deserted areas, and park your car under a street light or near an open business, because a criminal is less likely to attack you if you're in a well-lit area. At the same time, while walking home or to your car, always observe your surroundings carefully, and have your keys in your hand so you can open the door without fumbling. Make it a practice to interlace your keys through your fingers so if someone approaches and tries to hurt you, you can strike first with that hand and inflict some damage. It's also a good idea to carry pepper spray, which is legal in all fifty states, to disable robbers and other criminals. Just remember: it can be used against you if you drop it or it misfires. Please note, though, that pepper spray is illegal in Canada, and using it, even to disable someone who is threatening you, carries a $500,000 fine and up to three years in jail upon conviction.

If a thief confronts you and demands your wallet or purse, always surrender it immediately. No handbag or wallet is worth your life. However, toss it away from you rather than handing it over. Thieves generally are more interested in your money than in you, so they're likely to go after it and leave you alone. This also reduces the chance that a nervous robber will shoot you accidentally—or deliberately, for not complying fast enough or for looking at him or her. Once you throw your wallet or purse, run as fast as possible in the opposite direction and seek help.

Parking garages and open lots can be particularly dangerous places. Before you get into your vehicle, look around to make sure no one is lurking nearby, then peer into the car to see if someone is hiding inside. Once in the vehicle, lock the doors immediately so no one can reach in and drag you out of your seat or jump into the passenger seat. Also, watch out if there's a van or SUV parked next to the driver's side. Predators often hide in these large vehicles, then grab you when you're not paying attention. If possible, enter your car from the passenger side and slide over to the driver's seat. If it's not possible, find someone like a security guard to accompany you to your vehicle and wait until you get safely inside.

Once inside your vehicle, never remain there for long before driving off. Likewise, don't stay in your car after arriving at your destination, or after you've returned to your car after leaving work and shopping. Women, in particular, tend to do this—they commonly make phone calls, put on makeup, or attend to kids in the backseat. Predators watch for opportunities like this and make their move.

If someone threatening does approach your vehicle, put it in gear and drive off as fast as possible, even if that person gets in the way. He or she is likely to jump out of the way rather than be hit. If someone does manage to get into your car and orders you to drive, try to jump out, if it's safe to do so. If not, gun the engine and drive your vehicle into a parked car, a post, or anything stationary nearby. Your air bag should save you from injury, and the crash should rattle your assailant and cause him to flee.

Elevators can also be a source of danger. Always look into an elevator before entering to make sure someone's not trying to hide there, and don't get in with someone who looks suspicious or makes you nervous. Take the stairs instead.

Above all, trust your intuition. If something feels wrong, don't ignore that feeling—find help or get someone to walk with you. And never hesitate to call 911 if you believe you're in danger. Calling and finding out later that there wasn't a threat is preferable to ignoring an actual threat and getting into big trouble.

DOMESTIC VIOLENCE

The existence of domestic violence is a sad commentary on the state of our society. Domestic violence is the leading cause of injury to women, with one woman being assaulted or beaten every nine seconds in the United States. The situation isn't much better in Canada, where on average, a women is killed every six days by her intimate partner, according to a Statistics Canada report.

The United Nations defines domestic violence as "Any act of gender-based violence that results in, or is likely to result in, physical, sexual or psychological harm or suffering to women, including threats of such acts, coercion or arbitrary deprivation of liberty, whether occurring in public or in private life." Although domestic violence is commonly considered a crime against women, it can happen to anyone of any age and socioeconomic background. In fact, children, parents, elderly people, and even men, account for 15 percent of victims, according to the Bureau of Justice statistics. (Child abuse is covered later in this chapter.)

Domestic violence is not merely a physical act, however. It also includes such behaviors as sexual, emotional, and financial abuse, as well as neglect, threats, name-calling, insults, isolation, and other harmful psychological acts. The bottom line is that the abuser is manipulating, terrorizing, humiliating, and otherwise hurting someone for his or her own purposes.

If you're the victim of domestic violence, you need to know that you are not alone and you do not have to live with it. You have a right to live peacefully and without the threat of harm. There are many places that will help you escape the cycle of violence and give you resources and options to make a safe new life for yourself and your children. All information is kept completely confidential to protect you from your abuser. To find help, call the National Domestic Violence Hotline at (800) 799-7233 or TTY (800) 787-3224 in the United States, or go to thehotline.org.

In Canada, go to the Department of Justice's Family Violence website at justice.gc.ca/eng/cj-jp/fv-vf/help-aide.html, where you'll find links to family violence resources. You also can find help and protection through hospitals, religious organizations, battered-women's shelters, crisis lines, and the police.

Alternately, you may need help to avoid becoming an abuser or to break an existing cycle of abuse and abusive behavior. Rehabilitation and counseling that focuses on managing your anger, identifying violence triggers, and uncovering other undesirable behaviors are the first step. Here are other strategies that can help:

- Stepping back and considering how the abused person feels (known as empathy) when on the receiving end of physical, verbal, or other abusive behavior.
- Observing respectful couples and trying to determine what keeps them happy and non-argumentative.
- Postponing discussions when you are angry, which can defuse a potentially abusive situation.

- Talking to a religious leader or other trusted person about your feelings as a way to figure out why you exhibit abusive behavior.

But above all: an abuser needs help to break the cycle of abuse. When you are ready to take responsibility for your actions and change how you relate to people, contact your local domestic violence organization, which can direct you to perpetrator resources and services that can help.

Child Abuse

Any action that harms or directly puts a child at risk of harm is considered child abuse. The terrible cases we read in the paper about physical or sexual abuse are only the tip of the iceberg. Leaving a child in a hot car even for a short period of time, refusing to seek medical treatment for his or her injuries, not providing adequate and sanitary food and shelter, and otherwise neglecting and perpetuating acts of maltreatment are all forms of child abuse.

Some of the signs of child abuse include bruises, frequent injuries or broken limbs, depression, sudden changes in behavior, acting out, watchfulness (to prevent further abuse), a reluctance to be around a particular person, and even suicide. If you suspect a child is being abused or you need help for your own children, call the police or a local child welfare agency. You can do this anonymously. You may also call the Childhelp National Child Abuse hotline 24/7 at (800) 4-A-CHILD (800-422-4453). The organization serves both the United States and Canada.

Additional Help

So what do you do if you need help with a situation that falls short of domestic violence or child abuse? Your local department of social services or child welfare can help. (Please note that there is not one name for these organizations—it varies by state, province, and function.) One of the most important services these departments offer is investigations into reports of mistreatment or abuse. Child, elder, and disabled person protection services may include home inspections and removal of individuals from less-than-optimal living conditions.

If you believe a situation warrants attention, you can report it anonymously. Try Googling "child welfare" or "protective services" to find an agency that can help.

ATTA'S LESSONS

Even immigrants who have strong family values and strict cultural up-bringings can find themselves tempted by dangerous social challenges like drugs, alcohol, and promiscuous behavior when they immigrate to North America. This is especially a problem with young people. They may not know how to deal with the sudden freedom they have, or they may not be under the watchful eyes of parents and other family members any more. Sometimes, they're just weak when faced with temptation. And sometimes, their parents become so busy and distracted that they don't offer the proper guidance and support that young people need.

I recommend quickly creating and maintaining a disciplined, healthy environment for all family members so they can continue to have a productive life. Such a life should be filled with proper and ongoing support and association with family and close friends. It should focus on education, sports, and other acceptable social activities. Above all, parents must spend significant time with their children while managing their work schedule. Family and children must always come first.

CHAPTER 18: EMERGENCY PREPAREDNESS

Ever since the tragic events of September 11, 2001, life in America has changed dramatically. Some of Americans' breezy, carefree outlook on life has dimmed, and overall, society is much more vigilant and cautious, because people don't want to be caught unaware again as they were on that fateful September day.

Canada was also impacted by 9/11. A total of twenty-four Canadian citizens died in the World Trade Center disaster, and the country's military has assisted the other allied forces in the Middle East who have fought to bring those responsible for such terrible crimes to justice.

The U.S. government has always recommended that Americans be prepared for unexpected events, but no more so than since 9/11. And that doesn't just mean events like terrorist attacks—it also means being prepared for natural disasters like tornados, earthquakes, and floods. Every family should have its own disaster and emergency plan, and the time to create this plan is long before it's ever needed. This is good advice for American and Canadian residents alike.

Here are some things you should do to prepare for the unexpected.

CREATE A FAMILY EMERGENCY PLAN

Let's face it: emergencies are a fact of life. Besides natural disasters, emergencies can include an accident or job loss, and the time to figure out how to react in an emergency is *not* when it occurs and emotions are running high. Rather, it's important to sit down with your family and draw up a plan for dealing with emergency situations before you ever need it. The U.S. Department of Homeland Security (at Ready.gov) and the Government of Canada's "Get Prepared" site (at getprepared.gc.ca/index-eng.aspx) have lots of good information to offer.

The first thing to figure out is how you will touch base with each of your family members in an emergency. If your family is small, you can designate one or two people who will be in charge of checking on every family member.

But if you have a large extended family, a phone chain is a simple and efficient way to make contact with all your loved ones.

To create a phone chain, decide who will be the first responder. This should be someone who can remain calm in the face of an emergency. Then write a list *on paper* of all the people who should be contacted. List every possible means of contact, from phoning (via landline and cell) to texting. Divide the list of names into small groups or circles of perhaps three or four people each. Then give either a paper or an electronic copy of this master list to every person listed on it.

In an emergency, the first responder activates the phone chain by calling one person in each circle. In a perfect world, the first responder will reach someone in each group immediately, and it then becomes that person's responsibility to call someone else in the group. That person then calls another person in the circle, and so on, until everyone has been contacted.

Since the world is *not* perfect, it's likely that you won't be able to reach the first person in each circle. But to make the phone chain work, you must speak directly to a live human being. Don't just leave a voice mail or message on an answering machine, because that breaks the chain. Keep trying until you reach someone by phone and pass along your message orally.

Once you've established your phone chain and explained to everyone what to do when the chain is activated, hold an unannounced test to make sure it works and you are able to contact everyone. Pick a time when most people are available, such as on a weekend, so you can involve as many family members as possible. If you find there's a glitch, re-examine the process and iron out the problem.

Text and Internet Chains

Texting is another way to contact loved ones in an emergency. But as with a phone chain, you must make sure the person you've texted receives your message and responds. If you can't reach someone in a reasonable amount of time, go to the next person on the list.

Likewise, you can use Facebook or email to reach family members. But remember in an emergency that people are less likely to be online. Phones are almost always the best way to contact people in an emergency, assuming the landlines and/or cell phones are still operational during the crisis.

Power outages are one of the biggest obstacles you'll face when trying to connect with family members during a crisis. During the massive 2003 Northeast Blackout, for example, fifty million people were left in the dark. This is why you need an alternate plan for checking on the welfare of family members.

Establish a Gathering Place

During the Northeast Blackout, phone landlines worked for a while, but cell towers stopped transmitting signals right away, rendering cell phones useless. To prepare for the possibility that power will be disrupted, establish a central meeting place where family members can congregate once it's safe to move around.

Select a central place that most, if not all, your family members should be able to reach easily. Good places include a public park or a school or a church parking lot within walking distance of your home or office. During the winter, when it might be too cold to meet outdoors, or during a chemical or biological attack, you'll need an indoor or sheltered meeting place. Some places to consider include shopping malls, schools, and local government offices.

If your family is large or spread across the city, the state, and the province, establish more than one central meeting place. If there's no power, the groups won't be able to make contact with each other right away, but at least you'll know that everyone is accounted for.

Again, it's a good idea to practice your plan to make sure it works. You also should plan escape routes out of your own home, especially if you live in a multistory building.

Formalize Your Plan

Once you've decided on a plan, formalize it by writing everything down, and giving or sending a copy to each person in your family. And don't forget: an electronic copy of your plan is not going to be helpful if the power goes out. Keep a paper copy of the plan in a secure place, and keep another copy with your emergency supply kit.

If your plan requires you to travel very far or through a busy city, plan your route carefully using a program like Mapquest.com, then practice the route a couple of times, noting as many landmarks as possible along the way. It might seem silly to practice driving across town now, but if you ever need to use the route, you'll be glad you did, especially if a natural disaster wipes out many of the familiar landmarks.

Assemble an Emergency Kit

It's critical to have sufficient supplies on hand in case you have to evacuate your home during a disaster or if you are asked to "shelter in place" (that is, remain in your home until the danger passes). You should set aside certain supplies in an easily accessible place.

You can purchase ready-made emergency-preparedness kits online or at a sporting goods store. But you can easily make your own. According to Ready. gov, the U.S. government's preparedness website, a basic family emergency kit should include the following supplies:

Nutrition

- Water (1 gallon per person, per day, for at least three days, for drinking and sanitation)
- Food (at least a three-day supply of nonperishable food)
- Can opener for canned goods

Personal Care/Comfort

- Prescription medications (ask your doctor or pharmacist about storing prescription medications such as heart and high blood pressure medication, insulin, inhalers, and other prescription drugs)
- Pain relievers (such as aspirin or ibuprofen)
- Medical supplies/equipment (glucose and blood pressure monitoring equipment, and so on)
- Eyeglasses and/or contact lenses and supplies
- Denture needs
- Feminine supplies and personal hygiene items
- Sleeping bag or warm blanket for each person (consider additional bedding if you live in a cold-weather climate)
- Complete change of clothing (including a long-sleeved shirt, long pants, and sturdy shoes)
- Coat, scarf, hat, gloves, and boots for use in cold-weather climates

Baby/Child Care

- Formula
- Diapers
- Diaper rash ointment
- Bottles
- Powdered milk
- Medications
- Moist wipes

Safety

- Battery-powered radio with extra batteries or a hand-crank radio
- NOAA weather radio with tone alert and extra batteries
- Flashlight and extra batteries
- First aid kit (see page 264 for a list of items to include)
- Whistle (to signal for help)
- Fire extinguisher (check the expiration date)
- Protection/Sanitation/Direction
- Dust mask (to help filter contaminated air)
- Plastic sheeting and duct tape (to seal windows and doors when sheltering in place)
- Moist wipes, garbage bags, and plastic ties for personal sanitation
- Wrench or pliers to turn off utilities
- Household chlorine bleach and medicine droppers for use as a disinfectant (dilute one part bleach with nine parts water) and to treat water (16 drops of regular—not scented or color-safe—liquid bleach per gallon of water)
- Local maps with evacuation routes marked
- An emergency reference manual (such as a first aid book, or information fromready.gov and getprepared.gc.ca/index-eng.aspx)

Identification/Documentation

- Important family documents (copies of insurance policies and personal identification and bank account records placed in a waterproof, portable container). See page 265 for a list of items to compile.
- Cash or traveler's checks and change

MISCELLANEOUS

- Mess kits, paper cups, plates and plastic utensils, paper towels
- Matches in a waterproof container
- Paper and pencils/pens
- Books, games, puzzles, or other activities for children

PETS

Finally, don't forget your pets. Cats, dogs, and other pets cannot survive on their own and are likely to get lost or will die if you leave them behind. So if you have to evacuate your home, take your pets with you. Determine in advance where you can take them to be cared for, such as a kennel or a pet-friendly hotel or motel, since emergency shelters generally will not accept pets because of public health reasons.

Items to include in your pet survival kit include:

- Enough pet food, bottled water, and medications for at least three days, plus a manual can opener and food/water dishes
- Pet bed or blanket
- Veterinary records, cat litter/pan, first aid kit
- Phone number of your veterinarian and the local animal shelter
- A current photo of your pet for identification purposes
- A secure pet carrier, leash, or harness so your pet can't escape if it panics
- Finally, make sure your pet has up-to-date identification tags on its collar. You might also consider clipping a waterproof pet-identification container on its collar. Put your cell number and the address and phone number of the evacuation site you plan to use into the container.

FIRST AID SUPPLIES

Every household should already have a basic first aid kit, which you can buy at most drug stores, department stores like Target, and camping/outdoor stores. But you'll need a more extensive kit to keep with your preparedness items. Among the items your emergency kit should contain are the following:

- Two pairs of sterile gloves (non-latex, if you're allergic)
- Sterile dressings and adhesive bandages in various sizes
- Cleansing agent/soap and antibacterial wipes
- Antibiotic ointment
- Burn ointment
- Petroleum jelly or other lubricant
- Eye wash solution (to flush the eyes or for use as a general decontaminant)
- Nonprescription drugs like aspirin or nonaspirin pain reliever, antidiarrheal medication, antacid, laxative
- Thermometer
- Scissors
- Tweezers

Pack your first aid items in a portable container; preferably one that is waterproof. Make sure everyone in your household knows where it is stored. Ideally, it should be placed with the rest of your emergency supplies. You also should assign someone to be in charge of bringing the kit in case of emergency.

Important Personal Information List

During an emergency, you may be flustered and scared, so you don't want to rely on your memory when it comes to important contact information. So make a list of this important data now, before you need it, and give a copy to every family member.

This is the information you should note and store in a portable, waterproof case with the rest of your emergency gear:

- Local and out-of-town family members' contact information (home and business phone numbers and addresses, email addresses).
- Personal family information, including the full legal name of each family member, and his or her birth date and Social Security number.
- Addresses of local schools (as evacuation locations).
- Homeowners/rental insurance company name and phone number.
- Create a record of personal information specific to each person in the family. The list should include medical insurance names and policy numbers; medications and dosage information; physician names and phone

numbers; addresses of the closest medical facilities; and pharmacy name, address, and phone number.

- Finally, make a list of each person's past surgeries, dates, and locations; and note any known allergies.
- In addition to creating a master list of all this information, also prepare an individual card with information specific to each family member, and put that person in charge of keeping that list in a safe, accessible location.

Hopefully, you will never need to use any of the items discussed in this chapter in an emergency situation, but you never know. Since a natural disaster or other catastrophe can happen at any time, prepare for it now—just in case.

ATTA'S LESSONS

My family's first test of our disaster preparedness plan—or lack thereof—came during the 1989 San Francisco earthquake. I was working at the San Bruno branch of American Savings when minutes before closing time, a 7.8 magnitude earthquake shook the entire area, and all communication went down. Thanks to my car radio, I was able to learn about the earthquake and the fact that part of the (San Francisco-Oakland) Bay Bridge had collapsed, causing massive traffic jams and confusion all around the area.

Without any access to phones and a lack of an emergency plan, I spent the next twelve hours waiting in and crawling through a nightmarish traffic jam. Naturally, I was without news from my family. My son had been born only a month prior to the earthquake, which made my anxiety and anger about my lack of preplanning even worse. Once I got home, we started a search for my two sisters, who were working in the city at the time.

The comic strip character Pogo summed up my feelings at the time exactly when he said, "The certainty of misery is better than the misery of uncertainty." I vowed I would never be that unprepared ever again, which is also good advice for every immigrant.

Chapter 19: International and Domestic Travel

Now that you're a resident of North America, your homeland may seem very far away, both in terms of distance and ideology. But once your life here settles into an ordinary pattern, you'll probably find yourself longing for home. So when it's time to return to your homeland for a visit, you need to be fully aware of the various requirements the United States and Canadian governments have concerning foreign travel—and the time to learn about them is now, before you ever book your ticket.

North American International Travel Sources

The keeper of all the foreign travel knowledge in the United States is the U.S. Department of State, which you can visit at state.gov/travel. Its website is a treasure trove of information for travelers, covering everything from travel documents to weather advisories. Two of the most useful sections of the website are the foreign travel requirements and other country-specific information. You'll especially want to pay attention to the travel warnings. Not only does the Department of State issue alerts about dangerous places in the world; in some cases, the U.S. government prohibits or restricts American citizens and residents from visiting there. But most of the time, travel alerts come and go, especially during times of civil unrest. Even so, it's always possible that your homeland is on the list, so be sure to check well in advance of your travel date.

The Canadian government equivalent of this site is travel.gc.ca. It, too, offers tips on destinations and other information Canadians planning to travel abroad need to know.

Tips for Travel Abroad

Traveling outside the country can be confusing if you don't have the right information and know the requirements before you leave. Here are some important steps to take to enjoy a hassle-free international trip:

- Check to see if any particular immunizations are required.
- Register with the State Department's "Smart Traveler Enrollment Program," or STEP, to receive travel updates and other information. By registering with STEP, State Department personnel will be able to assist you better in case of an emergency, such as if your passport is lost or stolen while you're abroad. To enroll, visit travel.state.gov/travel, then search for "STEP." If you're traveling from Canada, register with the Government of Canada at travel.gc.ca/travelling/registration.
- Carry the following information with you for the American or Canadian consulate in each country you will visit:
  - Name and address of consulate
  - Phone and fax number
  - Email address
  - A list of required documentation
  - Name of a contact person
- Tuck a copy of your passport information page and travel itinerary in a safe place—a locking suitcase, your wallet, and so on. If your passport is lost or stolen, having a copy will expedite the processing of a replacement. Also leave a copy with family and friends as a back-up plan.
- Use the safe in your hotel or other accommodations to store your passport and travel documents. Never leave these important documents unattended in your room.
- Make sure your passport will be valid for at least six months after your anticipated date of return. That way, if you're detained for any reason, such as due to weather conditions or paperwork issues, you should have enough time left to get back home.
- Make sure your health insurance will cover you and your family while you're abroad, or apply for a new policy before you leave. Generally speaking, North American health insurance policies are not accepted on other continents.

- Take an extra pair of eyeglasses with you, and ask your physician for enough medication to last for your entire trip. Also take a letter from your physician listing all medications you take, their dosage, and the dosing frequency. Also, check with the consulates of the countries you plan to visit to make sure the medications you're carrying are not considered narcotics there (and thus would be illegal). You can find a list of foreign embassies and consulates in the United States at state.gov/s/cpr/rls/dpl/32122.htm. In Canada, go to w03.international.gc.ca/Protocol-Protocole/Consular-Consulats.aspx.
- Remember that you are subject to the laws of the countries you are visiting. Review and familiarize yourself with the laws and customs of each country you plan to visit, including your homeland. Things might have changed since you lived there.

Domestic Travel

With few exceptions, you can travel just about anywhere in the United States and Canada you wish to go (some exceptions include nuclear reactors, military installations, and Area 51, the secret military airfield that supposedly harbors alien technology like extraterrestrial spaceships). And there's plenty to see. America offers some fun and quirky sites, such as the world's largest ball of string (in Weston, Missouri), and a gravity-defying attraction where water runs uphill (Mystery Hill, Onsted, Michigan). If you need help figuring out which wacky and weird thing to see, check out the *Time* magazine article, "The Top 50 American Roadside Attractions," at content.time.com/time/specials/packages/article/0,28804,2006404_2006095,00.html.

AAA also publishes travel guides that contain information about these crazy sites, as well as more traditional tourist spots. It also offers travel discounts, travel insurance, international driving permits, roadside service, and much more. See aaa.com.

For Canadian roadside attractions, visit roadsideattractions.ca/province.htm for details on inexplicable attractions like the large chair and table in La Bostonnais, Quebec, and the Tin Man statue in the industrial town of Hearst, Ontario. AAA's counterpart north of the border is the Canadian Automobile Association (CAA) at caa.ca.

THE SIGHTS

For a couple of countries that are only a few hundred years old put together, the United States and Canada offer plenty to see. The Canadian population is much smaller than the U.S. population, relative to land mass, so the attractions are fairly spread out. In Canada, you're more likely to hit the urban centers like Edmonton, Alberta, with the world's largest shopping and entertainment complex; Vancouver, British Columbia; Toronto, Ontario; or Quebec City, Quebec. But if you're adventurous, there's nothing like the beautiful land and seascapes in places like Newfoundland and Labrador, the easternmost point in North America; or the rough-and-tumble Yukon Territories, known as the North American "Land of the Midnight Sun," where you can see the mysterious undulating Northern Lights (*aka* the aurora borealis).

America also has vast stretches of wide-open land in states like Wyoming and Montana, where there are more tumbleweeds than people. But the United States, with its population of 317 million-plus people in 3.7 million square miles (versus just 35 million people in Canada's 3.9 million square miles), has far more urban centers than Canada does. There are cosmopolitan centers like New York City and South Beach in Miami versus states like Nebraska, with nothing but corn for as far as the eye can see.

But no matter what you like, North America offers activities for everyone, from skiing, hiking, and golfing for sports enthusiasts to state, provincial, and national monuments, as well as battlefields and forts for history buffs. There also are many Native American sites that can be explored, as well as mining and ghost towns that offer glimpses of a long-ago past. Your kids will like the amusement parks such as Disney World (Florida), Cedar Point (Ohio), and Six Flags (Texas and other states), as well as water parks like SeaWorld (Orlando, among other places) and Wild Water Kingdom (Ontario). And, of course, there are plenty of urban activities, such as fine dining, shopping, and museums. The possibilities are endless.

Both AAA and CAA can assist with helping you find a great place to visit. The internet is also a great resource. Try Discover America, the official travel site for the United States at discoveramerica.com, or a commercial travel site like Expedia.com (Expedia.ca in Canada) or HotWire.com to start your search. Also, don't forget to check out the attractions in your own city. Many people look far afield for activities when there are wonderful places to visit right where they live.

Getting There

Chapter 9 discusses the many modes of transportation you can use to see the USA and Canada. But if you wish to see any of the wondrous oddities mentioned earlier in this chapter, the best way to get up-close-and-personal is by car or other motorized vehicle, because you can go at your own pace and spend as much time as you like. Busses, trains, and tours are other viable ways to get around, but you'll be on a stricter schedule.

Accommodations

Based on your budget, you have your pick of numerous types of accommodation across North America. Hotels are the most expensive, of course, just like throughout the rest of the world, and offer the best accommodations. Less expensive accommodation can be found in a motel (*aka* motor lodge), which is a type of accommodation designed for motorists. You'll know motels when you see them, because all their doors usually face a parking lot. Motels are often found along busy highways and airports.

If you want something cozier, check to see if your destination offers bed and breakfasts (B&B), which are establishments located in private homes. These homes have a limited number of bedrooms for guests, as well as a common seating area where breakfast is served. BedandBreakfast.com lists accommodations across the United States; BBCanada.com covers the north.

If you enjoy the great outdoors, a campground might be the right vacation spot for you. Campgrounds tend to be located in wooded and other natural areas, and you can pitch a tent, sleep in a motor vehicle like a camper or popup tent camper, or snuggle up in a sleeping bag right on the ground under the stars. Campgrounds generally offer only very basic services; there may be electrical hookups or bathroom facilities, but the most rustic sites may offer no modern conveniences at all. Naturally, it's very inexpensive to stay at a campground, and it's an experience your kids may especially like.

Alternately, you can rent (or buy) an RV (recreational vehicle) and enjoy more of the comforts of home right out in the wilderness. RVs generally have a living area, kitchen, bedroom(s) and onboard bathroom, making the RV experience like having a motel room on wheels. RV parks also have hookups for electricity and likely will offer high speed internet access (via satellite).

Travel Safety

Just like at home, it's important to be vigilant and cautious when traveling. Carry only as much money as you'll need, and don't flash it around. Preferably, convert most of your cash to traveler's checks, which are available from banks, credit unions, and the auto clubs. That way, if the traveler's checks are stolen, they can be replaced at no loss to you.

While in your hotel, motel, or B&B room, carefully lock the door, and instruct your children never to open the door to anyone while they're inside. If the accommodation offers a safe where you can store valuables, lock everything away for safekeeping. It's also a good idea to store your laptop computer and other electronic devices in the safe when you're not using them.

Carry hand sanitizer and environmentally safe cleaning products and paper towels with you when you travel, or buy them after you arrive. Although public accommodations like hotels and motels are cleaned daily, it never hurts to give the counters a quick swipe with a cleaning product to make sure everything is as clean as possible. A spritz of a product like Lysol will help kill off any lingering airborne germs.

Make sure someone back home knows where you'll be at any given time, especially if you're taking a trip into a national park or any other wilderness area. If the entire family is traveling and there's no one back home, at least inform the innkeeper or other personnel at your accommodations about where you're headed and when you'll return. Be careful about who you confide in, though; unscrupulous people could be listening in and may ransack your room while you're away.

Naturally, you'll stay connected with the folks back home. But since roaming charges can be quite high, you probably should stick to email or Skype and leave your cell phone at home.

Watch your credit card purchases carefully. It's easy to spend too much while traveling, which means you'll get a nasty surprise when the bill comes. Carry a small expenses log, or download an app to help you keep track. Also, be aware that when you check into a hotel or other accommodation, the facility probably will "reserve" an amount equivalent to the cost of your entire stay on your credit card to make sure it will get paid when you check out. That could reduce your spending limit significantly. For this reason, it's usually a good idea to carry an additional credit card so other purchases you try to make won't be declined by the credit card company because you've reached your credit limit. It's also a good idea to notify your credit card company about your itinerary so your foreign purchases aren't declined.

Rules of the Road

Before you ever leave home, plan your itinerary carefully and completely. North America is a vast place with many roads and byways that can be confusing to the uninitiated. Always consult maps or a website like Mapquest.com to plan your route and calculate distances, which may be a lot farther than they look on the map.

There are several different types of roads in the United States. The interstate system offers the most direct routes at the highest speeds (up to 75 miles an hour) and are called either "freeways" or "expressways." They're indicated by an "I" in front of the road number, as in I-5 in Southern California, or I-80, which runs west to east across America's heartland. Even-numbered interstate highways run from west to east, while odd-numbered highways run from north to south. Some of these roads require motorists to pay a toll to use them. Happily, there is generally another route that goes the same direction that is free to use, although it may be the longer way.

U.S. numbered highways are marked with the letters "U.S." in front of the road number, as in U.S. 101. They, too, are even-numbered if they run west to east and odd-numbered if they run north to south. The speed limit depends on whether the road runs through a populated area and can range anywhere from 25 mph (miles per hour) to 75 mph.

State highways have their own numbering system and have a letter designating the state name in front of the highway name, as in LA 3234 in Louisiana and PA 5 in Pennsylvania. The speed on these roads also depends on whether it traverses a populated area. Watch carefully for speed limit signs and adjust your speed accordingly so you don't end up having a personal meeting with a state trooper or "county mounty."

There are other smaller and less-traveled roads through the United States. Generally, you should stay off them, because they tend to be unmarked or even dangerous as they may be unpaved or could run close to the edge of a natural drop-off like a hill—or worse.

In Canada, the equivalent to the U.S. interstate system has various names, from "400-series" in Ontario to "Autoroute" in Quebec. The transcontinental provincial highway is called the Trans-Canada Highway and runs through all ten provinces that lie from the Pacific to the Atlantic Ocean.

Other Canadian road designations include provincial and territorial highways, and county and regional roads. The latter are marked with the name of the province and a number (as in Alberta 1X or NB 8; NB being short for New Brunswick). Locals usually refer to the highways by a name rather than a number, which can be confusing when you're asking for directions.

The speed limits in Canada are marked in kilometers (km/h) rather than miles per hour, which may be what you're more accustomed to from your homeland. The lowest speed limit is 30 km/h; the highest is 110 km/h. Naturally, the speed varies by province, so watch the speed limit signs carefully.

North America is a great place to explore and play. Take time to check out the sights and expand your horizons.

ATTA'S LESSONS

During some of the most difficult and depressing moments I experienced after leaving my homeland, I used to tell myself I should somehow enjoy the beauty of the new places I would see. So I made it a mission to always seek knowledge of and see new places. Since then, I have traveled through much of Europe, as well as to many U.S. states and Canadian provinces, both on business and for the pleasure of visiting relatives. No matter where I go, I explore and discover new things and places. This refreshes and energizes me so I can serve my loved ones and my fellow human beings better. We really do live in a big, beautiful world, and it's an absolute must to experience and enjoy travel and leisure as part of your plan to lead a successful life.

Chapter 20: Insuring Your Future

Insurance is actually a strange kind of product. Normally, you buy things you can use or enjoy. But you buy insurance to protect yourself and your loved ones against events you never want to happen, like death, injury, hazards, and loss.

As a result, it's easy just to ignore the need for insurance, especially because it tends to be expensive. There also will probably be a million other things you'll feel you need to pay for first, like car repairs, school clothes, and vacations. But insurance is all about risk and how much you can tolerate. Think about it: if something happened to you today, what would happen to your family? Do you have enough money saved so they can continue to live in the house, condo, or other place they now occupy? Would medical expenses wipe out any savings you have? Would a car accident lead to a lawsuit by the other injured party and take everything you own?

These are the types of questions you should ask yourself when it comes to buying insurance. Of course, some types of insurance are mandatory, so you have to buy them whether you want to or not. For example, almost every U.S. state (except Virginia, New Hampshire, and Mississippi), and all Canadian provinces require residents to have some form of basic auto insurance. Mortgage companies require borrowers to have home insurance. But other types, like life insurance, are completely optional.

In the end, it all depends on the amount of risk you're willing to take—and how much money you have for insurance plans to offset that risk. You can buy insurance for pretty much anything you can think of, but not all of it is necessary or makes financial sense. Also, it's possible that your employer may offer some types of insurance as part of your benefits package (Chapter 6 discussed the most common types). Generally speaking, it's usually less expensive to take advantage of those employer-offered insurance plans and only buy supplemental insurance if you don't think you have enough coverage.

This chapter discusses the basic types of personal insurance that are either mandatory or should be considered at the very least. You'll find worksheets on pages 217 to 222 where you can note the details of the plans you've chosen for future reference.

TYPES OF INSURANCE: UNITED STATES

Health Insurance (Mandatory)

All Americans are required to have health insurance as a result of Obamacare, the health insurance plan named somewhat irreverently for the president who signed the bill into law (and more correctly known as the *Affordable Care Act*, or ACA). According to the Henry J. Kaiser Family foundation, forty-seven million Americans were uninsured or underinsured before the ACA took effect, while the rest had traditional health-care plans, either through their employer or public health organizations like Medicare or Medicaid.

At the heart of Obamacare is the Health Insurance Exchange (HIX), which is an online marketplace where you can compare insurance plans in your state and find the one that's best for you and your budget. You can also call (888) 318-2596 if you don't have access to the internet, and a navigator will assist you in the enrollment process.

Obamacare offers four tiers of coverage, known as "metal plans," through the HIX. The main difference between them is the deductible (the amount you must pay before the insurance covers the rest) and the services they offer. The services vary by insurance company, so you'll need to address your questions about the depth of service directly to the company, either online or by phone.

The four metal plans include:

Bronze plan: This is the most affordable plan. It has higher deductibles (40 percent) and offers fewer services, but still must meet minimum coverage requirements set by the ACA. This might be a good choice if you're young, single, have few medical problems, and don't take prescription medication.

Silver plan: This plan has a 30 percent deductible and offers more services than the bronze plan. Naturally, the premium cost is also higher.

Gold plan: This plan is a step up from the silver plan and has a 20 percent deductible. Its premiums are higher than the silver plan.

Platinum plan: With a 10 percent deductible, this is the most expensive plan, but it also covers the most. It also has the highest premium. If you have a lot of medical conditions, see many doctors and specialists, and use a lot of prescription medications, this might be the best plan for you.

Plan prices depend on four factors: your age, whether you smoke, where you live, and how many people are covered in your family. In addition, despite the fact that the plans are divided into these metal categories, it's always possible that a gold plan chosen from one insurance company could be less expensive than the bronze plan from another company. For this reason, it pays to shop around before you select your plan.

All insurance plans are required to offer ten ACA-mandated essential health benefits, including ambulatory (walk-in) and emergency coverage, hospitalization, maternity and newborn care, mental health services, drug coverage, lab services and tests, rehabilitative services and devices, pediatric services, and prevention/wellness services. In addition, you can't be excluded from getting coverage if you have a pre-existing illness or medical condition, and you can't be turned away or charged more than other people.

Plans may be purchased directly from the HIX, from insurance companies, and from insurance brokers. And incidentally, if you have employer-provided coverage, you don't have to purchase your insurance from a HIX. However, you might want to check out HIX plans anyway. They could be cheaper than what you're paying now. However, you will not be eligible for an ACA plan subsidy (discussed below).

The ACA plans are complex, and this chapter covers only the basics. You're likely to have more questions. So go to healthcare.gov and search under "All Topics" for more information. You can also call (888) 318-2596, where you'll talk to a real person, not a machine. To compare health insurance plans, also go to healthcare.gov. Another easy-to-use website is HealthSherpa.com. Just plug in your ZIP code, and you can find plans and compare premiums.

ACA PLAN SUBSIDIES

Health care is mandated by the ACA, but there are still many underinsured and uninsured people in the United States who can't afford coverage of any kind. If you fall into one of these groups, there's still hope. The federal government offers subsidies (cost assistance) to those who can't pay for insurance. The current guideline is that if you earn an amount less than four times the federal poverty level (FPL), you will qualify for the subsidy or an advanced tax premium tax credit. For example, the poverty threshold for a single person in any of the forty-eight contiguous (mainland) states was $11,490 in 2013. (The FPL is higher in Alaska and Hawaii.) That person can earn up to $45,960 and still qualify for some assistance, although the higher the income, the lower the subsidy. On the other hand, if your household size is four (yourself, your spouse, and two children), the FPL in 2013 was $23,550 in 2013, and you can have an income up to four times the FPL, or $94,200, and still qualify for a subsidy.

To qualify, you must buy your health insurance through a HIX. You also must *not* be eligible for health coverage through your employer or another government plan. Finally, you must file a joint tax return if you're married, and you can't be claimed as a dependent on the tax return of another person (such as your parents or your spouse).

To get an idea whether you'll qualify for the subsidy, use the FPL calculator on the ABC for Health website at safetyweb.org/fpl.php. You can choose to have some or all the subsidies sent directly to the insurance company you've chosen, which will reduce your monthly premiums; or you can choose to wait to get the subsidy when you file your income tax return for the following year.

Medicaid and the Children's Health Insurance Program

Some people who have little or no income will be eligible for Medicaid instead of a metal plan. After entering your personal data at the HIX, you'll find out immediately if you qualify for free or low-cost Medicaid. It's also possible that your children would be eligible for the Children's Health Insurance Program (CHIP) coverage. You'll find more information about Medicaid and CHIP later in this chapter.

Final Notes on the ACA Plans

There are exceptions to the metal plan insurance-for-all requirement of the ACA. As mentioned earlier, if you have employer-provided insurance, or if you've purchased a private insurance plan, or have COBRA (group insurance purchased when you're separated from your job), retiree benefits, TRICARE (the U.S. military's health plan), VA (Veteran's Administration) health benefits, or any other type of insurance not named here, you don't have to do anything. Those plans remain in effect. But if you don't have insurance of some kind, you'll be fined a flat fee or a percentage of your income when you file your income tax return. That's how serious the U.S. government is about making sure all Americans have access to affordable, portable health insurance.

Traditional Health Care Plans

Employers in the United States usually offer traditional, managed care plans, which feature networks of providers, including physicians and hospitals, who agree to provide care at a reduced cost. While managed care plans focus on preventative care, they also provide a full range of medical, diagnostic, and hospital services. Under the terms of the ACA, these insurance providers also cannot refuse you coverage if you have a pre-existing condition, nor can they charge you more for the plan you choose. Following are the most common types of managed care plans.

Health Maintenance Organizations (HMOs) and Exclusive Provider Organizations (EPOs)

These plans offer a wider range of services through a network of select providers. They generally have lower out-of-pocket expenses, but you do have to stay within the network to get the lowest cost. An advantage is that these plans usually don't have a deductible that has to be met each year before they'll pay your expenses, and they have less paperwork. A disadvantage is that after selecting a primary care physician from the network, you have to get a referral to any specialists you may need to see.

Preferred Provider Organizations (PPOs) and Point-of-Service Plans (POSs)

These plans also have provider networks, and you can get care outside the network if you wish and don't mind paying more. But you don't have to select a primary care physician or obtain a referral to see a specialist. That can be a plus. However, PPOs usually do have an annual deductible and a copayment of $10 to $30 for office visits.

A point-of-service plan is a hybrid HMO/PPO plan. Like an HMO, you'll have to select a doctor from its network to participate. But like a PPO, you can go out-of-network, so long as you don't mind paying higher out-of-pocket costs.

High Deductible Health Plan (HDHP)

Also known as a "consumer-directed plan," this type of insurance plan has lower premiums and higher deductibles than traditional plans—often $3,000 or more. It can be a good choice for a young person in good health who probably won't use health care services very often, or an older person in good health who has sufficient savings to cover out-of-pocket costs. One warning, though: in addition to the deductible, you are likely to have substantial copay costs if you have a serious illness or accident. You can offset some of the cost by establishing a flexible spending account, which allows you to set aside pre-tax dollars for your expenses (discussed in more depth in Chapter 7). But you must spend all funds you set aside in the same year, or you'll lose them.

Catastrophic Health Insurance Plan

If you're looking for a plan that only covers unexpected/emergency medical costs, catastrophic health insurance might be a viable option. This is generally a hospitalization-only plan, with no coverage for ordinary health-care costs. If you're young (under thirty), you don't have any pre-existing medical conditions, you rarely see a physician, and/or you expect to obtain other health-care coverage soon (such as you'd get through an employer), then this might be a good choice for you. The monthly premiums for catastrophic plans generally are lower than other plans, but the deductible usually is much higher.

Medicaid

This is a state-administered social program for U.S. citizens and eligible green-card holders that provides health insurance coverage to low-income people and families who are unable to afford health care costs (including an Obamacare metal plan). Among the individuals covered are low-income adults, children, senior citizens, and people with disabilities. Medicaid helps pay for a range of medical expenses, including doctors' visits, hospital bills, prescriptions (although there are restrictions), vision and dental care, in-home care under the Community Alternatives Program, nursing home care, and mental health care. In addition, Medicaid may help pay for most medically necessary services for children under age twenty-one. If you're receiving Supplemental Security Income (SSI), Work First family assistance, and special assistance for the blind, you're automatically eligible for Medicaid.

While Medicaid does help, it doesn't necessarily cover all costs, particularly in the case of nursing home care. In addition, coverage varies according to income, resource limits, and need. But if it's the only coverage you have because of your financial situation, it can really help. For more information about Medicaid eligibility, refer to the Medicaid eligibility chart at ncdhhs. gov/dma/medicaid/Medicaid_eligibility_0713.pdf, or go to medicaid.gov.

CHILDREN'S HEALTH INSURANCE PROGRAM (CHIP)

Designed for families with incomes too high to qualify for Medicaid but who can't afford private coverage, the Children's Health Insurance Program (CHIP) provides comprehensive benefits for children up to the age of nineteen. Among these benefits are inpatient and outpatient hospital services, physicians' services; surgical and medical services, laboratory and x-ray services, and well-baby and well-child care, including immunizations. According to the CHIP website at medicaid.gov, CHIP also provides coverage for dental services "necessary to prevent disease and promote oral health, restore oral structures to health and function, and treat emergency conditions." Eligibility requirements vary by state. For more information, go to medicaid.gov and search for "CHIP."

MEDICARE

This federal health insurance program covers people aged sixty-five and up, certain younger people with disabilities, and people with end-stage renal disease (permanent kidney failure requiring dialysis or a transplant). According to the medicare.gov website, Medicare has four parts that cover different services:

- **Medicare Part A** covers inpatient hospital stays, care in a skilled nursing facility, hospice care, and some home health care. It also covers medically necessary appliances like wheelchairs and walkers.
- **Medicare Part B** covers certain doctors' services, outpatient care, medical supplies, and preventive services.
- **Medicare Part C** is a health plan that's offered by a private company that contracts with Medicare to provide Part A and Part B benefits. Examples

include Medicare Advantage Plans like HMOs, PPOs, private fee-for-service plans, special-needs plans, and Medicare medical savings-account plans. Most Medicare Advantage Plans offer prescription drug coverage.
- **Medicare Part D** covers prescription drug costs.

For more information about Medicare, go to medicare.gov, or call (800) MEDICARE (800-633-4227). TTY users may call (877) 486-2048.

Dental Insurance (Optional)

Both private and employer-provided dental insurance plans often fully cover basic services like routine checkups (including biannual cleanings and x-rays). If you need restorative work (fillings, root canals, crowns), you will usually have a copay of 50 percent or more. Non-employer-provided dental insurance tends to be expensive, and it may make more sense simply to set aside money in your monthly budget for future dental visits. The exception may be if the restorative work on your teeth is thirty to forty years old, since at some point, it will have to be replaced.

Orthodontic care (application of braces to straighten teeth) is usually not covered by dental insurance, and if it is, it usually has a lifetime maximum coverage cap. Likewise, dentures and bridges may not be a covered benefit, so ask before you buy.

Pediatric dental care for basic services like teeth cleaning, x-rays and fillings is included as one of the ten essential benefits under the ACA. Adults are not required to have dental coverage under the ACA, and the cost is not eligible for government subsidies.

Vision Coverage (Optional)

Vision insurance usually offers core benefits like routine eye exams, prescription eyeglasses, and contact lenses. It may also offer discounts on prescription and nonprescription sunglasses, as well as laser eye surgery like LASIK. If you don't have vision insurance through your employer, it may be more cost-effective to set aside funds every month to pay for an eye exam and glasses out-of-pocket. The cost of vision plans is set by law and start at $6 a month. If you choose to buy your own plan, make sure you check with your vision care provider to make sure he or she accepts the plan you've chosen.

Pediatric vision care is included in the ACA metal plans and at least partially covers eye exams and glasses. Adults have to obtain their own coverage and pay the premiums out-of-pocket.

Auto Insurance (Mandatory in Most States)

Despite the name, auto insurance covers all types of motorized vehicles, including passenger cars, SUVs, vans, trucks, motorcycles, and motor homes. Typically it includes all or some of the following coverage options:

- **Bodily injury liability:** This option covers bodily injury to the driver(s) and passenger(s) of other vehicle(s) in an accident for which you're responsible. Policies also often include coverage to defend you if you're sued as a result of the accident.
- **Property damage liability:** This pays for damages to another person's vehicle or property when you're at fault.
- **Medical expenses:** This option is for medical expenses incurred in an accident; it covers both you and your passengers. Some states have no-fault coverage instead, which pays for medical, funeral, and other expenses due to a car accident—no matter who is responsible.
- **Uninsured motorist:** Even though virtually every state requires some type of auto insurance, not everyone abides by the law. So this option pays for damages and bodily injury to both you and your passengers that are caused by another driver who has little or no insurance. This coverage varies by state.
- **Collision:** This is coverage that pays for damage to your car that's caused by a collision or rollover.
- **Comprehensive:** This option provides coverage if your car is stolen or damaged due to vandalism, fire, hail, or other reasons.

Some policies also include emergency road service coverage, which includes services like tire changing and towing to a garage so repairs can be made. It also typically includes car rentals for when your vehicle is in the shop for repairs and you need to get around. Both of these services cost extra.

It's usually a good idea to work directly with an insurance agent to find the best coverage for your situation. The cost of the policy will be dependent upon your driving record, the age of your car, the deductible, and the amount you are willing to pay as out-of-pocket expenses. You also should ask if your policy includes travel insurance so when you rent a car you won't have to buy the rental company's expensive car insurance.

Incidentally, you're not completely off the financial hook if you live in one of the states that doesn't require traditional auto insurance. In Ohio, Tennessee, Texas, and Washington, you can go without if you can prove that you have the means to cover liability losses. In California, you only need liability insurance, while in New Hampshire, you need liability insurance only if you've been in an at-fault accident.

LIFE INSURANCE (OPTIONAL)

The term "life insurance" is actually a misnomer—more correctly, it's death insurance, because this type of insurance pays the fixed dollar amount specified in the policy after the insured person dies. It's a way to leave behind enough money to take care of your loved ones after your death.

Life insurance can be divided into two basic categories:

Whole life insurance: This type of policy is a combination life benefit and investment fund. In addition to paying out a fixed amount after the insured person's death, a whole life policy accumulates cash value during its term, because some of the premiums you pay into it go into an investment account managed by the life insurance company. You can borrow against that cash fund without paying taxes on it, although you do have to repay the cash you take out.

Term insurance: As the name implies, this type of insurance is good for a specified period of time; say, anywhere from one to forty years. Term insurance policies don't have any investment value, and at the end of the term, the coverage ends and your money goes with it. But the good news is term life insurance is renewable and you're not required to take a medical exam each time you renew. The bad news is the cost of the insurance increases steadily as you get older.

One type of term life insurance to consider is universal life, which combines term insurance with money market-style investment capabilities. Other options include variable life and variable universal life, both of which are tied to stock or bond market performance. But be warned: none of these three will guarantee returns on your investment.

One of the most important things to consider when buying insurance is how much debt you'll be leaving behind after your demise. If you don't have sufficient savings to cover credit card, mortgage, and other debt, you'll need a larger insurance policy. Alternately, if you're looking for income replacement for your loved ones, you'll need to figure out how much they'll need.

To get an idea of how much insurance you should buy, try using an online life insurance calculator like the one found at Bankrate.com (bankrate.com/ calculators/insurance/life-insurance-calculator.aspx). Here's a sample calculation for a thirty-five-year-old man in Michigan who is the sole support for his family and has a net (after tax) income of $37,500 a year. He is a nonsmoker and has no significant health problems. He would like enough coverage to provide income replacement for thirty years (until his wife retires). He also plans to put his two kids through college. The calculations are based on the following facts:

- Annual net income needed to support the family: $37,500 a year for thirty years
- Estimate of college expenses for two children (now aged ten and twelve): $100,000
- Estimate of wedding costs for eldest child (now aged twelve): $50,000
- Estimated burial expenses: $10,000
- Amount in current liquid assets: $50,000

The estimated life insurance policy amount (per Bankrate.com) $829,903.84. That probably sounds like a scary figure. But according to the calculator at USAA.com, this healthy young man would pay $69.99 a month for thirty years for $1 million of term life insurance; or $678.29 a month for $1 million of simplified whole life insurance. If the numbers are too high for your bank account, scale back the amount of the policy to yield lower monthly premiums.

Picking the right life insurance can be confusing. You should consider talking to an insurance agent or broker to get enough information to make an intelligent decision.

Accidental Death & Disbursement (AD&D) Insurance (Optional)

This type of policy pays you or your beneficiaries if you are injured or killed in an accident. But insurance experts suggest getting this insurance as a rider (addition) to your life insurance policy rather than as a stand-alone policy. AD&D policies tend to have a lot of restrictions and exclusions, so shop carefully.

Homeowner's Insurance (Mandatory If You Have a Mortgage)

Even if you don't have a mortgage, you should have some type of homeowner's insurance to protect your home and property against structural damage and losses due to fire, lightning, windstorms, hail, vandalism, and theft. Policies also generally cover situations like frozen plumbing systems (which can happen if you don't winterize properly), sewer backups, and more. The policy usually covers dwelling replacement and some possessions. You may need a rider (additional policy) to cover your possessions fully.

Depending on the insurer, homeowner policies also often cover structures not attached to your house (like a detached garage or gazebo), personal liability, medical payments to persons injured on your property, and more. Some of these policies are discussed separately later in this chapter.

Property Insurance (Optional)

This type of policy protects against most catastrophic risks to your property, such as fire, theft, and weather-related incidents. This probably sounds just like homeowner insurance—which it is, in a sense—but it includes coverage against more catastrophic damage generally not covered by homeowner policies, including floods, earthquakes, nuclear accidents, and acts of terrorism. Alternately, you can purchase separate policies for these situations, as described below.

Flood Insurance (Optional)

Flood damage is generally not covered under homeowner insurance policies. Instead, you'll have to purchase separate insurance coverage (or a liability policy, as described above). Since flood insurance is very expensive, a lot of people forego coverage. But if you live in an area with elevated water tables, or if you live on a flood plain, in a coastal area that's prone to hurricanes, or even in a neighborhood that frequently floods, you might want to seriously consider spending the money. To help yourself decide, go to FloodSmart. gov at floodsmart.gov/floodsmart/pages/flooding_flood_risks/ffr_overview. jsp, where you'll find information about common flooding issues and assess your risk.

Earthquake Insurance (Optional)

As with flood insurance, not everyone will need earthquake insurance, but you'll sure be glad you have it when the Big One hits. You must have home-owner insurance, as well, to have earthquake coverage, which is so expensive that you might end up just taking your chances.

Private Mortgage Insurance (Mandatory in Some States)

If the down payment on your home was less than 20 percent on a conventional mortgage, your lender will require that you have private mortgage insurance (PMI). This insurance doesn't protect you; rather, it protects the mortgage company against loss if your home goes into foreclosure (that is, the bank seizes your home due to nonpayment) and the lender isn't able to recover its costs between the foreclosure and the resale of the house to someone else. It's not uncommon for banks to lose a lot of money when a house is foreclosed, so PMI helps them offset their losses.

Renter's Insurance (Optional)

Apartment dwellers need insurance, too, to protect their possessions. Renter's insurance is usually quite inexpensive (about a dollar a day) and is recom-mended because, although your landlord will (or should) have property insurance, it's not likely to cover your possessions in the event of a fire, vandalism, theft, or other situations, nor your liability for accidents. This type of policy will allow you to recover the value of your possessions, as well as protect you against liability lawsuit losses. You can also get earthquake and flood damage if you'd like the extra coverage. The insurance company definitely will be happy to take your money.

LIABILITY INSURANCE (OPTIONAL)

If you have homeowner's insurance, you already have a measure of liability coverage, which offsets legal claims made against you for falls or other accidents that happen on your property. You can buy extra coverage if you wish, but check your homeowner policy first to see whether the levels of protection are adequate. If they are, then save your money.

Estimate Your Insurance Costs

Contact an insurance agent or broker to get the fastest quotes on personal, home, and auto insurance. You also can check the following websites to estimate your costs:

United States

- Insure.com: insure.com, (800) 556-9303
- Insurance Quote: iquote.com, (800) 337-5433
- Quicken Insweb: insweb.com, (800) 467-8736
- Quick Quote: quickquote.com, (800) 867-2404
- Select Quote: selectquote.com, (800) 963-8688

Canada

- CarInsurance.com: carinsurance.com, (855) 430-7753
- Esurance: esurance.com, (800) 378-7262
- Insurance Hotline: insurancehotline.com, (800) 668-0128
- Kanetix: kanetix.ca, (888) 854-2503
- Navigators: navigatorsinsurance.ca, (905) 470-6040

TYPES OF INSURANCE: CANADA

Health Insurance (Mandatory Covered Benefit)

Canada has a publicly funded health-care system known as Medicare that provides access to physicians and medical treatments for all residents. There may be charges to the patient, depending on the province and your income level. Health care is covered in more detail in Chapters 12 and 20.

Dental Insurance (Optional)

Because dental services are not covered by the *Canada Health Act*, you must buy your own dental insurance if you want it. Employer-provided dental insurance will probably be less expensive, so check with your employer first to see if you're covered.

Vision Insurance (Optional)

Treatment for eye injuries and eye diseases like cataracts, glaucoma, and diabetic retinopathy are covered by Canada's universal health insurance. You'll need supplemental insurance to offset the cost of eye examinations, eyeglasses, contact lenses, and possibly laser correction surgery. If your employer offers vision insurance, there's no need to purchase private insurance.

Auto Insurance (Mandatory)

Basic insurance is required throughout Canada. British Columbia, Manitoba, Quebec, and Saskatchewan have public auto insurance systems, and the premiums are said to be less expensive than in provinces with private auto insurance. Types of coverage include the following:

- **Accident benefits coverage (***aka*** "Section B"):** This covers medical care and provides income replacement benefits to those injured in a car accident. It's required everywhere in Canada except Newfoundland and Labrador.
- **No-fault:** A type of policy that pays damages in an auto accident regardless of who is at fault.

Life Insurance (Optional)

Life insurance is intended to be a way to provide for your family's needs when you die. Funds can be used for any purpose, but usually go toward living expenses (food, mortgage payments, etc.), college tuition, and other costs like burial expenses.

There are three types of life insurance policies:

- **Term Life:** This is the least expensive protection available. A term policy expires at the end of a specified term, typically five, ten, or twenty years. It pays only if the insured person dies within the coverage period. There's no accumulated value at the end of the term.
- **Universal Life:** This type of policy is more expensive than a term policy and has an investment component. In addition to insuring your life, a portion of your premiums is deposited into an account, where it can earn interest. You can decide where the funds will be invested, and the accumulated value is paid to your heirs after your death.
- **Whole Life:** This policy is similar to universal life but is more expensive and less flexible. For example, the insurer decides where to invest the deposited funds rather than you. It does have a pay-out value after your death.

Accidental Death Insurance (Optional)

According to ScotiaLife, which is—you guessed it—an insurance company, accidents are the second leading cause of death in Canada. That may be enough to scare you into purchasing accidental death insurance, which pays your survivors a tax-free benefit following your demise from a covered accident. However, financial experts generally agree that it's better to purchase additional term life insurance rather than accidental death coverage, especially since term life insurance is usually less expensive. But it's up to you.

Mortgage Loan Insurance (Mandatory on a Case-by-Case Basis)

If you made a down payment of less than 20 percent on your home, your mortgage holder will require you to have mortgage loan insurance. Its purpose is to protect the lender, not you, in case you default (stop paying) on the loan. The good news is that with mortgage loan insurance, you can make a down payment of as little as 5 percent and still qualify for rates comparable to those offered to people who have made 20 percent down payments.

There are three mortgage insurance providers in Canada: CMHC, Genworth Financial Canada, and Canada Guaranty. You can learn more about each at mymortgage.ca.

Home Insurance (Recommended)

Although home insurance isn't mandatory in Canada, your mortgage company is likely to require it anyway. The types of standard home insurance policies include the following:

- **Comprehensive:** This type of policy covers both the home itself and its contents.
- **Optional Coverage:** This insurance covers things not covered by a comprehensive policy, including natural disasters (earthquakes, tornados, hail), sewer backups, and so on.
- **Basic/Named Perils:** This policy covers against specific risks (perils) for which you are willing to carry some of the financial risk as a way of keeping the policy cost down. For example, you might insure for named perils like fire and theft, but exclude hurricanes and earthquakes.
- **Broad:** This policy provides comprehensive coverage on the building and named peril coverage on the contents.
- **No Frills:** This is insurance for a home that doesn't quite meet an insurer's standards. For instance, perhaps the foundation is crumbling, or the home is in need of extensive renovation. This type of policy will keep you covered until the home is remodeled or restored, at which point you'd move into one of the other policies named above.

Most of these policies also include personal liability coverage, which covers you if you're sued due to bodily injury or property damage sustained while someone is on your property. If you'd like additional coverage, you can add optional umbrella liability coverage to your policy.

Once your home is paid off, you could opt out of home insurance. But that's risky. If something happened to your home (fire, natural disaster, etc.), you'd have to pay to rebuild or restore out-of-pocket.

Condo and Tenant Insurance

Although your condominium corporation or apartment building management company will have insurance on the building in which your home is situated, their coverage won't cover your possessions in case of loss nor your personal liability if someone sustains an injury in your home. For this, you need condo or tenant insurance.

When buying this insurance, make sure your policy includes sufficient coverage to replace your furnishings, computer equipment, clothing, jewelry, and other possessions. In addition, you may also wish to consider having all-perils coverage, which provides protection against the widest range of risks; or specified perils, which covers you in case of the most common risks, such as fire, lightning, falling objects, smoke, vandalism, and so on.

For more information about the various types of insurance policies available to Canadians, visit the Insurance Bureau of Canada website at ibc.ca/en/Need_More_Info/Glossary/A.asp.

Insurance Worksheet: United States

Use this worksheet to organize the details of the various insurance plans you've purchased or have through your employer.

Type of Insurance	Insurance Company Name	Monthly Premium	Policy Number	Policy Amount	Maturation Date (if any)
Health					
Dental					
Vision					
Auto					
Life (whole)					
Life (term)					
Death and Disability (rider or policy)					
Homeowner					
Property					
Private Mortgage					
Renter					
Liability					
Other					
Other					

Insurance Worksheet: Canada

Use this worksheet to organize the details of the various insurance plans you've purchased or have through your employer.

Type of Insurance	Insurance Company Name	Monthly Premium	Policy Number	Policy Amount	Maturation Date (if any)
Health					
Dental					
Vision					
Auto					
Life (whole)					
Life (term)					
Life (universal)					
Accidental Death					
Homeowners					
Mortgage Loan					
Condo/Tenant					
Other					
Other					

Life Insurance Worksheet

Use this worksheet to log additional details about the life insurance policies you carry.

Type of Insurance	Name of Insured/Policy Holder	Company Name	Monthly Premium	Beneficiary	Face Value	Maturity Date
Life (whole)						
Life (term)						
Life (universal); Canada						

Chapter 21: Legal Matters

When you think back over your life, the memories that probably come to mind first are closely tied to your loved ones. For example, your marriage would be one of those memorable life events. The birth of your children, the joyous birthday and anniversary celebrations, and the deaths of treasured loved ones are also milestones you remember.

There's no question that family is your most precious "possession." So it should make sense that you need to make plans and take the appropriate steps to protect both your loved ones—and yourself—as you travel through this life. For this reason, this chapter covers the various legal matters you should consider and documents you should have drawn up, either now or in the immediate future. Many of these legal matters require the services of a lawyer, but the time and expense is worth it to protect those closest to you. Please also note that this chapter provides just a general overview of various legal matters. Seek the services of an attorney experienced in the legal area you're interested in, to make sure you get the latest and most accurate counsel.

UNITED STATES

WILL

A will is a legal document that indicates how you wish to have your estate distributed after your death. Your estate consists of various assets, from money you have in cash, stocks, bonds, and other financial instruments, to any personal possessions you have, such as your home. It also states your wishes concerning any minor children (under the age of eighteen) you have.

The term for when a person dies without a will is *intestate*. If you are married and you die intestate, your estate usually will go to your spouse, or possibly to your spouse (50 percent) and your children (50 percent), depending on which state you live in. While this may be fine with you now, you must consider that your spouse and children could die at the same time as you do. It's much better to draw up a will that states exactly where you want your estate to go, rather than to leave it to chance.

If you are not married and you die intestate, the state where you live will determine where your estate will go. According to LegalZoom.com, the state will distribute your estate to the following people in this order: your children, or if they are not alive, their children; your parents; your brothers and sisters or, if they are not alive, their children; your grandparents or, if they are not alive, their children (i.e., your uncles and aunts); the children of your deceased spouse; any relatives of your deceased spouse. If there are absolutely no heirs, then the state where you live acquires your assets.

There are several types of wills. The testamentary will is the most common, and consists of a document that is drawn up by an attorney, then signed in front of witnesses.

The second type is a holographic will, which is a written document signed without witnesses. The problem with this type of will is that it rarely holds up in court, which is where your estate will end up. The result could be challenges to the will and fights over how your estate should be divided. Finally, the oral will is given in front of witnesses, but like a holographic will, it doesn't stand up in court very well.

As a result, you should spend some time thinking about how you would want your estate divided. Make a list of every asset you own, including anything that's stored in a safe deposit box, any family heirlooms, and anything else you'd like to go to a particular person. Then seek the assistance of an attorney to record your wishes. After you've signed the will in the presence of witnesses, your attorney will take care of having it filed correctly.

You'll receive a copy of your will after it has been executed (signed). Store it in a safe place, like a fireproof box in your home. You should also give a copy of the will to the executor of your estate, who is the person you select to carry out your wishes after your death. Finally, make sure all your loved ones know where the original is stored.

It's possible that you may wish to change your will after it has been executed. All you have to do is write a new will to replace the old one, or have your attorney make a change, known as a *codicil*, to the previous will.

LIVING WILL

This type of will has nothing to do with your assets. Rather, it's a way to indicate the type of medical care you wish to have if you are unable to speak for yourself. For instance, you might indicate that you want everything medically possible done for you. Or you could ask for a "do not resuscitate" (DNR) order, meaning you don't want a medical provider (doctor, nurse, emergency medical technician) to do cardiopulmonary resuscitation (CPR) or provide other advanced cardiac life support if your heart stops or you stop breathing.

To make sure others respect your wishes, your living will should be signed, witnessed, and posted in a visible location, such as on your refrigerator. Also be sure to discuss your wishes with your family.

Advanced Directive Patient Advocate

Another document you should have to let medical professionals know who is authorized to speak (advocate) for your care if you are unable to do so yourself is the advanced directive patient advocate form. The document is used to appoint the person of your choice (your advocate or proxy) to act on your behalf and make medical decisions concerning your care, custody, and treatment. Your named patient advocate must be at least eighteen years old and of sound mind (mentally capable). You also may designate one or more additional people to act as your advocates if the first is unable to do so. Additionally, you'll indicate specific instructions regarding care you do wish and don't wish to receive. This will include the DNR order you may have given in your living will. Finally, you'll indicate any other special instructions you may have, including religious requests (e.g., allowing medical care provided by a person of only one specific gender) and instructions regarding anatomical gifts (organ donation).

The advanced directive should be signed, witnessed, and stored in a safe place until it is needed. Make sure several people know where to find it.

The advanced directive form is specific to your state. For clickable links to your state's form, go to caringinfo.org/i4a/pages/index.cfm?pageid=3289.

Trusts

In addition to writing a will, another way to bequeath your assets to the person or persons of your choice is by establishing a trust fund. Trust funds are not just financial tools for the wealthy; they're a good way for you, the grantor, to leave a legacy to someone you love.

Trust funds are legal entities that are usually established for minor children (including grandchildren) who are inexperienced with handling money.

However, you can set up a trust for anyone, including a charitable organization. (Trusts can even be set up to take care of a beloved pet after your death.) The trust is managed by a financial institution, and the proceeds avoid probate court upon your death by having named beneficiary(ies).

There are two types of trusts: the living trust is set up by the grantor while he or she is still alive, while an after-death trust is established through the terms of a will after the death of the grantor. Living trusts can be designated as revocable (able to be changed) or irrevocable (not able to be changed). Both types of living trusts have tax shelter benefits, but irrevocable trusts are the most advantageous. Grantors typically set up a revocable living trust to benefit a charitable organization.

As the grantor, you have the right to tailor the trust at any time to meet the needs of the person named to receive it (the beneficiary). To set up a trust, determine how to transfer your assets into it, and change the trust as you see fit, engage the services of an experienced estate and trust attorney.

POWER OF ATTORNEY

If a situation arises where you need someone to act legally on your behalf, then you can give that person or persons power of attorney over your affairs. You might do this for a number of reasons. For instance, maybe you need to return to your homeland for an extended period of time and would be unable to take care of your financial affairs and other responsibilities from afar. If you're in the military, you could be deployed for a long period of time and need assistance. Or maybe you're facing treatment for a serious illness. All these situations, among others, may warrant a power of attorney (POA).

The POA is a written legal document, but it doesn't have to go through a court. Rather, you'll draw up the document (use a state-specific template found online or ask your attorney for one), have it signed by two adult witnesses not related to you, and then have it notarized. In North Carolina and South Carolina only, you must also have the document recorded in the office of your county recorder. Keep the original copy in a safe place, and give a copy to the person who will see to your affairs. Be sure to include language in the POA stating that a copy is acceptable when presented.

The POA becomes valid as soon as you sign it, and the person who acts on your behalf is called the "attorney-in-fact." However, he or she does *not* have to be a legal attorney to be your proxy. You don't lose control over your own affairs when you have a POA agreement, and you can revoke (take it back) any time you wish. You also can give POA rights to more than one person, but be careful, they'll all have access to your bank accounts and other financial matters.

In addition, you can help another person set up a POA as long as that person is of sound mind. If he or she is mentally incapacitated, a guardianship or conservatorship (described later in this chapter) will be necessary instead.

Besides the general POA described above, there are other types of POAs:

- **Durable POA:** This continues indefinitely rather than ending when you recover or otherwise retake control of your affairs. Some people do this so it's not necessary for their family to establish a conservatorship if they become incapacitated at a later date. Any of the POAs mentioned in this section can be made durable, if you wish.
- **Health Care Limited POA:** This gives the attorney-in-fact permission to make health-care decisions for the grantor, including terminating care and life support. For this reason, some grantors amend the POA to prevent his or her representative from having this power. Incidentally, the health care limited POA is different from an advanced directive patient advocate (discussed earlier), because it doesn't grant any financial rights to the person who administers it.
- **Limited POA:** This gives the agent the authority to handle certain transactions on your behalf for a set period of time. This could include tasks like check writing or managing savings-account deposits, entering a safe deposit box, or buying and selling real estate, to name just a few. It's entirely up to you which rights you wish to grant and the length of time for which these rights are in effect.

CONSERVATORSHIPS

Sometimes the people in your life need someone to advocate on their behalf to ensure their good health, safety, and security. In those cases, it may be necessary to establish a conservatorship, which is a legal arrangement that puts someone in charge of handling another person's day-to-day affairs while incapacitated (due to an illness or an accident, for example) or unable to handle matters by himself or herself (due to dementia, for example). That person is known as a conservator and is entrusted with the right to make legal decisions on someone else's behalf. Things a personal conservator may handle include arranging for care and a living space, being in charge of personal and medical care, and making sure the person eats and takes medication. An estate conservator is given the right to handle financial matters and make financial decisions.

To establish a conservatorship, a petition must be filed at probate court and contain relevant facts regarding the need for a conservatorship. A court investigator will speak to the prospective conservatee, after which a hearing will be held to select a conservator. A conservator is usually a family member, although a friend or financial professional may also be appointed. You may need an attorney if there are any disputes about who should be named the conservator. The conservatorship lasts as long as the person needs it, or until his or her death.

There are two basic types of personal conservatorships: the general probate conservatorship (or guardianship in some states, regardless of the age of the person), which is for adults who are unable to tend to their own needs, as discussed previously; and the limited probate conservatorship, which is set up to care for a developmentally disabled person.

One type of probate conservatorship is the mental health conservatorship. This is set up for a person who is so gravely disabled by a severe psychiatric disorder that he or she is unable to handle day-to-day activities. These disorders may include (but are not limited to) bipolar disorder, clinical depression, obsessive compulsive disorder, or schizophrenia.

For additional information about conservatorships, contact a conservatorship attorney.

GUARDIANSHIP

In this type of arrangement, a person (the "guardian") is designated to look after the needs of another individual (the "ward"). As with a conservatorship, the guardian makes decisions related to the health and safety of the ward, much like he or she would do for a minor child, although it's possible to be named a guardian for a mentally or physically incapacitated adult. A court oversees the establishment and administration of a guardianship, and an investigator will visit the ward and gather information about the guardian. If approved, the guardian is required to provide an annual accounting of income and expenses to the court.

CANADA

WILL

A will is a legal document that tells people after you've died exactly where you want your money and your possessions to go. You may choose to leave everything to your spouse or your children; or you may want bequests made to a favorite university, charity, or other organization. In any event, you need to do some advance planning to make sure everything you've worked for so hard in your life goes to the people or organizations you have chosen.

If you die without a will, you are said to be *intestate* (literally, without a will). This is not an optimal situation for you or your heirs, since the province/territory in which you resided will step in and decide how to distribute your assets for you. This will happen even if you've told someone to expect an inheritance or if you have written some notes about who should get your assets. In addition, it can take a long time to get the will processed and the estate released to your heirs.

Here's what usually happens. Your province/territory of residence will award the first $50,000 of your estate to your surviving spouse. Whatever remains is divided up between your spouse and children. If you don't have a spouse or children, your parents are next in line to inherit your estate, followed by your brothers and sisters. If no heir is found, then your entire legacy will be escheated, or forfeited, to the province or territory. That means a worthy organization that you might have wanted to support would get nothing.

The way to avoid all these problems is to create an estate plan, which will include a will. You should do this even if your estate is very modest. After all, your heirs may be counting on having your assets to survive after you're gone. You don't want the government to take something your heirs are entitled to.

Always engage the services of an attorney to draw up a will for you so you can be sure it is valid and your heirs will not have any trouble claiming your assets. He or she will make sure the will contains the proper wording and is signed properly.

The three types of wills that are recognized in Canada are the following:

1. **Last Will and Testament:** This document details your bequests and must be typed and signed by you in front of two witnesses who are not your beneficiaries or the spouses of your beneficiaries.
2. **Notarial Will:** This will is just like a last will and testament but is used only in Quebec. It must be prepared by a notary, then is signed before the notary and at least one witness.
3. **Holographic Will:** This type of will is prepared by you in your own handwriting and is signed without the presence of witnesses. If you are about to take your last breath and don't have a will, this is better than nothing. But some provinces/territories don't even recognize a holographic will as valid, so it's always better to do some advance planning and have your will created and executed properly before you need it.

TRUSTS

A trust is a legal document used in estate planning that transfers some or all of your assets to your heirs either while you're alive or after your death. It's more ironclad than a will, because it can't be legally challenged. A trust also lets you avoid probate, which can be advantageous if you don't want the particulars about the size of your estate to become known publicly.

There are several types of trusts. Among them are the revocable living trust, which can be changed or revoked (cancel) at any time while you're alive. If your spouse is also named as an administrator of the trust (as in the case of joint ownership of a business), he or she can continue to manage the trust after your death.

Living trusts are beneficial, because they allow you to see how your heirs are benefiting from your money, like grandchildren who use the money for college. However, the income from this type of trust is taxed at the same rate as your personal income tax rate, which is the highest marginal rate of tax possible (usually 39 to 47 percent). That can take a hefty bite out of the proceeds. For this reason, Canadians often opt for a testamentary trust instead, which is a personal trust that operates after the death of the person who establishes it. It's taxed at the personal provincial tax rate, which is much lower than the federal tax rate.

Two more trusts include the alter-ego trust and the joint-spousal trust. They're advantageous, because they allow beneficiaries to avoid capital gains taxes altogether. Speak to your tax advisor for more information.

POWER OF ATTORNEY

A power of attorney (POA) is a legal document that designates who can make decisions for you if you are physically or mentally incapacitated and unable to speak for yourself. The POA doesn't prevent you from taking care of your own affairs while you're still capable; rather, it's a contingency plan, or something that exists just in case it's needed.

There are two types of powers of attorney (POAs) granted in Canada (although please note that the names may differ depending on which province/ territory you live). The power of attorney for personal care is set up so someone can make personal care decisions for you if you are mentally incapacitated and unable to speak for yourself. This person is usually a spouse, relative, or friend, and some of those decisions may relate to deciding where you'll live, who will take care of you, and what type of health care you'll receive.

The person you appoint is known as your attorney for personal care. He or she does not have to be a lawyer and does not act as your legal counsel in any way. He or she can make decisions only about your personal care, and only if you are unable to make those decisions yourself. It's always a good idea to put your wishes in writing so the attorney for personal care will have some guidance about how to act on your behalf.

The second type of POA is the power of attorney for property. This POA gives permission to the person of your choice, called the attorney for property, to make decisions about and manage your finances on your behalf.

You can select anyone to be your attorney for property. Most commonly, a spouse, other relative, or friend is designated, but you also can choose your accountant, lawyer, or solicitor (someone who actually practices law), or your trust company if you wish. (There may be a fee for this service; always ask in advance.) You may appoint more than one person to act as your joint POA attorney, but each person must agree with the others' decisions, so having more than one could be a problem.

Your POA for property can do everything from paying bills and managing your bank accounts, to filing tax returns and selling your home on your behalf. However, your POA for property doesn't have the authority to make decisions about your personal care. If you wish to have the same person look after your finances and your personal care, you must create a separate POA for personal care, except in New Brunswick, where only a single form is necessary.

The POA agreement must be signed and witnessed by two people unrelated to you. Unless your financial affairs are complicated, you don't need a lawyer to create a POA for you. You can find a booklet with more information about POAs and the forms you'll need to set them up at the Ontario Ministry of the Attorney General's website at attorneygeneral.jus.gov.on.ca/english/justice-ont/estate_planning.asp. (Select your language, then search for "power of attorney kit.") You also can call (416) 314-2800, (800) 366-0335, or TTY: (416) 314-2687. The information and forms are generic enough to be used in any province/territory.

Advance Health Care Directive

Also known as a living will or a power of attorney for health care (not to be confused with a power of attorney for personal care, discussed above), an advance health care directive is a document that records your wishes if you become ill, incapacitated, or mentally incompetent and unable to communicate your wishes about the medical treatment you consent to receive. The advance directive usually covers such issues as whether you wish to be kept alive by artificial means (resuscitative intervention) in the case of a catastrophic cardiac event or brain injury.

You don't have to name anyone to look after you when you have an advance directive. Rather, you just need to sign and date an advance directive form, have it witnessed by two people not related to you, then give copies to your spouse, family, doctor, and other trusted individuals. You can find a free copy of the form online at ag.ca.gov/consumers/pdf/AHCDS1.pdf.

Proxy Directive

This is a document that combines both an advance directive and a power of attorney. Refer to the previous discussions about advance directives and powers of attorney for more information.

Adult Guardianship

Sometimes, it's necessary to legally name a person to look after the welfare of an adult (usually elderly) who has become physically or mentally incapacitated. If he or she hasn't named an attorney for personal care or property (as discussed earlier), the court can be petitioned to create an adult guardianship to care for that person.

There are two types of guardianships: guardianship of the person (to handle personal care, living arrangements, and health care), and guardianship of the estate (to handle finances, manage investments, and so on). Typically, the same person fulfills both roles. The guardian usually is a spouse, family member, or other responsible adult, but if no one is available to assume the role, a judge may designate a person or an organization instead. Alternately, a trust company may be appointed to look after the financial needs of the person.

Guardianship of a Minor

A guardianship of a minor arrangement is Canada's way of protecting minors from abuse and exploitation. An adult may apply to act as the guardian for a child under the age of majority who does not have or is unaccompanied by his or her parents. This includes children under the age of seventeen who come to Canada to study, as well as refugees who land in Canada and are separated from their parents. In addition, a parent or parents who can no longer care for their minor child(ren) may also request a guardianship.

The age of majority varies by province/territory. The age of majority is eighteen in Alberta, Manitoba, Ontario, Prince Edward Island, Quebec, and Saskatchewan; and nineteen in British Columbia, New Brunswick, Newfoundland, Nova Scotia, Northwest Territories, Nunavut, and Yukon.

The court usually first tries to place such children in the home of a close relative. If that's not possible or if the child's parents reside in his or her country of origin, the child becomes the ward of a children's aid society until the court makes a placement that is in the best interests of the child. However, the minor child is consulted and is allowed to express his or her opinion about the proposed living arrangements.

This is just a brief summary of the types of legal documents and arrangements in both the United States and Canada. For specific advice about your particular situation, consult with a qualified attorney.

Naming an Executor Best Practices

Being named the executor of someone's estate is a matter of pride and honor, but it's also a lot of work and requires a substantial time commitment. Therefore, when you're considering who to name as the executor of your estate, ask yourself:

Will the person I've chosen have enough time to take on the task, especially on top of his or her other work and family commitments?

Is he or she organized enough to prepare the required documents and records accurately and completely?

Does he or she have the patience, temperament, and tact necessary to deal with the people involved in the estate, as well as all the hassles and frustrations inherent in handling diverse legal and financial matters?

Chapter 22: Retirement Strategies

When most people think about retirement planning, they think of retirement accounts, and scrimping and saving now so they'll have enough money to live on later. This can be a challenge for people who are in the "sandwich years"—a time when they're paying college tuition for or otherwise supporting one or more children, while helping aging parents with their costly medical needs.

But while the savings part of retirement planning certainly is of paramount importance, there are other issues you'll face when retirement age looms. In this chapter, you'll read about the savings issues, resources, and decisions you'll have to make when you finally decide to say goodbye to your work life. After all, you want to ensure your golden years—*aka* your retirement years—don't end up being made out of lead instead.

THE REALITY

According to the U.S. Department of Labor:

- Fewer than half of Americans have calculated how much they need to save for retirement.
- In 2012, 30 percent of private industry workers with access to a defined contribution plan (such as a 401(k) plan) did not participate.
- The average American spends twenty years in retirement.

The situation isn't any better in Canada. Statistics Canada says that just 24 percent of eligible tax filers contributed to an RRSP account, a type of retirement account, in a recent year. In addition, they're saving only 4 percent of their personal disposal income.

Financial experts in both the United States and Canada estimate that people will need 70 percent of their preretirement income—or up to 90 percent for low-income earners—to maintain their standard of living when they do finally retire. On the other hand, Fidelity Investments recommends having a minimum of eight times your salary in various savings vehicles before moving into retirement. Either way you look at it, that's a scary figure considering the low levels of savings among baby boomers on both sides of the border. But the good news is, by saving and cutting expenses now, you can at least improve your chances of having money to support yourself after retirement.

WHEN TO RETIRE

The full retirement age in the United States is sixty-six for people born after 1938, and sixty-seven for people born after 1957, although it's possible to start claiming reduced Social Security benefits beginning at age sixty-two (more on that later). In Canada, the retirement age is sixty-five. Generally speaking, retirement is voluntary, although there are exceptions. In the United States, for example, the mandatory age of retirement is sixty-five for airline pilots, while air traffic controllers must retire at age fifty-six. In addition, most federal law-enforcement officers, national park rangers, and firefighters have a mandatory retirement age of fifty-seven.

For everyone else, though, the age at which you retire is a matter of choice. Sometimes that choice is driven by personal or family medical issues; sometimes a need to relocate may force retirement. But more often than not, people are retiring later, because they simply haven't saved enough to retire comfortably.

If you're in that position, you may end up holding on to your full-time job for many years past the official retirement age—perhaps as late as age seventy or beyond. That's fine as long as you're physically able, but it's not unusual for people in their sixties to start experiencing health-care problems, which makes working difficult, if not impossible. So you may find yourself in a position where you have to retire to attend to your own or your spouse's health-care needs.

If that day comes, but you still need a paycheck to make ends meet, you might consider taking a part-time job instead. Just keep in mind that landing a job is not necessarily a sure thing, and, in fact, can be more difficult as you age. Alternately, you might start your own business. This is an especially good option if you have a skill from your work life that can be parlayed into self-employment.

The bottom line is it might be wiser to retire later rather than sooner so you have more time to save and otherwise prepare financially. In addition, a paper presented recently at the Alzheimer's Association International Conference suggested that the risk of getting dementia decreased by more than 3 percent for every year worked past retirement age. It's something to think about.

RETIREMENT FUNDING OPTIONS

In addition to accruing savings from a full-time job or other sources, planning for your financial future is key to a solvent retirement. Here are some of the sources of income you may have already or could establish to build a retirement nest egg.

Company-Sponsored Pension

It wasn't so long ago that the majority of employers, large and small, offered a company-sponsored pension to reward employees who stayed with the company for a set number of years. Those who met the length of stay requirement—most often a minimum of five years—were said to be vested in the company's retirement plan. But in the United States, at least, all that changed when new pension rules were put into place in 2003 by the Clinton Administration. This led to the phasing out or the total elimination of pension benefits by many companies.

North of the border, Statistics Canada reported in a recent year that just 38 percent of Canadians had company-sponsored pension plans. That leaves almost two-thirds of Canadians without a pension and makes them responsible for saving for their retirement in other ways.

As a result, if you have a company-sponsored pension in either country, you're one of the fortunate few. It may be a good idea to hold onto your present job longer for that reason alone.

There are two types of pension plans: the defined benefit plan, in which the employer contributes a set amount each month to an employee retirement fund, which is managed by a plan administrator; and the defined contribution benefit plan, in which employees make investment decisions about the money in their own retirement account. In effect, this puts the onus on employees to make the right investment decisions, something they might not be qualified to do.

If your retirement plan is set up so your employer will match your contribution, by all means maximize the amount you contribute, if at all possible, so your money will grow twice as fast.

SOCIAL SECURITY (UNITED STATES)

Social Security is a government-run system that serves as a source of income for retirees and disabled Americans. It also serves as a source of income for the beneficiary of a retiree who dies. It is not meant to be the primary source of income, however; it is meant to supplement a person's personal savings and investments.

According to the National Academy of Social Insurance (NASI), approximately 158 million Americans pay Social Security taxes, and 57 million people collected monthly benefits in 2013. The Academy estimates that about 25 percent of the households in the United States receive income from Social Security.

The program is key to keeping people out of poverty, although the amount paid out may just keep their heads above water, so to speak. NASI says that in 2013, the average monthly benefit for retired workers was $1,264 a month. The maximum benefit for someone retiring at the full retirement age of sixty-six in 2013 was $2,533 a month.

The amount you receive is calculated on your lifetime earnings. Social Security uses the thirty-five years of your life in which you earned the most money to arrive at this number. The resulting figure is the amount you would receive if you wait until your full retirement age to start collecting. That could be sixty-five, sixty-six, or sixty-seven, depending on the year you were born.

Social Security has a retirement estimator you can use to get a general idea of how much you might receive in benefits after you retire. Calculations are based on your age at retirement, income, and factors such as military service, railroad employment, or benefits earned on work for which you were not required to pay Social Security tax. The estimator tool can be found at ssa.gov/estimator. You'll need your Social Security number to access the estimator.

It's possible to start collecting Social Security as early as age sixty-two. However, if you do start collecting early, your benefits will be reduced a fraction of a percent for each month before your full retirement age—and you never recover the lost benefit amount.

If you were born in 1943 through 1954 with a full retirement age of sixty-six, the retirement benefit would be reduced a full 25 percent if you started collecting early. To see the effect of collecting early on a $1,000 monthly retirement benefit, see the chart at socialsecurity.gov/retire2/agereduction.htm. To maximize your benefit, you should defer collecting benefits as long as possible. You may defer applying for benefits until as late as age seventy.

Another thing that can reduce your benefit amount is if you have a pension for work you did that was not covered by Social Security. Federal civil service jobs as well as some jobs at the state and local level (such as law enforcement jobs) may fall into this category.

Continuing to work while you are collecting Social Security benefits may also reduce your benefit amount. In 2013, Americans were allowed to earn $15,120 in gross wages or net self-employment wages and still earn the full benefit amount. Any income earned above that amount reduces benefits by $1 for every $2 earned. To get an idea of the effect of your earnings on your Social Security benefit, use the retirement earnings test calculator at ssa.gov/ OACT/COLA/RTeffect.html.

Although many people don't pay federal income tax on their Social Security benefits, you may have to if you have substantial taxable income like wages, self-employment income, interest, and dividends on investments. Form SSA-1099 will show the amount of the benefits you received in a tax year, and will help you determine whether you must pay federal income taxes. Generally speaking, however, if your Social Security benefits are your only source of income, you won't have to pay income taxes on them.

Although you can apply in person at any Social Security office, it's easier to apply online at ssa.gov/planners/about.htm. The entire process takes about fifteen minutes. When you are within three months of age sixty-five, you can apply for Social Security and Medicare (discussed later in this chapter) at the same time.

OLD AGE SECURITY (CANADA)

People who meet Canadian legal status and residency requirements are eligible to receive an Old Age Security (OAS) pension in Canada. It's available to most people over the age of sixty-five and is not based on employment history. In fact, even if you have never worked or you are currently working, you are still eligible for OAS. However, you must have lived in Canada for at least ten years after the age of eighteen to qualify. If you currently reside outside Canada but lived in the country for at least twenty years after the age of eighteen, you'll qualify to receive OAS.

You can defer receiving your OAS pension for up to sixty months after you become eligible to receive it. Delaying payments may be advantageous, because you'll be eligible for a higher monthly premium.

For more information about OAS benefits, go to the Service Canada website at servicecanada.gc.ca/eng/services/pensions/oas/pension/index.shtml.

MEDICARE (UNITED STATES)

This is the government's health insurance program for people age sixty-five and older. It helps with the cost of medical care but doesn't cover everything. For an in-depth discussion of Medicare, see Chapter 20, or go to socialsecurity.gov/pubs/EN-05-10043.pdf and download a booklet that should answer all your questions.

MEDICARE (CANADA)

Canada's Medicare system covers people of all ages. There is no need to apply for benefits when you retire; you're automatically covered.

Retirement Best Practices

It's crucial to plan for your "golden years" so you have as many years as possible to save the funds you'll need for a comfortable retirement. Here are some tips to get you started:

Find a financial advisor you can trust. This can be a registered investment advisor at a brokerage firm or an independent financial planner. If you choose the latter, it's usually best to work with a certified financial planner (CFP), since he or she has specialized training in personal finance. Ask relatives, friends, and coworkers for referrals, or contact your bank or attorney for leads, then check references.

Take the advice of your financial advisor. Naturally, you may not always agree with what he or she proposes. But if you knew everything there was to know about finances, you wouldn't need financial guidance. So listen carefully and make rational decisions based on the advice you receive.

Start with small investments if that's all you can afford to set aside. Over time, even small balances grow nicely due to interest compounding, which means interest is paid on accumulated interest. Depending on the rate of interest, compounding can result in some serious increases in your savings.

Increase the amount you invest when your income goes up. In fact, when you get a raise, consider putting the entire extra amount right into savings.

Pay yourself first. When your paycheck comes in, make sure a set amount flows right back out into your investment accounts. If you wait until after you've paid your bills, taken that trip to Paris, or otherwise earmarked those funds, you'll find that there's nothing left at the end of the month and you won't save anything. Set up recurring electronic transfers from your account right to your investment accounts to guarantee that saving is always going on.

Diversify your financial holdings. While 401(k) plans and IRAs in the United States and RRSPs in Canada (all discussed later) are safe investments, you may be able to grow your retirement money faster by investing in the stock market, buying municipal bonds, or making other investments. Just be aware that not all investments have a guaranteed rate of return, which is another reason why it's good to diversify.

Never cash out a 401(k) when you change jobs. Instead, preserve your retirement assets by leaving them in your previous employer's plan, or rolling over (transferring) the funds into a new account or the plan offered by your new employer (if it's an option). Always roll funds over directly to the new financial institution to stay on the IRS's good side.

RETIREMENT ACCOUNTS

UNITED STATES

The U.S. has a wide range of financial instruments to help you save for retirement. Four of the most common types of retirement plans are listed here:

- Individual Retirement Arrangements (IRAs): These are accounts created specifically for retirement savings. There are four types of IRAs: traditional IRAs, Roth IRAs, SIMPLE IRAs, and SEP IRAs. Any taxpayer can establish a traditional IRA and/or a Roth IRA. Contributions made to a traditional IRA are usually tax-deductible, but distributions (withdrawals) are taxed. However, since funds are intended to be withdrawn after a person retires and is earning less, they're usually taxed at a lower rate. Roth IRA contributions, on the other hand, are not tax-deductible, so eligible distributions are tax-free.

- The amount you can contribute annually to a traditional or Roth IRA varies depending on factors like whether or not you are covered by a retirement plan at work. For more information, contact your tax advisor, or visit the IRA deduction limits page at irs.gov/Retirement-Plans/IRA-Deduction-Limits.

- SEPs and SIMPLEs: These are IRAs that are established by employers who are typically small business owners. Both allow you to contribute a set percentage of your income, up to a certain amount every year. The limit for a SEP is 25 percent of your compensation, or $52,000, in 2014. The limit for employee contributions to a SIMPLE IRA is $12,000 in 2014.

- If you set up an IRA, you should treat it like a piggy bank, not a cash machine. Although it's always possible that some life event could come along that would require you to tap into your IRA, the penalty for withdrawing funds before the age of 59 ½ is steep—10 percent at publication time—plus you'll immediately have to pay income tax on the amount you withdraw. So it's best to deposit only the funds you know you won't need immediately.

- To learn more about IRAs, talk to your tax advisor or go to the IRS website at :
  www.irs.gov/Retirement-Plans/Individual-Retirement-Arrangements-(IRAs)-1
- 401(k) plans: This is a type of profit-sharing plan that allows employees to contribute a certain amount of their earnings for long-term growth. In some cases, employers contribute to employees' accounts in lieu of contributions to a traditional pension plan. The amount you contribute annually is excluded from your taxable income, thus reducing the amount of tax you'll pay on your annual tax return, but the distributions are fully taxable when you start making withdrawals after retirement.
- Consider 401(k) plans as hands-off savings vehicles. But if you really must tap into your account to cover an emergency situation, it's almost always best to see if your employer offers a loan option so you don't have to take a hardship distribution. If you borrow against your 401(k), you can repay the funds over time just like you would a bank loan. But you don't have to pay taxes on the funds as long as the full amount of the loan is repaid. If you take a hardship withdrawal, you're liable for income taxes on the distribution and you can't replace the money in your account.

There are other types of accounts created for general purposes that you can still use to save for your retirement, although they may not have the same tax advantages. They're discussed in Chapter 13.

CANADA

Canada offers three types of retirement-friendly savings plans. They include:

- **Registered Retirement Savings Plan (RRSP):** This plan allows you to contribute pre-tax funds, which reduces your income tax. The income earned on your account remains tax-exempt as long as the funds remain in your account. You'll pay tax when you start receiving payments from the plan. You can contribute to an RRSP until December 31 of the year you turn seventy-one-years old. The amount you contribute depends on what the Canada Revenue Agency (CRA) refers to as your "contribution room." You can find your contribution limit on form T1028, which you receive after your current year tax return is processed by the CRA.

- If you're game, you can calculate your contribution room manually in Chapter 3 of the guide RRSPs and Other Registered Plans for Retirement, available from the CRA at cra-arc.gc.ca/E/pub/tg/t4040/t4040-e.html#P1168_40407, or by calling (800) 959-8281.

- **Tax-Free Savings Account (TFSA):** Touted as an easy way to save for both short- and long-term goals, the TFSA allows you to save tax-free money throughout your lifetime. If you start at age eighteen, the magic of compounding can really make the dollars in your account add up. The annual TFSA dollar limits are low—$5,500 in 2013, for example—and contributions are not tax-free. But the income earned and withdrawals are usually tax-free. There are restrictions. For more information, see the CRA website at cra-arc.gc.ca/tfsa.

- **Pooled Registered Pension Plan (PRPP):** This is a large-scale, low-cost deferred income plan that was established in 2013 for both employed and self-employed people who don't have an employer-sponsored pension plan. Funds are pooled with those of other qualified individuals across the country, which results in greater investment opportunities at lower administrative costs, according to the CRA. The fund is also portable, meaning it moves with you when you change jobs.

- **It's possible that your employer will establish a PRPP to which you can contribute.** But if you're going solo, you can open your own PRPP account at a financial institution like a bank. The amount you can contribute annually depends on your unused RRSP contribution room (discussed earlier in this chapter). Because PRPP contributions are tax-deductible, direct withdrawals are taxable.

- At the time this book was published, PRPPs were available only to employees "whose employment falls under federal jurisdiction, including banking and inter-provincial transportation, [as well as] Canadians who are employed or self-employed in the Yukon, Northwest Territories and Nunavut," according to the CRA. However, it's expected that more provincial governments will enact PRPP legislation, making plans available to more people. Check with the CRA or your financial institution to find out where things stand in your province. In the meantime, you can find more information about this savings vehicle at: www.cra-arc.gc.ca/tx/prpp-rpac/prppqa-nd-eng.html#q1.

OTHER RETIREMENT TACTICS

Maximizing the amount you contribute to retirement accounts is a reliable and sensible way to build retirement equity. But there are additional things you can do to prepare yourself for retirement. They include the following tactics:

- **Adopt the 4 percent withdrawal habit.** Financial experts say that withdrawing just 4 percent from your retirement savings for living expenses in your first year of retirement, then adding just 3 percent to that figure every year to cover the cost of inflation, will help you stretch your savings farther and prevent you from running out of money. This assumes, of course, that you have a good-sized nest egg to begin with. If your retirement savings are more modest, you'll need a different strategy.

- **Cut spending.** You may have had a great time gleefully buying whatever you wanted while you were employed. But now that you're facing retirement, it's time to put the brakes on nonessential spending. You don't have to save every nickel from now on, but if you spend wisely, you'll have more money to pay your household bills, buy groceries, and enjoy life for a longer period of time. In addition, you should make a budget and stick to it so you don't overspend.

- **Pay down debt.** Consumer debt is more like consumer death —the only ones thriving are the credit card companies. High interest charges erode your savings and worse yet, if all you pay every month is the minimum balance, it literally can take you a decade to pay off even small debts. So if possible, use some of your savings to pay off your high interest credit cards. The 1.5 percent return you'll get on money parked in the bank is no match for the 18 percent or more you're paying on revolving debt. Pay it off and you'll keep more of your money in the long run.

- **Convert nondeductible debt into deductible debt.** In the United States, the only deductible interest option you have is on your mortgage. So if you have a lot of unsecured loans or credit-card debt, consider getting a second mortgage or line of credit and using those funds to pay off higher interest debts. But if you do this, you absolutely must cut up the credit cards, close your other revolving credit accounts, and resist opening new accounts. If you don't, you run the risk of racking up charges all over again, and you'll be even farther behind than before.

- **Downsize your life.** Cut expenses ruthlessly. Reduce your cellular phone bill by dropping data plans and use calling cards instead to make long-distance calls. Drop premium channels and DVRs (digital video recorders) from your cable service. Borrow best-sellers from the library rather than buying them, or buy Kindle versions, which generally are as much as 25 percent less expensive. Lease a smaller car when your current lease expires, or buy a well-maintained used car. Physically downsize your possessions by purging your home of things you don't use or wear anymore. Sell new and gently used items in a garage sale or on eBay or Craigslist (where you'll earn a little pocket money), and then donate the rest.

- **Downsize your home.** If you're now an empty nester (meaning the children have all moved out), you probably don't need that four-bedroom house anymore—not to mention, you probably don't want to clean and otherwise maintain such a leviathan anyway. Find a smaller home more suited to your smaller family. In fact, you may even find that renting an apartment or condo is a better choice for you now. If you free up all the money you used to sink into a big mortgage and taxes, you can save more money while having enough disposable income for living expenses.

- **Move to a city with a lower cost of living.** This can be a good option for reducing costs, although the emotional cost of leaving family and friends behind may not be worth the savings. But if this is a viable option, start your search on the internet. You can find plenty of information related to the cost of living in major cities so you can make an informed decision.

- **Reassess your retirement dreams.** Maybe you had big plans to travel or build a new house when you retired. But you may find that these dreams are no longer as tempting. Quiet afternoons spent reading, volunteering at a hospital, or visiting friends may hold more appeal now. Consider what's really important to you now and adjust your dreams.

- **Start your own business.** If you have a skill from your former profession that can be spun off into a freelance or consulting job, consider using it to create a business of your own. Project management, writing, graphic design, website development, and bookkeeping are just some of the skills you can use to keep busy, earn some cash, and feel needed.

- **Work part-time.** Many people retire, then find they're completely bored. Think about it—if you're in reasonably good health, you probably can expect to live another twenty to thirty years in retirement. How much golfing can you reasonably do in the next two decades, or how many years of reruns can you watch on the SciFi channel? A part-time job doing something you enjoy can keep you energized and revitalized. It doesn't have to be a professional job. If you'd enjoy greeting people at Wal-Mart or serving Egg McMuffins at the drive-thru window, then that's better than sitting at home with nothing to do. And of course, some part-time jobs come with health care benefits that are much appreciated in retirement. If that's not an option, at the very least you can use your earnings to help cover the cost of the health-care benefits you are probably now paying yourself.

ATTA'S LESSONS

There's an expression that growing older isn't for the faint of heart. Most of the time, we only think about the physical limitations that come with advanced age, but for immigrants, it goes much deeper than that. Think of it this way. People in their native, secure environment can carry on and plan for retirement with relative ease. But it's a totally a different ball game for immigrants who may have to leave their native countries during middle age or their senior years and start life over in a brand-new environment without any financial security. It can be very scary.

The answer is to plan for the future, which can be difficult if you're starting a new life from scratch. I know this from firsthand experience. When I first came to the United States, I talked to the financial consultant at my bank branch right away about the various retirement fund options available to me. This was at a time when I was struggling financially and trying to rescue my big family from refugee conditions. I started with the minimum automatic deductions despite being in a very difficult financial situation. This is why I talk so much about and promote the idea of saving and planning for retirement. Immigrants and millions of other people in this country cannot and should not count on retirement support from the government. It's up to us to fund our retirement years on our own.

Retirement Account Worksheet

Note the details about all your accounts here for easy reference.

Pension	Balance	Investment Types
1.		
2.		
3.		
401(K) Accounts		
1.		
2.		
3.		
4.		

Chapter 23: The Elder Years

Some people refuse to face reality and prefer to ignore it completely. Others attempt to change their faces and sculpt their bodies through surgery to look more youthful. But the reality is, every day you're growing older, and one day, you're going to be a senior citizen.

The game changes when you reach your elder years. Not only will you be unable to do or may be disinterested in things that always came easily to you in your younger days; eventually, you're also going to need services and assistance with daily life. This chapter addresses some of the social needs you, your spouse, and possibly your aging parents may already have or will have in the future, and presents strategies for dealing with them. The U.S. and Canadian resources are discussed separately. For information about financial and legal preparation for your senior years, refer to Chapters 13 and 21.

LONG-TERM CARE: A DEFINITION

Many people mistakenly believe that "long-term care" refers only to medical insurance that covers you if you get sick or become disabled in your later years. But while medical insurance certainly is part of the long-term care model, the term actually refers to the range of daily services you may need to manage your day-to-day activities, legal matters, and social status, in addition to your medical care.

Here are the basic personal tasks the U.S. Administration on Aging (AoA) says you need to consider as part of a long-term care plan:

- Bathing
- Dressing
- Using the toilet
- Transferring to or from a bed or chair
- Caring for incontinence issues (inability to hold urine or feces)
- Eating

The AoA says you also need to make plans for assistance with what it calls "Instrumental Activities of Daily Living"; these include the following activities:

- Doing housework
- Managing money
- Taking medication
- Preparing and cleaning up after meals
- Shopping for groceries and clothes
- Using the telephone and other communication devices
- Caring for pets
- Responding to emergency alerts, such as fire alarms

Deciding who will help with these tasks is part of the long-term-care process. And, of course, you also may need to make the same decisions for your parents, spouse, and other loved ones.

If you or your loved ones haven't done any long-term-care planning, you're not alone. But the fact is, the AoA says that 70 percent of people aged sixty-five and up will one day need some form of long-term care in their senior years. (In Canada, the figure is estimated to be 40 percent.) Chronic conditions like diabetes and high blood pressure make you even more likely to need help and at an earlier age. In addition, if you're female, you'll need care for a longer period of time (since women outlive men); people who live alone also tend to need help sooner. Finally, if your diet is poor or you don't exercise, your chances of needing long-term-care services increase significantly.

HAVE "THE TALK" WITH RELATIVES

If you have relatives at or beyond senior citizen age already—or you're facing that milestone yourself—now is the time to discuss long-term-care-planning ideas and instructions. It's usually difficult to discuss these matters with loved ones, because they're such emotional issues. Older people are afraid of losing their independence and using up their remaining assets, so they may prefer to ignore anything related to elder care. So you should reassure your loved ones that you have their best interests at heart and initiate a discussion about their long-term care and expectations. Following are some issues you should address.

Who Will Provide Care?

When a person first needs long-term-care services or doesn't require a lot of assistance yet, it may be possible for him or her to rely on community support services. These services may include meals-on-wheels programs, low- or no-cost senior transportation, and adult day care. (Adult day care is a place where older adults can go for meals and socialization during the day before returning to their own homes at night.) These programs also may provide physical and psychological assistance to disabled and mentally challenged adults, particularly those who can't be left unsupervised in their home. Family members who are the primary caregivers for an older adult may find a day care to be particularly helpful, both when they are at work and when they need a break from the rigors of long-term care.

In fact, unpaid family members and friends who are not medically trained often provide the front-line care for elderly persons, both in North America and around the world. Some estimates place the percentage of people who rely on unpaid home care providers at 80 percent. Among the tasks they undertake are food preparation, bathing, transportation to and from medical appointments, pet care, and other unskilled care.

A person who needs more advanced care may be able to rely on in-home skilled providers to attend to their daily needs. Providers may include home care nurses, who can render a higher level of medical care, including giving injections of daily medications, changing catheters, and monitoring blood-glucose levels. Home care nurses generally don't provide basic living care; rather, those services are usually provided by unskilled in-home caregivers if the elderly person doesn't or can't get assistance from a family member or friend, as discussed earlier.

Naturally, with the exception of benevolent family members and friends, all these services are fee-based. The amount the elderly person pays will depend on location and the depth of services necessary.

Where Will Care Be Provided?

Optimally, care that's delivered in the senior's home is preferable, both because he or she is more likely to feel the most comfortable and safe there, and because many seniors have mobility issues. In addition, even fee-based home care is generally less expensive than live-in programs. But when it's no longer possible for a person to live on his or her own, the next step usually is assisted living.

"Assisted living" is the term for a wide range of residential care services for senior citizens and disabled people. Choices include standalone facilities and continuing care retirement communities (CCRC), which is a term used in the United States that refers to retirement communities that provide various levels of care at the same campus. Following are the different types of assisted living situations in the United States.

INDEPENDENT LIVING RETIREMENT COMMUNITY

This is not an assisted living community per se, because its residents usually have minimal care needs, but when it's part of a CCRC, it acts as the gateway to assisted living when the need arises. Independent adults aged fifty-five and up, with few or no health care needs, often choose this lifestyle when they longer wish to take care of a home or condominium, yet want the safety and security of living in a community with the feel of a neighborhood. Residents generally live in their own private apartment (although some communities also offer single-family homes and condos), and enjoy communal services like meals, transportation, and recreational activities. They may also have access to concierge-style services (things like having dry cleaning picked up and delivered, or purchasing tickets to sporting events and cultural activities, and so on).

In Canada, this type of living situation is called independent supportive living (discussed later in this chapter).

ASSISTED LIVING

The next step in the retirement community continuum is assisted living, which combines housing for seniors, along with any support services and health care they may need. The individuals in assisted living may still be quite independent but may need help managing everyday activities like bathing, dressing, preparing meals, taking medications, and so on. They, too, reside in their own apartment, or may simply have a room in a larger residential building devoted entirely to senior citizens. Care generally is delivered right in the person's living space.

In the United States, assisted living facilities are licensed and regulated at the state level, and the services they offer may vary. Check with your state's department of health to see what services are provided.

Elder Care Best Practices

Here are some of the things you can do to ensure your elder care needs are handled properly:

- **Plan for your long-term care needs sooner rather than later.** One good option is to purchase a life insurance policy that has long-term care benefit riders. These riders cost more but definitely will help pay the cost of future long-term care.
- **Remain in your home as long as possible.** It's usually at least a little cheaper to hire home health aides to come to your home than it is to move to a retirement community.
- **Look for long-term care insurance that includes a 100 percent home-care benefit.** If you can afford it, this type of policy will preserve more of your estate. But please note that it is an expensive option.
- **Check with your tax advisor to find out which tax deductions or credits are offered by your state,** since they can help offset the cost of long-term care.
- **Talk with your financial advisor about your options if you have waited too long to plan for long-term care.**

'SPECIAL CARE UNIT'

This is an assisted living arrangement for a person with Alzheimer's disease and other types of dementia. While the person has his or her own living quarters, it generally is in a special section of an assisted living community and has additional security, like locked doors or closed circuit monitoring to protect the resident from wandering. The caregivers are specially trained to manage the care of people with these types of cognitive diseases. In Canada, these services are known as memory care (discussed later in this chapter).

'Nursing Home'

This is a facility that provides the highest level of medical and nursing care outside of the hospital setting for a group (usually three or more) of unrelated elderly people with chronic medical conditions. (Nursing homes also offer temporary convalescent care to people of all ages in the same facility.) In addition to accepting Medicare (discussed in Chapter 20), these facilities also accept private funding and long-term-care insurance.

Nursing homes generally are for the sickest senior citizens who are not expected to recover. Terminally ill people may receive hospice care while in the nursing home, which is a form of health care meant to provide pain relief and comfort (palliative care) rather than curative care during a patient's last days.

How Much Will It Cost?

In most cases, long-term care is an out-of-pocket expense. Care that is delivered 24/7 will cost the most, no matter whether it's delivered in an assisted living setting or in the senior's own home. In the United States, Medicare will pick up some of the cost of care in certain situations. For example, Medicare may cover up to a hundred days of skilled nursing home care per benefit period, but will not pay for in-home unskilled care unless you are homebound and also receiving skilled nursing care. As a result, you will have to use your savings and investments, up to and possibly including the equity in your home to pay for your care.

One way to offset some of the cost of long-term care is to purchase private long-term-care insurance. Unfortunately, this type of insurance tends to be quite expensive, and therefore may be beyond the means of many people. Supplemental insurance is less expensive, but covers far less. Still, they're worth checking into. One place to start is AARP, which offers a free Medicare supplemental insurance decision guide at golong.com (once there, click "Get a free decision guide").

OTHER SENIOR SERVICES

LONG-TERM CARE THROUGH THE U.S. DEPARTMENT OF VETERANS AFFAIRS

If you are an honorably discharged veteran of any branch of the U.S. military, you are likely to be eligible for a variety of extended care services through the U.S. Department of Veterans Affairs (VA). These services may be rendered in your home, at community sites, in residential settings, or in nursing homes. Services are paid for through VA, federal, and state funding (such as Medicare), personal insurance, and savings. For more information, visit the VA long-term care site at va.gov/GERIATRICS/Guide/LongTermCare/Paying_for_Long_Term_Care.asp, call (877) 222-VETS (8387), or contact your VA social worker.

LOW-INCOME/SUBSIDIZED HOUSING

Low-income senior citizens may qualify to live in a senior housing complex subsidized by the U.S. Department of Housing and Urban Development (HUD). You have to meet certain income requirements, and the rent is paid directly to the landlord for you. For more information about low-rent apartments, go to hud.gov/apps/section8 and search for your state. You also may call (800) FED-INFO (800) 333-4636), or TTY (800) 483-2209.

Subsidized housing is just that—a place to live. If you need assistance with daily tasks or any of the other types of nursing care discussed here, you must make separate arrangements.

MEDICAL MONITORING

You've probably seen the TV commercials where a senior citizen is shown on the floor in obvious distress, and calls out, "I've fallen and I can't get up!" What those commercials are selling is a personal home emergency response system consisting of a necklace with a panic button that can be pushed to call for help. Technology like this, as well as services like Xfinity Home Control (available through Comcast), which allow you to view real-time video of the activities in your home from a remote location, are good ways to help seniors shelter in place for as long as possible. As you can imagine, these services are not inexpensive, but they can give you a lot of peace of mind if you're a concerned relative, or if you need the assistance yourself.

ELDER CARE IN CANADA

Canada offers basically the same services and options as those found in the United States, although they may have different names or vary by province/territory.

HOME CARE

Rendered in the senior's home, this type of care can include everything from unskilled assistance with daily tasks (housekeeping, meal preparation, errands, and so on) to skilled nursing care. In-home care tends to be less expensive than independent living, the next level of long-term care, unless care is required 24/7. Then the cost of care may rival that of independent living.

INDEPENDENT LIVING/INDEPENDENT SUPPORTIVE LIVING

Seniors who have minimal health care needs but wish to eliminate the burden of home ownership while remaining active in a community may enjoy an independent community. Available services like housekeeping, meals, and laundry, coupled with a full slate of activities, make this an ideal situation for active seniors. Independent living communities usually offer apartment-style living in tranquil settings.

ASSISTED LIVING

Also known as retirement care, assisted living care is rendered to individuals who need assistance with daily tasks. Typically, the resident starts out in an apartment or suite in a retirement home, but as health-care needs increase, he or she eventually moves to an area designated specifically for people who need additional assistance. Living and dining areas are shared spaces, while the senior lives in a room of his or her own where medical care can be given.

LONG-TERM CARE

Other terms for long-term care include continuing care, residential care, extended care, and nursing care. These types of care are available to people who are much more dependent on outside assistance. Services offered include personal care, eating assistance, skilled nursing, and skilled medical care.

Since long-term care falls under and is funded by the provincial/territorial governments, it's not covered by the *Canada Health Act* (discussed in Chapter 12). Private pay long-term care is allowed in some provinces, and copays for room and board vary by jurisdiction.

MEMORY CARE

This is a type of long-term, residential care for persons with Alzheimer's and other forms of dementia who need a safe, supportive environment. The level of care increases as the resident's condition progresses, and the ratio of caregivers to patients is much higher than with other types of assisted living. The residences feature secured exits and visual cues like pictures and signs to orient the person with dementia to his or her surroundings. This is one of the most expensive forms of long-term care.

OTHER SENIOR SERVICES

VETERANS INDEPENDENCE PROGRAM AND LONG-TERM CARE

According to Veterans Affairs Canada, military service pensioners who are residents of Canada are eligible for "VIP services of home care, ambulatory health care, home adaptations, or immediate care in a community facility other than a contract bed." They also may be eligible for long-term care, provided it is rendered in Canada in a community facility rather than only in a contract bed, and an assessment shows this is the best type of care for his or her condition. Other conditions apply. For more information, visit the "Eligibility for Health Care Programs—Military Service Pensioner" page at veterans.gc.ca/eng/department/policy/document/1024.

RENT SUBSIDIES

At the time this book was written, the Canadian government had ended funding for rent-geared-to-housing-assistance subsidies and was considering a move to a cost-share rent program for low-income persons who live in co-op and nonprofit housing. Subsidies began expiring in 2013 and are expected to disappear completely by 2015. The details about what, if anything, might replace this type of social housing are not firm. Until decisions are made, you can monitor the situation by visiting the Canada Mortgage and Housing Corporation website at cmhc-schl.gc.ca/en/corp/about.

MEDICAL ALERT SYSTEMS

These systems consist of a small, waterproof pendant worn around the neck that sends a wireless signal to a monitoring station when the alert button is pressed. They're a good way to help elderly people who shelter-at-home feel more secure that they'll get help and medical attention if they fall or are otherwise injured.

ADDITIONAL GOVERNMENT RESOURCES

The Canadian government offers a variety of federal, provincial, and territorial resources for seniors. To find out what services are available in your area, visit seniors.gc.ca/eng/sb/ie/index.shtml and click on your province or territory. You can download a free senior living guide at the same site that covers everything from senior services to Old Age Security and the Canada Pension Plan. Alternately, you may call 211 locally for information in more than 150 languages, or (800) O-Canada (800-622-6232) to speak to a senior services agent.

ELDER ABUSE

It's an unfortunate reality that because the elderly are frailer and may not have full possession of their faculties as they age, they can easily become victims of abuse. This abuse may come in the form of physical abuse inflicted by a family member or paid caregiver who takes out frustrations on the elderly person; it could be in the form of an attack like a robbery or carjacking; or it may be due to a scam or other type of fraud perpetrated by someone who wishes to steal money and possessions from the elderly person, or defraud them of their life savings. Elder abuse may also manifest itself as sexual, verbal, emotional, and psychological abuse.

One way seniors can be protected is by securing a guardian arrangement (discussed in Chapter 21) that puts a responsible and caring individual in control of their care and finances to safeguard them.

Another way to protect seniors is to be vigilant and report your suspicions that abuse, neglect, or exploitation are happening to the Department of Human Services or other protective services agency in your state or province/territory, an elder-abuse hotline, or the local police. Hotline calls and other referrals are completely confidential.

Allegations of abuse are investigated promptly by an authorized inspector who will recommend a course of action to protect the individual. Actions may include removal from the abusive situation, making alternative living arrangements, counseling, providing medical and mental health assessments, offering financial management assistance, and more.

Self-neglect is another type of elder abuse, even if it's self-inflicted. If you notice that an elderly person lacks personal hygiene, lives in an unsanitary or dirty environment, or otherwise appears to be failing to take care of himself or herself, you should consider getting help for that person. However, please note that the elderly person may refuse assistance, at which time the only things you can do are to make sure he or she has access to medical services and to continue to check on his or her well-being regularly. If the home situation deteriorates significantly, it may be necessary to seek a court-appointed guardianship so the person may be taken care of properly.

Finally, if you personally need help to stop abusing an elderly person, please seek counseling, which can help you deal with being a caregiver and its stressors better. In addition, respite care that allows you to be relieved of your responsibilities as a caregiver for a while (even for just a few hours a week) can help you cope. Taking your elderly charge to adult day care or arranging for the services of a visiting nurse are ways you can lighten the burden of care and safeguard the person for whom you're responsible.

ATTA'S LESSONS

Rapid aging, constant deterioration, and lack of proper elderly care for our parents, ourselves, and future generations, combined with an increasing influx of immigrants worldwide, makes elderly care one of the most pressing challenges facing current and future generations.

Immigrants tend to care for their elderly family members to the end, but it can be an impractical and exhausting task here in the United States and Canada. With busy lifestyles, and the rising costs of housing, medicine, and other support, even immigrants with traditional values find it difficult to keep up with the rigors of elder care. Yet our elders and their wisdom are a source of inspiration for us all. Their positive energy and spirit keeps us connected.

The next time you feel challenged to care for your elderly relatives, remember that each and every one of us faces the same fate—we will all age. The question is: how will we be treated during our elder years? The answer is it's up to you. You must roll up your sleeves and make preparations now while you're still able to. So save as much as possible, make plans for the future, and offer love and care to your elders, because one day, that will be you.

Final Words

While wealthy immigrants have the luxury to choose when to emigrate and often can select exactly where they wish to go, forced immigrants like refugees constantly find themselves as victims of long-lasting circumstances. Often, through no fault of their own, they are forced to leave their homeland, then fight an uphill battle to establish themselves in a new environment that's different from everything they know. In many cases, they cope with frustrating challenges, unfamiliar conditions, and a lack of language skills, and find themselves aimlessly maneuvering their way around in search of answers to questions they don't know how to ask.

I look at life as an immigrant as being in the wilderness in the dark, not knowing where you are, yet realizing that you're just a few hours away from town and the welcome feel of the sun shining on your face. I look at the guide you're holding as a trail map that will not only help you find your way out of that wilderness but will help direct your journey onto a path that will lead to a successful future.

Regardless of why you are in North America, where you are located, and how you want your life to turn out, your task now is to cope with the challenges of life as an immigrant in a new environment, as well as to deal with the big changes that still lie ahead. Ignoring these new realities as though they don't exist will slam you backwards and leave you without real balance in your life. What's more, getting angry about your situation or indulging in wishful thinking is a big waste of time.

Since arriving in the United States as an immigrant more than thirty-five years ago, I have seen many other immigrants thinking and talking a lot about the "the good old days," with the hope that those day will return. But, my friend, they never will. In fact, no one—not immigrants, not native-born people—can run away from the reality of change, nor is there a place to hide that is beyond the range of change. And even though we may not like change, the reality is that we are very fortunate to be here in North America. Realistically speaking, there are no better places on earth to live than the United States and Canada, where we have enormous opportunities if only we reach out for them.

One welcome change in your life is that you no longer have to dream about coming here someday. You are here! Your life now is about not having enough education or money, or about not having a good enough job. But even though there are plenty of legitimate challenges like these to overcome in your new life, there is honestly no room for excuses. The truth is, excuses are fatal to your future success. Either you move and take action now, or you sit back and waste the wonderful opportunities that will come your way.

It is a good idea to be humble in this life, but you have to be realistic, too. Not many people begin with many advantages these days. Personally speaking, I only finished high school, but I have never stopped learning and working hard since my high school days. I faced lots of frustration and hardships, just like you are facing now, but none were severe enough to stop me from accomplishing my goals. My only regrets are the occasional excuses I made and the time I may have wasted due to procrastination. Even today, I continue to make up for those lost moments and play catch up.

As a matter of fact, I remember reminding myself shortly after my arrival in the United States that every individual here, including some of the wealthiest people on earth, must have started with very little or nothing, just like me.

The bottom line is that I wrote this guide to help you make the best of your own journey. You will always be in the driver's seat. The way you think and the way you act will set the tone for the way things turn out. You may not have control over every situation you encounter, but you are indeed in control of how you respond to what happens to you next.

It is YOUR LIFE. Make it happen.

Glossary

9-to-5: a term used to signify a typical work day (9 a.m. to 5 p.m.).

911: phone number to dial to summon emergency services.

24/7: 24 hours a day, 7 days a week.

Affordable Care Act: a law that mandates that all Americans have health insurance.

Bait-and-switch: a dishonest practice in which a retailer advertises a product at a bargain price; then when a customer tries to buy it, a salesperson tries to convince the customer to buy a more expensive product instead.

Bankruptcy: a proceeding in a federal court in which a debtor's assets are liquidated and the debtor is relieved of further liability.

Beneficiary: person named to receive the proceeds of a trust, a will, or an insurance policy.

Big-ticket item: an expensive item; it can be anything from gemstone jewelry to a pricey automobile.

Biometrics: a process that uses human characteristics or traits for identification purposes; fingerprinting is an example of biometrics.

Blended family: a family that includes children from the previous marriage or relationship of one or both of the spouses (or significant others).

Boutique: a type of small store that specializes in fashionable, one-of-a-kind, often expensive items like wedding gowns, designer clothing, and jewelry.

Bricks-and-mortar store: a store with a physical location; compare with online store.

Carjack: unlawful seizure of a person's vehicle by a criminal, often when the owner is actually sitting in it.

Credit score: a measurement—usually a number—given by creditors reflecting your ability to pay back a loan.

Deductible: the amount of money you must pay out-of-pocket before an insurer will cover the rest of the approved amount.

Deportation: the act of removing an undesirable foreign national from a country against his or her will.

Depreciation: the decrease in an item's value over time.

Dual Citizenship: having legal citizenship in more than one country.

Emigrate: the act of leaving one's homeland to go to another country; compare with "immigrate."

Enhanced license: a driver's license with an endorsement that allows the bearer to travel between the United States, Canada, Mexico, and the Caribbean by land or sea; however, it cannot be used to travel by air.

ESL: an acronym for English as a second language.

Executor: a person designated to carry out the wishes and instructions of a deceased person.

Financial planner: an individual who helps you manage your investments, as well as make decisions about insurance, taxes, college, planning, retirement planning, and all other aspects of your financial life.

FAFSA: acronym for "free application for federal student aid," which is an application for student aid.

Footprint: the amount of space something takes; used to describe the amount of space a computer system takes on a desktop.

Franchise: a business that operates under a special license that allows it to use the franchisee's business model and other tools to market itself; a franchise owner is the owner of record and handles all management responsibilities, from hiring to operations.

Furniture mount system: a type of TV support system that allows a flat-screen TV to be mounted to a stable piece of furniture if a wall mount is not possible.

Graduated driver's license: a system used in North America in which drivers gain experience and skill on the road in steps; typically, new drivers earn a learner's permit, then a restricted license, then a full license.

Green card: a U.S. government-issued card given to lawful permanent residents; the card is not actually green.

Guardianship: legal arrangement in which a person is designated to look after the care and welfare of another person (and possibly pets).

HIPAA: an acronym for Health Insurance Portability and Accountability Act, a health-care privacy law that allows people to transfer and continue health-care coverage when a person changes or loses a job.

Identity theft: the act of illegally posing as another person to commit theft or fraud.

Immigrate: the act of settling in a new country; compare with "emigrate."

Internal Revenue Service (IRS): the U.S. government agency responsible for collecting federal taxes.

Jury: a group of people who listen to testimony in a civil or criminal case in a court of law and provide a verdict; most juries are composed of twelve citizens.

K-12: a term signifying kindergarten through grade 12 in the American public school system.

Lemon history: information about a vehicle's history of defects that were discovered only after it was sold.

McMansion: a negative term for a large luxury home built on a plot of land that's really too small to accommodate it.

Mess kit: a kit that contains eating utensils, cookware, plate, and dishes for use during camping trips or an emergency.

Medicaid: a joint federal and state program that helps with medical costs for some people with limited income and resources.

Medicare: the federal health insurance program for people who are sixty-five or older, as well as for certain younger people with disabilities.

Medical tourism: term used to describe those who seek medical treatment outside the country.

Mom-and-pop shop: a small business that is independently owned and operated; usually has just a few employees (often the owner and a few helpers).

Mortgage: a loan taken to purchase a home that is secured by the value of the home.

NOAA weather radio: a radio designed to monitor the National Oceanic and Atmospheric Administration for weather bulletins.

Odometer rollback: a procedure in which a person tampers with a vehicle's odometer by rolling back, or changing, the mileage to make it appear that the vehicle has fewer miles on it than were actually driven. Dishonest sellers do this to get more money for the vehicle. This is a fraudulent and illegal act in both the United States and Canada.

Online education: a way to earn an educational degree via internet classes.

Online store: a store on the internet that does not have a physical location; compare with "bricks-and-mortar store."

Outbuilding: a building separate from but associated with a main residence; in North America, outbuildings like former horse stables have been converted into carriage houses for use as homes.

Out-of-pocket: paid out of personal funds.

Peephole: a small opening in a door (usually an exterior door) that allows a person to look out without being seen.

Power of Attorney: giving another person legal authority to do transactions in your name.

Powertrain: a term for the engine, transmission, and driveshaft assembly in a vehicle.

Probate: a court order giving one or more persons the legal authority to administer the estate of a deceased person in order to distribute inheritance to the beneficiaries.

Pro bono: professional work done on a voluntary basis.

Realtor: a sales professional who specializes in home sales.

Resume: a document used to summarize your accomplishments and qualifications for a potential employer.

Revenue Canada: the Canadian agency responsible for collecting federal taxes.

Reverse chronological order: placement technique that presents events from most recent to oldest; commonly used in resume writing.

RFID: an acronym for "radio frequency identification," a type of data-collection technology that stores data.

Rush hour: the peak driving time of the day when there are a lot of vehicles on the road at the same time. Typically, the hours of 6 a.m. to 10 a.m. and 4 a.m. to 7 p.m. are considered rush hour, although in cities like Boston and Los Angeles, it may seem like rush hour is 24/7.

Sedan: a passenger vehicle with three separate sections: an engine compartment, a passenger section, and a cargo space; can be two-door or four-door.

Shelter-in-place: remaining in your home during an emergency until it is safe to venture outside again.

Shopaholic: person who shops as a fun recreational activity that in some cases resembles or becomes an addition.

Smoking cessation program: professional assistance for helping to quit the smoking habit.

Social Security card: a U.S. government program in which monetary contributions made by younger workers are used to provide money to older people.

Social Security number: the unique nine-digit number that appears on a Social Security card and is used for employment, income tax, and banking purposes.

Social Insurance: a Canadian program in which pooled money collected from younger people is distributed to older people after they retire.

Turnkey operation: a business model in which everything you need to operate the business is provided to you by a second party. This might include the building, tangibles such as inventory, or intellectual property such as business models, marketing, and sales techniques.

Immigrant Planning Resources

Use this list of handy resources to find additional information about the various topics explored in this book.

AUTOMOTIVE PURCHASES

Autotrader.com
Carfax.com
Cars.com
Craigslist.com
Edmunds.com
KBB.com

BANKING

Canada

Credit Score: ic.gc.ca/eic/site/oca-bc.nsf/eng/ca02179.html
Understanding Banking in Canada:
rbc.com/canada/welcometocanada/pdf/understanding-banking-in-canada.pdf

United States

Bankrate.com
Budgeting:
practicalmoneyskills.com/personalfinance/savingspending/budgeting
Credit Score:
experian.com/credit-education/what-is-a-good-credit-score.html
Investopedia: investopedia.com/university/banking

CITIZENSHIP RESOURCES

Canada

Birth certificate: servicecanada.gc.ca/eng/subjects/cards/birth_certificate.shtml
Come to Canada: cic.gc.ca/ctc-vac/cometocanada.asp

Driver's license: servicecanada.gc.ca
Passport: ppt.gc.ca/index.aspx

UNITED STATES
Application for Naturalization: uscis.gov/n-400
Becoming a U.S. Citizen: An Overview of the Naturalization Process (video): uscis.gov/citizenship/learners/study-test/study-materials-civics-test/becoming-us-citizen-overview-naturalization-process
A Guide to Naturalization: uscis.gov/natzguide
Ten Steps to Naturalization: uscis.gov/us-citizenship/citizenship-through-naturalization/path-us-citizenship

CREDIT RESOURCES
UNITED STATES
Bankrate.com
Federal Trade Commission: ftc.gov
Opt-out of pre-approved offers: Optoutprescreen.com

DOMAIN EXTENSIONS BY COUNTRY
domainit.com/domains/country-domains.mhtml

DOMESTIC VIOLENCE ASSISTANCE
CANADA
justice.gc.ca/eng/cj-jp/fv-vf/help-aide.html

UNITED STATES
thehotline.org

DRIVER'S LICENSE RESOURCE
Service Canada: servicecanada.gc.ca/eng/subjects/cards/drivers_licence.shtml

DRIVING DIRECTIONS
Highway Conditions (U.S., Canada): Highwayconditions.com;
National Traffic and Road Closure Information (U.S.): fhwa.dot.gov/trafficinfo;
Mapquest.com

EMERGENCY PREPAREDNESS

Contact information for disaster survivors: (800) 621-FEMA, TYY: (800) 462-7585, fema.gov

Ready.gov

National Contact Center: (800) FED-INFO

ENGLISH GRAMMAR AND USAGE RESOURCES

Academic English Café: academicenglishcafe.com

Purdue Online Writing Lab: owl.english.purdue.edu/owl

ENTITLEMENT PROGRAMS

CANADA

CanadaBenefits.gc.ca

UNITED STATES

Social Security Administration: ssa.gov

HEALTH CARE RESOURCES

CANADA

First Nations People Health Benefits:
  hc-sc.gc.ca/fniah-spnia/nihb-ssna/index-eng.php

Health Care, Refugees:
  cic.gc.ca/english/refugees/outside/arriving-healthcare.asp

Provincial/Territorial Ministries of Health:
  hc-sc.gc.ca/hcs-sss/delivery-prestation/ptrole/index-eng.php

UNITED STATES

Department of Health and Human Services: hhs.gov

HealthCare.gov

HealthSherpa.com

Long-Term Care: longtermcare.gov/the-basics/finding-local-services

Medicaid: medicare.gov/your-medicare-costs/help-paying-costs/medicaid/medicaid.html

Medicare:
  medicare.gov/sign-up-change-plans/decide-how-to-get-medicare/whats-medicare/what-is-medicare.html

HOME SCHOOLING INFORMATION
Canada
Home School Canada: homeschoolcanada.ca

United States
A2Z Homeschooling: a2zhomeschooling.com

IDENTITY THEFT INFORMATION
Identity Theft Resource Center:
  idtheftcenter.org/Protect-yourself/id-theft-prevention-tips.html

INCOME TAX AGENCIES
Canada
Canada Revenue Agency: cra-arc.gc.ca

United States
Internal Revenue Service: irs.gov

INCOME TAX PAYMENTS
Canada
My Account for Individuals: cra-arc.gc.ca/myaccount

United States
Electronic Federal Tax Payer System (EFTPS): Eftps.gov.

INSURANCE INFORMATION (GENERAL)
Canada
Insurance Bureau of Canada: ibc.ca

United States
Insurance Information Institute: iii.org

INSURANCE RATE COMPARISON TOOLS
Canada
CarInsurance.com
Esurance.com
Insurancehotline.com

Kanetix.ca
navigatorsinsurance.ca

UNITED STATES
Insure.com
iquote.com
Insweb.com
Quickquote.com
Selectquote.com

JOB HUNTING SITES (ONLINE)
CANADA
Ca.indeed.com
Eluta.ca
Monster.ca
JobBank.gc.ca
Workopolis.com

UNITED STATES
Careerbuilder.com
Geebo.com
Glassdoor.com
Indeed.com
Monster.com

LEGAL ASSISTANCE
CANADA
Service Canada: servicecanada.gc.ca/eng/subjects/law

UNITED STATES
LegalZoom.com

NATIONAL DO NOT CALL REGISTRY
CANADA
lnnte-dncl.gc.ca

UNITED STATES
Donotcall.gov

PHISHING INFORMATION
CANADA
Royal Canadian Mounted Police:
  rcmp-grc.gc.ca/scams-fraudes/phishing-eng.htm

UNITED STATES
Snopes.com
US-Cert: us-cert.gov/report-phishing

RETIREMENT
Canada Retirement Pension:
  servicecanada.gc.ca/eng/services/pensions/cpp/retirement/index.shtml
U.S. Social Security Administration: ssa.gov

SALARY COMPARISON WEBSITES
Glassdoor.com
Payscale.com
Salary.com

SEX OFFENDER REGISTRY
fbi.gov/scams-safety/registry

SMALL BUSINESS RESOURCES
CANADA
Canada Small Business Financing Program:
  ic.gc.ca/eic/site/csbfp-pfpec.nsf/eng/Home
Guide for Canadian Small Businesses: cra-arc.gc.ca/E/pub/tg/rc4070
Small Business Association Canada: sba-canada.ca

UNITED STATES
Internal Revenue Service: irs.gov
Small business and Self-Employed Tax Center (U.S.):
  irs.gov/Businesses/Small-Businesses-&-Self-Employed/
  Small-Business-and-Self-Employed-Tax-Center-1
U.S. Small Business Administration: sba.gov

STUDENT FINANCIAL AID
CANADA
Student Loans Canada: finaid.org/otheraid/canadian.phtml

UNITED STATES
Federal Student Aid: fafsa.ed.gov; studentaid.ed.gov/types/loans

U.S. Security and Exchange Commission, 529 Savings Plan:
  sec.gov/investor/pubs/intro529.htm

TRAVEL INFORMATION/MAPS
CANADA
Country Travel Advice: travel.gc.ca/travelling/advisories

Mapquest.com

UNITED STATES
Federal Highway Administration: fhwa.dot.gov

MapQuest.com

U.S. Department of State: state.gov/travel

UNEMPLOYMENT BENEFITS
In the United States, contact the unemployment agency in your state

In Canada, contact Service Canada: servicecanada.gc.ca

VEHICLE HISTORY REPORTS
Autocheck.com

Carfax.com

Appendix A

Homeschooling in North America: A Viable Option
By Marcia Williams

It is a fact that the quality of public schools in the United States has deteriorated over the course of the last few decades. Parents today would be the first to tell you that the education system is no longer the same as it was when they were going to school.

Statistics back this up. According to the Broad Foundation, a philanthropic organization dedicated to helping urban school students succeed, American public school students are seriously lagging behind. Nearly three out of four 8th and 12th grade students cannot write proficiently. More than 1.1 million students drop out every year, and the drop-out rates are close to 40 percent for African American and Hispanic students. In a recent year, the United States placed 22 out of 27 industrialized nations in terms of graduation rate. After World War II, the United States was number one.

There are many reasons why the public school system is failing our children, from a lack of resources to unqualified teachers. But boredom is another significant reason why children drop out of school. Children who don't feel challenged will stop trying and may get so far behind on their work that they can't catch up, no matter how smart they are. Creative students get frustrated when their school doesn't provide an outlet for their talents.

Our children face significant social challenges at school as well. Some really scary stuff runs rampant in public schools today, from drugs and alcohol abuse, to negative peer pressure, bullying, fights, gangs, and weapons. These things, coupled with substandard teachers, curricula that don't meet today's needs, outdated materials, and low state standards, are other reasons why traditional schooling doesn't work.

This must stop. A lack of adequate education causes myriad social problems among our children, including crime, teen pregnancy, unemployment, and dependency on welfare. Small wonder, then, that some parents choose not to put their children in government-run public schools. Instead, some pay for private schooling, while others choose to home school.

Home schooling is legal in every state and every Canadian province, although the laws that govern it vary by location. Parents who home school are free to offer a typical school curriculum or totally change things up and let their children make their own choices about their education plan. It's an awesome responsibility but one that yields major benefits for children.

The states and provinces offer various homeschooling guidelines to help parents and other home schoolers succeed. In California, for instance, parents must file an R-4, or Private School Affidavit, which essentially gives them permission to start a private school in their home, and thus keeps them from being prosecuted for truancy (illegally keeping their children out of school). Parents can also enroll in a private school satellite program (PSP), which is a type of R-4 institution that helps by handling administrative work, offering curriculum packages, and more. The fee for this type of home school program generally ranges from $250 to $400 per school year.

There are other resources available to assist new home school families, from support groups to newsletters, classes, park days, websites, and legal assistance, all of which are intended to help parents make the home schooling experience successful.

But it's the parents themselves that drive the home schooling experience. Usually, after the first few months, they get a successful routine going and need very little help. They use prepackaged curricula or rely on the internet or the library. They can set up classes in small groups with other home schooled children or keep their kids at home to study. They also can encourage their kids to volunteer, play sports, learn to dance, or play a musical instrument, among other activities. They also can choose to test their children's knowledge, assign papers, or simply give oral feedback. It's all up to them.

In the end, the beauty of home schooling is that parents, in partnership with their children, can choose what's important to them. This, coupled with learning in a safe environment in which parents can instill good values in their children, makes the home schooling experience rich and rewarding.

For more information about home schooling, including tips and ideas, search online for "home schooling" plus the name of your state or province.

Marcia Williams homeschooled her youngest son, now twenty-four, his entire school life. She is a writer, speaker, and mentor to anyone who wants more information on the subject of education.

Contact her at williamsacademy12@yahoo.com.

Appendix B

Financial Terms

401K: an employer-sponsored retirement plan.

Annual Percentage Rate (APR): the interest rate charged on a loan, credit card, or other financial instrument.

Asset: something you own, including possessions and investments.

Average daily balance: a method used to calculate finance charges on an account.

Bankruptcy: a legal state in which a person or company is unable to repay debt.

Broker: a person or company licensed to sell financial investments like stocks, bonds, and mutual funds.

Cash advance: money withdrawn against an account.

Credit report: a document that show a person's credit purchase and repayment history.

Debit card: a card used to withdraw funds directly from a checking or savings account.

Default: failure to repay a loan, like a mortgage.

Delinquency: state of being late on two or more payments to a financial institution.

Depreciation: progressive decrease in an item's value over time.

Dividend: a payment paid to stockholders as a return on their investment.

Finance charge: the interest fee on a revolving charge account.

Financial planner: an individual who helps you manage your investments.

Fraud: criminal act intended to result in financial gain for the criminal.

Gross income: income before taxes are taken out.

Interest rate: rate charged for the use of money.

IRA: individual retirement account; funded with pre-tax funds.

Minimum payment: the lowest amount of money that must be repaid on a credit account.

Net income: income remaining after income taxes and other deductions have been deducted.

Net worth: overall value of assets minus liabilities (amount owed).

Online banking: a system that allows people to use the internet to conduct banking transactions.

Origination fee: a fee for processing a mortgage.

Roth IRA: a type of individual retirement account funded with after-tax money

Secured credit card: a credit card backed with collateral; used to rebuild credit.

Stock: a share of a publicly traded company.

Transaction fee: a fee charged to the user of a financial service.

Appendix C

Common Home Mortgage Terms

Amortization: the process of paying off a debt (often from a loan or mortgage) over time through regular installment payments.

Annual percentage rate (APR): refers to the entire rate cost of mortgage plus all fees.

Balloon payment: a huge sum due at the end of a brief mortgage term; usually set up so mortgage payments are as low as possible.

Buy down: process of paying an amount to a mortgage lender to obtain a lower rate and lower payments.

Buyer's agent: a licensed real estate agent who represents home buyers.

Closing costs: the amount charged to close a mortgage loan, which includes numerous fees, as well as property taxes and escrow amounts.

Credit score: a rating given by scoring agencies to reflect an individual's use of credit.

Down payment: a cash payment required at the time of closing a loan by a lender.

Escrow: a fund held by a third party to collect funds due from a home buyer for another party, such as a mortgage insurance provider or property tax collector (like a state government).

Good faith estimate (GFE): a preliminary report listing the loan terms, costs, and fees for a new mortgage.

Home inspection: a visual evaluation and inspection of a property by a bank representative to determine a property's overall condition so a price can be set; also an inspection by a qualified professional estimating safety and efficiency of current home conditions carried out as a safeguard for a new home buyer.

Homeowner's insurance: a type of insurance that reimburses a homeowner for property damage due to theft, fire, liability, and disasters.

Interest rate: the cost to borrow money for a home loan; expressed as a percentage.

Loan origination fee: the amount charged by lenders and brokers to originate a mortgage.

Mortgage insurance: insurance that protects a mortgage company against loss in case the homeowner defaults on the mortgage.

Point: 1 percent of the principal amount of a mortgage; also referred to as a discount point.

Principal loan balance: the mortgage loan amount, not including interest. Rate lock: a fixed-rate guarantee for a limited period of time.

Realtor: a person licensed to sell real estate on behalf of a home owner and to buy real estate on behalf of a buyer.

Seller's agent: the real estate professional who represents the seller of a property.

Settlement costs: the fees associated with selling or purchasing a home.

About the Authors

Atta Arghandiwal was born in Afghanistan but has spent over half his life in the West. He left Afghanistan shortly after the Soviet invasion and became a refugee in Germany. He immigrated to the United States in December 1981. Two weeks after his arrival in the United States, he started work as a bank teller, where he built a successful twenty-eight-year career, earning the status of senior vice president and regional manager. With deep passion for his heritage, Arghandiwal published his first book, the award-winning memoir Lost Decency: The Untold Afghan Story, while tending to his life-long dream of writing Immigrant Success Planning.

Eileen Figure Sandlin is an award-winning writer and author of twenty-one books, including eighteen small-business start-up books. She has published more than eight-hundred magazine and newspaper articles, as well as thousands of newsletter articles. Her writing specialties are health care, small business issues, and education. Sandlin holds a master's degree in journalism and is a professor of business communication at a major Midwest university.

OTHER BOOKS AND FURTHER INFORMATION ON THE AUTHOR:

Through his first award-winning moving memoir *Lost Decency: The Untold Afghan Story*, Atta Arghandiwal shares his own turbulent journey as well as the stories from the people of Afghanistan as they escape their war-torn country. *Lost Decency: The Untold Afghan Story* spans a history of fifty years in order to increase awareness about political upheaval and the innocent people who have been caught in chaos.

As a keynote motivational speaker and financial services professional, Arghandiwal shares thought-provoking, heart-warming, and practical life journeys' best practices through inspiring real stories and insight as an immigrant.

Specialties: Keynote motivational speaking on Afghanistan Issues, Banking, Leadership, Talent Development, and Management in Service Industry.

To learn more about Atta Arghandiwal, please visit attamoves.com

Facebook: www.facebook.com/attamoves
Twitter: @attamoves
LinkedIn: www.linkedin.com/in/aarghandiwal

If you want to get on the path to be a published author
with **Influence Publishing** please go to
www.InfluencePublishing.com/InspireABook

Inspiring books that influence change

More information on our other titles and how to submit
your own proposal can be found at
www.InfluencePublishing.com

CPSIA information can be obtained at www.ICGtesting.com
Printed in the USA
LVOW10s0325220314

378442LV00012B/58/P

9 781771 410236